Uppity

Uppity

*My Untold Story About The
Games People Play*

BILL WHITE

with Gordon Dillow

Foreword by Willie Mays

GRAND CENTRAL
PUBLISHING

NEW YORK   BOSTON

Grand Central Publishing
Hachette Book Group
237 Park Avenue
New York, NY 10017
www.HachetteBookGroup.com

Printed in the United States of America

First Edition: April 2011

10 9 8 7 6 5 4 3 2 1

Grand Central Publishing is a division of Hachette Book Group, Inc.
The Grand Central Publishing name and logo is a trademark of
Hachette Book Group, Inc.

The publisher is not responsible for websites (or their content) that are not
owned by the publisher.

Library of Congress Cataloging-in-Publication Data
    White, Bill, 1934–
    Uppity : My Untold Story About The Games People Play / Bill White with
Gordon Dillow.
        p. cm.
    Includes index.
    ISBN 978-0-446-55525-8
  1. White, Bill, 1934–   2. Baseball players—United States—Biography.
3. African American baseball players—Biography.   4. Baseball—United
States—History.   5. Discrimination in sports—United States.   I. Dillow,
Gordon.   II. Title.
    GV865.W45W45 2011
    796.357092—dc22
    [B]
                                                        2010038025

To my grandmother, Tamar Young,
who taught me to have pride in who I was,
and to my mother, Edna Mae Young,
who gave me confidence in what I could become.

ACKNOWLEDGMENTS

Writing a book is like playing a baseball game. You can't do it alone.

There are a number of people who helped make this book possible. First and foremost I would like to express my thanks and gratitude to my lady, Nancy McKee, for encouraging me to put my life on paper.

My agents, Eric and Maureen Lasher of the LA Literary Agency, guided this project from the beginning. Rick Wolff, vice president and executive editor at Grand Central Publishing, never stopped believing in it. Carolyn Kurek, Laura Jorstad, Tom Whatley, and Giraud Lorber were all instrumental in getting the book copyedited, manufactured, and produced. Thanks also to Meredith Haggerty.

My co-author, Gordon Dillow, helped me mold a lifetime of memories into book form. I'm grateful for his hard work, good humor, and wise counsel. Jerry Bembry provided valuable assistance in organizing an early version of this book.

My thanks to those who helped me remember events that happened over the years: Willie Mays, Dave Garcia, Monte Irvin, Valerie Dietrich, Earl Robinson, Ernie Banks, Art Adler, Marty Appel, Ralph Wimbish Jr., and Mickey Morabito. Katy Feeney, Lee Butz, Phyllis Collins, and Lew Klein also took the time to read the early drafts and offer helpful comments and corrections. Any errors that remain are mine, not theirs.

The story of a man's life is not his story alone. It is also the story of many people, living and departed, who made him what he is. I will always be grateful to my family members who made sure I stayed out of trouble and got the best education possible: my grandmother, Tamar Young; my mother, Edna Mae Young; my aunts, Molly Bell Bennett and Leola Anderson; my cousin Lilly Mae Anderson; my uncles, Wilmer Young and his wife Loretta, Willie Young, Marvin Young, Charles Young, Felix Young, and James Young. My thanks also to the people of the old Benton Homes public housing project in Warren, Ohio, who treated me like family, and to my high school and Hiram College buddies, Dr. John Vlad and his wife Mary Alice, and Dr. Roger Bryant and Dave Rogers.

There will always be a special place in my heart for my children—Edna, Debbie, Tom, Steve, and Mike—and my grandchildren, Jordan and Kendall White. I am proud of all of them.

Good teachers have an impact that lasts for a lifetime. I would like to offer a lifetime's worth of thanks to my teachers at Warren G. Harding High School—Latin teacher Clara K. Webb, world history teacher Ruth LaPolla and English teacher Ruth Partridge—and to my mentor at Hiram College, Mary Louise Vincent. There were teachers outside the school buildings as well, including Lemuel Young and Charlie Caffee of Warren, Ohio, who taught me how to play baseball.

The struggle against racial discrimination in Major League Baseball was the work of many people. Some of my personal heroes in that struggle were Jackie Robinson and Larry Doby, who led the way; Mal Goode of ABC-TV, the nation's first black network correspondent; journalists A. S. "Doc" Young, Sam Lacey, Joe Reichler, Bob Boyle, and other sportswriters, black and white, who saw injustice and refused to remain silent. I will always remember the late Dr. Ralph Wimbish, and his equally courageous wife, Bette, who steadfastly encouraged me, George Crowe, Bob Gibson, Curt Flood, and many others to stand up for our rights as Americans.

There were many people who guided and shaped my Major League Baseball career, people who were on my side when I was hitting .300 and remained on my side when I was batting .160. In addition to those already mentioned, they include Harry Walker, Johnny Keane, Bing Devine, Eddy Stanky, Al Fleishman, Bob Bauman, Leo Durocher, Jim Tugerson, Charlie James, Dick Ricketts, Alex Pompez, Frank Forbes, and Danville Leafs outfielders Charlie Allen and Bob Knight.

My eighteen-year-career in broadcasting would have been much less successful—and probably a lot shorter—without the help and encouragement of many people. Harry Caray and Bob Hyland of KMOX radio in St. Louis gave me my start in the business. Mike Burke, Howard Berk, and Bob Fishel of the Yankees took Howard Cosell's suggestion and hired me as a Yankees broadcaster and then backed me up when the going was rough. Ernie Harwell, Jack Buck, Dan Kelly, Vin Scully, Lilyan Wilder, Bob Neal, Herb Score, Joe Garagiola, Frank Messer, Tommy Villante, Gene Shalit, and Stu Schulberg helped me learn how to be a broadcaster. Frank Miller of CBS gave me the chance to call a World Series, and John Chanin of ABC Radio Sports sent me to the Olympics. George Steinbrenner and our friends Bill Roesch and Dick Kraft, the legendary Bob Sheppard, Debbie Nicolosi, and Pearl Davis of the Yankees gave me their support, even though I wasn't a "homer." The incomparable Phil Rizzuto gave me eighteen years of friendship and fun, for which I will always be thankful.

Commissioner of Baseball Bart Giamatti generously gave me his guidance, support, and friendship when I became president of the National League; his untimely death left a void that would never be filled. Former National League president Chub Feeney, Cathy Davis, Nancy Crofts, Eddie Vargo, Don Marr, Brian Burns, Anita Rice, Lou Hoynes, Bob Kheel, American League president Dr. Bobby Brown, and John McSherry all shared their years of baseball experience with me and made my job easier. My thanks also to Peter O'Malley, Doug Danforth, Fred Kuhlman, Wayne Huizenga, Bob Lurie, Paul Beeston, Lee MacPhail, Roland Hopkins, Dave and Pamela Beaubien, Bill Hewitt, and Bill Bowen.

There were many others who helped me in my three careers in baseball. They include Davey Williams, Yogi Berra, Billy Martin, Elston Howard, Willie Stargell, James "Cool Papa" Bell, Joe Black, Roxy Campanella, Butch McCord, Cora Rizzuto, Johnny Pesky, Dr. Hans Kraus, Jocko Conlan, Rusty Staub, John Roseboro, singer Joe Willliams, Ed Arrigoni, Celtics star Bill Russell, Mike Shannon, Jim Kaat, Ken Coleman, Sherm Feller, Dorothy McConkey, Betsy Cohen, George Michael, Judge Robert Cannon, John McHale Sr., Dick Wagner, Tina Sloan-Green, Paul Guenther, Phil Kind, Walter Conti, Bill Eastburn, Bill Werndl, "Dandy" Don Meredith, Jack Frazee, sportswriters Frank Dolson, Bob Broeg, and Allen Lewis, the Harris family, the Sciss family, and Sandy and Jane Koufax.

My appreciation and gratitude to all of them. It was an honor to play on their team.

FOREWORD

When I saw Bill White play in his first major league game, I knew he was a good baseball player. But it was something he said after the game was over that let me know he was also a good man.

It was May 1956, and my team, the New York Giants, was in the last game of a three-game road series against the Cardinals in St. Louis. Bill was just a kid then, a young college student who had spent three years in the minors, including one season as the only black player in the Carolina League. Just that morning, Giants manager Bill Rigney had called Bill up from the AAA Minneapolis Millers to take over at first base.

I'd seen Bill play a few times in the Giants' spring training camp in Phoenix, so I knew he could play ball. But playing in the minors or in spring training was one thing; playing in the majors was something else. You're out there in that big stadium, in front of all those people, and the other players are sizing you up—it can put a lot of pressure on you.

That was especially true for black ballplayers. There weren't a lot of us in the majors back then, so you kind of stood out. That first time you stepped up to the plate in the majors, you felt like the whole world was watching you.

The pressure could throw some guys off their game. I know it did me. Before I was called up to the Giants in 1951, I had batted .477 in the AAA minors, but I went 0-for-5 in my first major league game, and in my first two weeks with the Giants I was 1-for-26 before I finally settled down to business. So I knew what kind of pressure a young ballplayer could face out there.

But Bill White was different.

He was a quiet kid, the sort who didn't say much until he got to know you. He kept his emotions inside himself. I knew that like a lot of black ballplayers in those days, he'd had a hard time playing in the minors in the segregated Deep South. Folks today may not realize it, but back then black ballplayers had to deal with people in the stands calling them racist names, and with having to eat and sleep apart from their teammates. Bill never got used to it, never accepted it—but he never let it throw him off his game.

And he didn't let the pressure of being called up to the majors throw him off his game, either.

It showed in his first time at bat. He was the Giants' leadoff batter at the top of the second inning, and he was behind in the count until Cardinals pitcher Ben Flowers missed with a curveball and filled out the count. Then Flowers challenged Bill with a fastball right up the middle.

And Bill crushed it. That ball soared over right field and landed on the roof over the right field stands. In his first major league at-bat, Bill had hit a home run.

And he didn't stop there. Bill hit a double in the fourth inning and a single in the ninth, going 3-for-4 in the game, and his level of play at first base was outstanding. We lost the game to the Cardinals anyway, 6–3, but it was a heck of a first major league game for any young ballplayer.

Some young guys might have gotten cocky about it, let themselves get all puffed up. But when I saw Bill in the locker room after the game, he didn't seem all that excited. Fact is, he actually looked kind of disappointed.

"That's a good start," I told him, giving him a pat on the shoulder. "You're going to be all right."

Bill didn't smile. Instead he looked at me and said, "Thanks, Willie. I just wish we had won the game!"

That was Bill White. He could take a quiet sort of pride in his own accomplishments, but he never forgot that he was part of a team. That's the kind of guy you knew you could count on.

I kind of took Bill under my wing after that, trying to help him along. He lived with me for a while in my home in the East Elmhurst section of Queens, and when I'd drive him to the Polo Grounds for a game I'd try to teach him things about the team we were going to play. I'd been around for a while, so I knew what their pitchers threw, who you could steal off of and who you couldn't, how to play their batters at first base. Bill learned fast; I never had to tell him anything twice. Sometimes after a game we'd go to Harlem and I'd take him around to places like the Red Rooster and Small's Paradise and introduce him to people.

We had a lot of good times together, so I was upset when Bill asked to be traded by the Giants in 1959 and went to the St. Louis Cardinals. For me it was like losing a little brother.

But we always kept in touch. Bill played thirteen seasons in the majors, then went on to become the first full-time black broadcaster in the major leagues. After that he became the first African American president of the National League.

But even as he got older, and his jobs changed, in some ways Bill was always the same as that young player in his first major league game way back in 1956. He was never loud or flashy about what he did, never thought that he was bigger than whatever team he was playing for or whatever job he had taken on. He just went out every day and did his best—and he was never afraid to speak out for what he thought was right.

Now, I don't want you to get the wrong idea about Bill. Most of the time he was a pretty laid-back guy. He loved to laugh and have a good time, and we could always joke around together. We still do.

But the thing people had to understand about Bill was that when it came to something important, something he believed in, you couldn't push him. Because if you pushed him, he'd push you right back.

And that's what he's doing in this book.

My friend Bill White is pushing back.

—Willie Mays
September 1, 2010

Uppity

CHAPTER 1

It was a hot, muggy night in the summer of 1954 when the team bus pulled into the gravel parking lot of a run-down burger joint just outside Wichita, Kansas. As usual, Dave Garcia, the team manager and part-time second baseman, got off the bus first to see if I could eat there.

My team, the Sioux City Soos, part of the New York Giants organization, had just played a night game against the Wichita Class A minor league team, the Indians, and now we were looking at a long, all-night bus ride back up Highway 77 to Sioux City. This roadside restaurant wasn't exactly a fine dining establishment—a few badly scuffed tables, dirty linoleum floors, a skinny cook hunched over the grill—but it was late, and the road ahead was dark, and we were all hot and tired and hungry. It was here or nothing.

So while the rest of us waited, Dave climbed down off the bus, one of those old, round-topped Greyhound Scenicruisers, and walked inside to ask if the manager would be willing to serve the team's first baseman—that is, me. The reason it was a question is because I was a young black man, the only black player on the team.

Earlier in the season, when I had first joined the Soos, the entire twenty-man roster, me included, would have just walked into the restaurant and waited to see what happened. After all, we weren't in the Deep South, where blacks and whites were never allowed to eat together, where roadside restaurants that served black people, and only black people, were clearly marked with signs that said COLORED. We were in the Western League, with teams in Iowa, Kansas, Nebraska, and Colorado—but still, you never knew.

Sometimes they would serve us—or, more specifically, me—without a word, although I could usually count on getting some sideways glances from some of the white customers. Sometimes I could hear them say things like "Oh, they're serving them in here now?"—and everybody knew who the *them* was. Sometimes the restaurant manager would let us eat, but only in a separate back dining room where the other patrons couldn't see us. And sometimes they would flat-out refuse to serve us, at least not together, in which case the team would have to get up from the table and file back onto the bus and look for another place to eat.

Finally Dave decided it was easier to ask first.

More than half a century later, it's hard for some people, especially young people, even young black people, to believe that this happened in America, that the racism was so open and raw. But it was.

True, change was in the air. The Supreme Court had recently ruled on *Brown v. Board of Education of Topeka, Kansas,* which decided that "separate but equal" segregation in public schools was unconstitutional, setting the stage for numerous civil rights battles, not only in the South but across the country. The year after that, Rosa Parks would refuse to give up her seat on a bus to a white man in Montgomery, Alabama, prompting a bus boycott and introducing the nation to a man named Martin Luther King Jr. The civil rights movement was just starting to discover its own power.

In sports, meanwhile, it had been seven years since Jackie Robinson, with great courage and dignity, had broken the so-called color line in baseball, taking the field with the Brooklyn Dodgers as the first black man to play in the modern-day major leagues. Jackie had broken the color line, but he had not erased it on the playing field or in the hotels, restaurants, and spring training camps where Jim Crow still ruled. Baseball, America's pastime, could never be fully desegregated until all of America was desegregated—and that would be a long time coming.

Which is why in the summer of 1954 a young black ballplayer still had to wonder if some dingy roadside restaurant in Kansas would allow him to sit down and eat a hamburger.

When I saw Dave Garcia come out of the restaurant and climb back aboard the bus, I could see on his face what the answer had been. He was pissed.

Dave was a good guy, old enough at thirty-three to be kind of a big-brother figure for me. We were roommates on the road, at least in the nonsegregated hotels, and we often hung out together. He understood some of what I was going through. While he was a native of East St. Louis, Illinois, Dave's mother and father had been born in northern Spain, and although ethnically he was the whitest of white guys, sometimes at road games people in the stands would see his name on the roster and call him a "greaser" or a "spic."

Dave looked at me and shook his head.

There was an awkward silence on the bus. My teammates were for the most part decent guys. They didn't like what was happening, but it was a long road ahead and they were hungry. It was 1954 and that was just the way it was.

I mumbled something like, "Go ahead, you guys. Don't worry

about it." After a minute, they started to stand up and file off the bus. They didn't look at me. Dave said he'd get a hamburger and fries and a milk shake and bring it out to me. He followed the team into the restaurant, and I sat in the bus, alone.

It certainly wasn't the first, or the worst, indignity that I'd experienced in my young baseball career. The year before, my first season in the minors, I was playing first base for the Danville (Virginia) Leafs, a Class B affiliate of the Giants that was part of the Carolina League—only the second black player ever in the league, and at the time the only black player in that Deep South league. On road games, it was routine for people in the stands to shout out "Hey nigger!" or "Hey darkie!" or "We're gonna use your black ass for 'gator bait!"

For a teenage kid who grew up in the North, in the relatively benign racial climate of Warren, Ohio, the anger and hatred in the Deep South was a shock. And it made me angry right back. I had always been taught to take pride in myself, and I did. I was proud of my heritage, proud of my family, proud of my academic accomplishments—in the off season I was attending college as a pre-med student—and proud of my abilities on the baseball field. And now some rednecked, tobacco-chewing Carolina cracker with a fourth-grade education was calling me "nigger"?

When that happened, there was nothing I wanted more than to climb into the stands and start kicking some ass. But I couldn't. I couldn't fight them all, so I just had to take it. And taking it was the hardest thing I'd ever had to do.

Now, a year later and a thousand miles away, the racism was still there—not as overtly as in the Deep South, perhaps, but just as hurtful. And I still had to take it.

I don't know why I reacted the way I did on the team bus that night outside Wichita. Maybe it was because I had hoped, naively, that once out of the South and into the Midwest I wouldn't be wrong.

treated that way. Maybe it was because I had kept my anger bottled up inside for so long. Or maybe it was just because the Kansas sky was so big and so dark and so empty, and I was young and so far from home.

But whatever the reason, as I sat on that bus and watched through the window while my teammates sat down to eat, I did something that I had never done before in my life, and have never done since.

I held my face in my hands and cried.

Four decades later, I was at my home in Pennsylvania when I got a call from Leonard Coleman, the president of the National League.

A few months earlier, Len, a onetime Princeton football and baseball player with a master's degree from Harvard, and formerly Major League Baseball's director of market development, had succeeded me as the National League president. He was the league's second African American president; I had been the first.

"Bill," he said, "I just want to let you know that the quarterly baseball meetings are going to be in Detroit in August, and the owners would like you to come. They don't think you had the proper send-off when you left, so they'd like to have a dinner in your honor as a way to acknowledge your years in the league office."

I didn't say anything at first. I liked Len, although he hadn't been my first choice as league president, and I didn't want to hurt his feelings. But I was going to be honest with him.

I had spent thirteen seasons in the major leagues with the New York/San Francisco Giants, the St. Louis Cardinals, and the Philadelphia Phillies. I had won seven straight Gold Glove Awards and was selected for the All-Star Game five times. I had a career batting average of .286, with 870 RBIs and 202 home runs—including a home run in my first major league at-bat in 1956—making me one of the top five hundred home run hitters of all time.

I had also spent eighteen years as a professional sportscaster, first in St. Louis and Philadelphia and then calling games on radio and television for the New York Yankees—the first African American to do regular play-by-play for a major league team. After that I had spent five often tumultuous years as president of the National League—again, the first African American to hold such a position.

Some people have called me a pioneer. And I suppose I was.

But while I had always respected the game of baseball, after thirty-one years I could not respect the business of baseball, or the politics of baseball.

Major League Baseball had always prided itself as being in the forefront of racial and ethnic equality, and on the playing field that was true. If a player was batting .300, no one could argue that he was actually batting only .200 and thus wasn't up to the job.

But it was a far different story off the field, in the coaching positions and in the executive offices and certainly in the owners' boxes. There, where performance and ability were more difficult to quantify, Major League Baseball had lagged disgracefully far behind even the rest of American society in breaking the color barrier.

Four decades after Jackie Robinson debuted with the Brooklyn Dodgers, and almost as long after I helped integrate the Carolina League, Los Angeles Dodgers general manager Al Campanis had gone on television and wondered aloud if blacks had the "necessities" for a front office job. At about the same time, Cincinnati Reds owner Marge Schott allegedly told some other team owners that she "would never hire another nigger" for an executive job. Although both were more or less punished for what they said—Campanis by losing his job, Marge by being banned from baseball for a brief time—I knew that they had only said aloud what too many people in the upper levels of the baseball business quietly thought.

Some years earlier, during my tenure as National League president, *The New York Times Magazine* had done a cover story on me, the headline for which was "Baseball's Angry Man." But I didn't think that was accurate. I was never a shouter or a desk pounder; I kept my emotions under control. I think what some people mistook for anger was the fact that I have always been a direct man, and that I always said exactly what I thought.

I wasn't a lonely young black kid sitting on a team bus in Kansas anymore. And I didn't take any nonsense from anyone.

So when Len called to invite me to dinner with the baseball owners, and I thought back to all the lies and deceit and manipulation I had experienced with some of them, to the dishonor and disservice of the game, I knew immediately what my response would be.

"No disrespect to you, Len," I said, "but I'm not going to that dinner. You can tell the owners I said the hell with them."

CHAPTER 2

In the fall of 2004, I steered my motor home off Interstate 10 in the middle of the Florida Panhandle and up a two-lane strip of blacktop called Highway 331. My destination was a little town called Paxton, near the Florida–Alabama border, the place where I was born.

There wasn't much to Paxton—there never had been—just a gas station and a diner and a couple of churches and an old schoolhouse set down amid long-abandoned cotton fields and scrub pine woods. I'd been invited there by a local minister, the Reverend James Williams, to speak at a get-out-the-vote rally for the upcoming presidential election. I was a local kid who'd made good, and the reverend thought I could get the crowd fired up.

I wish I could say that my speech at the tiny Paxton library building tipped the electoral balance in the state of Florida that year. Unfortunately, to the reverend's embarrassment, only a few people showed up.

But after my speech was over, the reverend, a lively man in his eighties, loaded me in his car and gave me a tour of the town—which didn't take very long. Eventually we drove down a dirt road behind the schoolhouse, past a threadbare baseball diamond, and then stopped at a rusty metal gate. As we got out of the car, the reverend pointed down the road to two weather-beaten old gray wood shacks collapsing in on themselves amid choking, knee-high weeds.

"That's it," the reverend said. "That's where your family lived. That's where you were born."

I had been back to Paxton only once, for a brief visit almost half a century earlier, and at the time I hadn't even visited the old family homestead. So my memories of this place were uncertain and vague.

I remembered the hard-packed red clay dirt, with scrawny chickens scratching at it, and the stand of pecan trees along the road. I knew that even when the shacks were new, going on three-quarters of a century ago, they hadn't amounted to much, just some huts thrown together with green pine so warped that it barely kept the weather out, with rough lumber floors and an outhouse in the back. Of course there had never been any electricity or running water. It had been a place of grinding, desperate poverty.

And seeing it now made me feel uneasy.

My grandparents, the children of former slaves, had come to Paxton from a little town in Georgia called Hog Wallow—and no, I'm not making that name up. The rumor in our family was that Grandpa James had killed a man in Georgia—possibly because the man had tried to trifle with James's young wife, my grandmother, Tamar Young—and although such things were treated more casually back then, he still thought it was best to put a state line between him and the scene of the crime.

Grandpa James had worked in a lumber mill in Paxton for a while, and on the railroad, and for a time he even ran a boardinghouse and restaurant in Flowers Quarters—for black people only, of course. But like most of the black men in Paxton, Grandpa mostly worked as a sharecropper on a cotton plantation, which meant he raised a crop on someone else's land and then had to give the owner a large share of the proceeds to pay for the use of the land and the "rent" on the crude shacks they lived in. It was a system guaranteed to keep the tenant farmers stuck in poverty.

My grandparents had nine children—my mother, Edna Mae Young, being the second youngest—and while they were poor, they had pride. Their children's clothes might have been old and much-mended, but they were never dirty.

Of course, all of their children had to work from a young age—and in Paxton, work for black people meant hoeing and picking in the cotton fields. An efficient cotton-picking machine had not yet been invented, so cotton harvesting was all done by hand. It was hard, hot, exhausting labor, especially for children. But there was no other choice.

My grandparents were determined that their children would have a better life than they had—and that meant getting an education. Although the children had to work for the family to survive, between cotton-picking time and cotton-planting time, they made sure their kids were in school.

But in Paxton, that was a problem. Although they lived across the road from a school, my mother and her sisters and brothers weren't allowed to go there. The Paxton school was for whites only. Instead, they had to take a "school bus"—actually it was an old flatbed truck—to the black school way down the road in a town called DeFuniak Springs, which was seventeen miles away. On old dirt country roads, that meant a forty-five-minute drive each way.

Despite that, all but one of their children learned to read and write, an exceptional accomplishment among black families in the South back then. My mother, Edna Mae, even became the valedictorian of her high school class.

She managed to do that even though at a young age she faced an additional roadblock—which was me. My mother was just sixteen when she gave birth to me in 1934. My father was named Penner White, but he left town shortly after I was born and played no role in my upbringing or my life. The only thing he ever left me was his last name.

I never lacked for male role models. My uncles were there to set an example, but sadly, I never got to meet my grandfather. In 1931, a few years before I was born, he was killed when a mule wagon rolled over on him, and the leadership of the family fell on my grandma. Fortunately, although she was a physically tiny woman, standing just four foot eleven, she was a true matriarch, strong, resourceful, and tough.

Maybe too tough for some. Grandma always made it a point to look people straight in the eye—black people, white people, it didn't matter. That may not seem particularly remarkable now, but back then, and especially in the South, for a black person to look directly at a white person was a sign of insolence, of being what was known back then as "uppity." That could be difficult, even dangerous, but Grandma didn't care. It was a trait she passed on to my mother, and to me.

Grandma was a churchgoing Christian lady and never preached hate, but I could tell from the way she acted and the things she said that if you were white you already had two strikes against you in Grandma's book. Maybe even three. When I was growing up, Grandma would tell me stories about how our ancestors in Africa had vibrant, culturally advanced societies long before white people did, and how things might have been if the slave catchers hadn't come, and how black people had built America. Grandma didn't just think that black people were as good as white people; she thought we were better than white people.

In any event, my grandmother knew that her children could

never achieve their full potential in Paxton, or anywhere in the Jim Crow South. Even those Southern black people who somehow managed to rise in the world—as preachers or doctors—would still be regarded as black preachers or black doctors, with all the suffocating limits that segregation placed on them.

And so like so many other black people, Grandma was determined to find better opportunities for her family elsewhere.

What happened in the first half of the twentieth century is known to history as the Great Migration, the mass movement of black people out of the Deep South and into the North and Midwest. They left by the millions, searching for better jobs and better lives—and, most important, freedom from the hopelessness that Southern segregation forced upon them. They didn't always find those things—the mythical North, it turned out, was not a paradise—but at least they had hope.

Today the South has made some progress. But I can't help but wonder how much better it would have been, how many decades of anger and strife and misery could have been avoided, if the South had simply given its black citizens greater freedom and opportunities instead of driving so many of the most hardworking and ambitious among them into flight. Still, you can't change history. I'm just grateful that when the Great Migration was happening, my family was a part of it.

After my grandfather died, my grandmother started planning our exodus from Paxton like a military campaign, first sending one of my uncles up north to get established, followed by an aunt, then another uncle, and so on. In 1937, when I was three years old, it was my mother's turn. She and I climbed aboard a train—in the "colored" section, of course—and headed north forever.

Almost seventy years later, as I stood there in Paxton with the Reverend Williams, by the rusty gate near the dilapidated shacks that had once been my family's home, I thought about that history.

"Would you like to go back there for a closer look?" the reverend asked, gesturing toward the shacks. I shook my head.

"No, that's okay," I said. We got back into his car and drove away.

I didn't tell the reverend this, but I knew that the only thing my mother and grandmother had wanted from those miserable share-cropper's shacks, and from the town of Paxton in general, was to leave them far, far behind.

The place "up north" where my family settled, the place I would always think of as home, was Warren, Ohio, a small city of about forty thousand people in the far eastern part of the state near the Pennsylvania border.

Warren was a pleasant enough little town, but it wasn't exactly a Garden of Eden. While it was originally an agricultural center, by the late 1930s it had turned into an industrial hotbed, dotted with slag heaps and belching smokestacks and soot-filled skies. I remember my grandmother complaining that the sheets she hung on the outside clothesline to dry always came out gray from the falling soot.

The town's biggest employer was the Republic Steel plant, and that was where five of my uncles worked. In those pre-OSHA (Occupational Safety and Health Administration) days, working in a steel plant was hot, dirty, and dangerous. And although my uncles worked side by side with white people, mostly European immigrants, there was still some racial discrimination. For example, black workers weren't allowed to use the plant locker room showers after they finished a shift. Instead, they had to wash up at home. Still, none of my uncles quit the steel industry to go back south to the cotton fields.

Our entire family lived in an all-black public housing project called the Benton Homes. The white public housing project was across the road. Although public housing has taken on a negative connotation these days, with images of urban high-rises awash in drugs and crime, Benton Homes wasn't like that. The units were one-story, wood-frame and tar-paper-roof structures, each divided into half a dozen two- or three-bedroom apartments. They were more than modest by today's standards, but each apartment had electricity and a bathroom and running water—which made them seem like mansions compared with a sharecropper's shack.

(Years later I took my oldest daughter, Edna, who was eight at the time, to Warren to see the Benton Homes projects before they were torn down, to give her an idea of her roots. Raised in the comfortable suburban environment that came with being the child of a major league baseball player, she could hardly believe it. "No way, Daddy," she said. "No way you could have grown up here." But I did.)

Although for most people the projects were temporary way stations—eventually every one of my aunts and uncles saved up enough to move out and buy their own homes—there was still a sense of community there. People looked out for one another, and for one another's kids. If you got caught making trouble, you could count on a spanking from whatever adult caught you. And then you could count on another one from your folks when they found out what you'd done.

But the best thing about Warren, as far as my mother and grandmother were concerned, was the public school system and the opportunities it offered.

Denied admission to college in the South because of her race and her family's poverty, my mother never lost the drive to better herself and her position in life—and mine. When she had first arrived in Warren, like most working black women in town she had taken a job as a domestic servant, cleaning up other people's houses. She lasted only a week. Such work was, she felt, beneath her. And she was right. She also thought that the work my uncles did, though honest and honorable, was beneath me. I remember her telling me, "You will never work in the steel mills. You will never do what my brothers have to do." She was determined that her only child would do better.

Eventually my mother enrolled at Warren Business College, where she was one of only two black students, and she graduated at the top of her class. Warren, Ohio, wasn't Paxton, Florida, but there was still resistance to giving a black woman a white-collar job. Unable to put her skills to work in town, she took a federal job as an air force procurement administrator in Dayton, Ohio. The job kept her away from home for long periods of time, leaving me in the care of my grandmother and my aunt Molly. But even from afar, by letter and phone call, my mother insisted that I excel at school.

And I did. Maybe it was because I was smart, or maybe it was because I just worked harder than the other kids. To me, being smart and working hard have always meant pretty much the same thing. I was always at or near the top of my class and always made the honor roll. I was even the president of the high school Latin Club.

The public schools in Warren were fully integrated, and even though all the teachers were white, there was very little friction between the races. Until they are taught otherwise, children don't look at race as an issue—but adults sometimes do. During my senior year at Warren G. Harding High School, the only high school in town, I decided to run for student body president, the first black student to do so. I was a popular student, and had what I thought was a great campaign slogan: "White Will Treat You Right!" I had a pretty good chance against my only opponent, an Italian kid, but then the school administrators urged another black kid to get into the race, which divided the vote and sent me down to defeat.

Later I was elected senior class president, but there again race became an issue with some of the school administrators. Traditionally the senior class president had the first dance with the prom queen, and at Harding the queen had always been white. Again, Warren wasn't the Deep South, but this was still the early 1950s, and black boys simply did not dance with white girls. Rather than face a potential scandal, the school administrators abandoned the tradition that year so that I didn't dance with the prom queen.

In my senior year I was called in to see a school counselor, a prim, spinsterish woman who looked over the first page of my academic record and shook her head in disgust. By this time, I had already fulfilled almost all of the courses required for graduation, and even some advanced college prep classes, so my schedule showed that I was taking five "study halls" and one civics class. Without looking any farther, the counselor had decided that I was lazy.

"Look at all these study halls you're taking," she said. "You'll never amount to anything."

After all my hard work and academic accomplishments, her words were like a slap in the face. I felt that she had taken one look at my black skin, and a superficial look at my record, and had simply written me off. She wasn't expecting anything from me, and so she assumed I had nothing to offer.

That's the worst thing you can do a child, any child—not to expect or demand anything of him. If you expect nothing from a youngster, nothing is exactly what you'll get. Fortunately, unlike that school counselor, my mother and grandmother always expected a lot from me. And they made sure I delivered.

I was an honor student and graduated second in my class of 120 students in 1952. The only sad part was that my grandmother wasn't there to see it. That remarkable woman died of cancer when I was in my junior year.

So as my senior year concluded, I thought my path was set. I would go to college, and then medical school, and I would come back to Warren as a doctor. This child of a Southern sharecropping family would be a distinguished and respected member of the community.

That was my dream.

But then somehow, baseball got in the way.

CHAPTER 3

That's a nice bit of power you've got down the line there, kid," Giants manager Leo Durocher told me one day in August 1952. "We'd sure like to see you hit some balls like that for us in New York."

We were in Pittsburgh, where the Giants were playing a three-game series against the Pirates at Forbes Field. Earlier that day I'd been out on the field, taking batting practice while the Giants' coaching staff looked on. I'd been nailing pitches, ripping shot after shot down the right field line and into the stands.

Now Leo Durocher himself, one of the best managers in baseball history, was asking me, an eighteen-year-old kid from Warren, Ohio, if I wanted to become part of the New York Giants organization.

For millions of American kids, it would have been a dream come true, the answer to a thousand youthful prayers.

But I wasn't at all sure if playing baseball, for the Giants or anyone else, was what I wanted to do.

You have to understand that I hadn't come naturally to sports. I was a small kid when I started high school, barely standing five feet tall. It wasn't until I graduated that I made it up to six feet. Although I was a pretty fast runner and had excellent eyesight—a key factor in hitting a fast-moving round ball with a cylindrical bat—I wasn't naturally quick or agile. Whatever success I achieved in high school sports—and my successes were extremely modest—was the result of hard work and determination more than any natural ability.

The biggest problem I had with sports came from the people I loved most—my mother and grandmother. Maybe it would have been different if instead of people saying that you *played* baseball or *played* football, they said that you *worked* at baseball, or *studied* football. Work and study were things that my mother and grandmother understood and respected; playing was not.

"You'd just be wasting your time when you could be studying," my mother said when I told her I wanted to play sports in junior high school. She also worried that being so small, I might get hurt.

Eventually she relented, on the condition that playing sports didn't cause my academic studies to fall short. At Warren G. Harding High School, I lettered in three sports—football, basketball, and baseball. But I excelled at none.

I'm not being modest. I wasn't All-American, All-State, or even All-Conference in any of my high school sports. In baseball, I was so average that I warmed the bench until my senior year—and the only reason I was a starter then was because another, better player had graduated. To tell you the truth, baseball was never my favorite sport. I didn't love the game; for me, it was something to pass the time until football season started.

There was also a practical reason why I gravitated toward football. Back then, as it is today, football was where the most athletic scholarship money was. For the sons of steelworker families, a football scholarship was often the only ticket to a college education.

A college diploma, not a professional sports contract, was what I dreamed about.

I was a good enough high school football player and had a strong enough academic record to earn full-scholarship offers from Columbia University in New York and Western Reserve (now Case Western) University in Ohio. They were both fine schools, and the scholarships made them financially attractive.

But then I visited Hiram College in the town of Hiram, twenty miles away from Warren. It was a small—about four hundred students—but highly prestigious liberal arts college with an excellent science and pre-med program. The people there were friendly and welcoming, and I decided it was perfect for me. The only problem was that while I was able to get a grant to cover half the yearly cost for tuition and room and board—which came to precisely $759.11—I had to come up with the rest of the money myself. My mother was able to help me, but I knew that unlike most of the other students, who came from prosperous families, I would find paying for four years of college, not to mention four years of medical school after that, to be a struggle.

That's where baseball came in.

Hiram didn't have a baseball team when I first enrolled there in the winter of 1952, but they promised they would start one. They cobbled together a fifteen-man team, outfitted us with worn-out old Cleveland Indians uniforms, and let us play baseball on a high school football field. I barely hit .200 and hit just two home runs during the ten-game season. I wasn't exactly a standout.

That summer one of my friends, Roger Bryant—a Western Reserve student who later became a successful dentist—and I were playing on the Warren team of the National Amateur Baseball Federation's (NABF) eighteen-and-under league. I played first base, Roger played shortstop. In August, our team went to Cincinnati for the annual NABF tournament. In the championship game, which was played in the Cincinnati Reds' Crosley Field, I managed to muscle a couple of home runs into the right field bleachers.

At that time, I batted and threw left-handed, although I wasn't a true lefty. I wrote left-handed on paper but right-handed on a blackboard, threw balls overhand with my left arm but underhand with my right arm, like in softball. (Today I swing a golf club right-handed. I don't know why; it just feels right that way.)

Although I didn't know it, as I was hitting those homers into the right field seats, a guy named Alan Fey was watching from the stands. Fey was a "bird dog" for the New York Giants—that is, not a full-time scout but someone who occasionally earned small commissions by tipping off big league scouts about promising young players. After the game Fey came up to me, introduced himself, and said, "You looked pretty good out there hitting the ball. You might actually be good enough to give this game a shot."

I appreciated the kind words, but I didn't think much of it. I just didn't think of myself as a promising young baseball player.

But then a couple of days later, after I'd gone home to Warren, I got a call from Tony Ravish, the Giants' chief scout in the Northeast. Tony, a former catcher in the minors and for the Toronto Maple Leafs of the International League, was a fast-talking New Yorker and a classic baseball scout. In fact, the next year he would actually play a scout in the Hollywood movie *The Big Leaguer*.

"Bill," Tony said, "the Giants are interested in you. They're going to be in Pittsburgh this weekend and they want you to come down so you can work out for them."

Again, I should have been bowled over. But I wasn't. I just didn't see myself playing professional baseball.

Still, I didn't want to pass up any opportunities, so I took the train to Pittsburgh. In the morning, before the Giants–Pirates game began, I took batting practice and starting hitting home runs while Tony and Leo Durocher looked on.

For a left-handed pull hitter, the right field line at Forbes Field was a relatively short 320-foot shot. I took dead aim on the foul pole and started hitting balls that easily cleared the fence. Fortunately, the pitches were all fastballs, which I could hit; if they'd thrown me breaking balls, which I couldn't hit, my baseball career probably would have ended right there.

Strangely, after only a couple of dozen swings I heard a loud voice. Durocher yelled, "Okay, that's enough. Let's get him off the field." I was quickly hustled into the clubhouse. I thought I must have disappointed them somehow, but Tony later told me that Pirates general manager Branch Rickey had come to the stadium early that day. Durocher was afraid that if Rickey saw me hit, he might try to grab me for the Pirates. The Giants had decided that they wanted to sign me.

All of this probably sounds a little too fast, a little too easy. A kid with marginal baseball skills hits a few balls out of the park and suddenly a major league club wants to sign him up? It certainly wouldn't happen that way today.

But you have to remember that back then, major league baseball organizations were a lot bigger than they are today. Major league teams had not only Class AAA, Class AA, and Class A minor league teams, but also Class B, C, and D teams below that. In 1952, the Giants alone had fourteen farm teams at all levels. Almost every Podunk in America had some level of major league farm club. And the pay for minor league players, and even major league players, was only a fraction of what it is today.

With hundreds of players in their organization, a team could afford to take a young player with one bankable skill and hope that with time and practice he could develop into an all-around competent major-league-level player. My one bankable skill was hitting fastballs over the right field fence. The Giants figured that if I could do that at 320 feet in Forbes Field, maybe someday they could use me to hit home runs down the 258-foot right field line at the Polo Grounds.

When Giants scout Tony Ravish stopped by my hotel room that night, he started right in trying to sign me—ideally for as little money as possible. Initially, Tony wanted to sign me up with no signing bonus—that is, no money up front. I told him no. Then he upped it to $1,000, and I still said no. Tony, exasperated, called Leo Durocher.

"The kid wants more dough," Tony said. I could hear Leo's voice coming through on the other end. He was cussing so loud that Tony had to hold the phone away from his ear.

A few minutes later, Leo showed up at the room. He was pissed off.

"Whaddaya want, kid?" he demanded.

So I told him. I wanted enough bonus money to pay for my four years of college at Hiram—that was $2,500 up front. I wouldn't take less.

This may seem almost unbelievable. An eighteen-year-old kid bargaining for more money with one of the toughest managers in baseball? But I had a powerful negotiating tool, which was my own ambivalence. I wasn't dying to go pro. If the money was good enough to pay for my top priority, which was college, then fine. But if it wasn't, I could walk away without a qualm.

I wasn't being cocky or arrogant. I just knew what I wanted, and what I had to do to get it, and I wasn't afraid to say so. I've been that way all my life.

Looking back, Leo might have booted my butt out of the hotel room and out of Pittsburgh and out of baseball forever. But he didn't.

Durocher and I couldn't have been more different. Leo was a loud, tough, profane, big-city guy who was married to a movie star, Laraine Day. He was the one who famously said, "Nice guys finish last." It was a sentiment that, although taken out of context when he said it, summed up the way he approached not only baseball, but life. He was also the guy who, as manager of the Dodgers in 1947, told the white players this about Jackie Robinson: "I don't care if the guy is yellow or black, or if he has stripes like a zebra. I'm the manager of this team and I say he plays."

Meanwhile, I was a quiet, reserved—not shy, but reserved—teenager from a small town in Ohio. And of course, Leo was white and I was black. But for some reason Leo had taken a liking to me. I guess he saw some potential there.

"Okay, kid, you got it," Leo finally said. I left Pittsburgh that day with a $2,500 signing bonus offer and a promise that I could go to spring training with the Giants the next year. And Leo even threw in a new pair of baseball spikes.

Now the only hurdle standing between me and playing baseball for a major league organization was my mother.

Back then you couldn't vote or sign a binding legal contract if you were under twenty-one. For me to accept the contract, my mother had to sign for me—and she was completely against it.

"What do you want to do that for?" she demanded. "You can't make a living playing baseball. And they aren't going to give black folks a fair shot anyway."

She had a point. Although Jackie Robinson broke the on-the-field color line in baseball in 1947, and Wally Triplett became the first black player to be drafted into and play for the National Football League in 1949, and Earl Lloyd took the court as the first black National Basketball Association player in 1950, big league professional black athletes were still relatively rare in 1952.

The salaries earned by even major league baseball players back then weren't close to what they are today. (In 2010, the average MLB salary was $3.3 million.) In 1950, near the end of his career, Joe DiMaggio was paid $100,000 a year, the highest baseball salary up to that time. Jackie Robinson, in 1950 the highest-paid Dodgers player, was making $35,000, the equivalent of about $300,000 today. But the major league minimum salary at the time was just $5,000, and the average major league player made about $10,000 to $15,000.

Sure, fifteen thousand dollars a year was okay money in the early 1950s, but it wasn't life-changing wealth. Most ballplayers wound up as ordinary working stiffs after their baseball careers were over, especially if they lacked education. One of my future teammates on the Giants, a solid player for eight years in the majors, wound up driving a cab and eventually went to prison for robbery. Another spent seven years as a star pinch hitter with the Giants and then spent the next twenty-five years of his life working on a New York Harbor tugboat.

Professional baseball may have been exciting and fun, but it wasn't a ticket to lifetime financial security.

Despite all that, my mother eventually relented and let me play, but only after I promised her that I wouldn't let baseball interfere with college and that whatever happened, I would get my degree.

As it turned out, that was the only promise I ever made to my mother that I didn't keep. Until the day she died in 2001, despite all my accomplishments in professional baseball and beyond, my mother never quite forgave me for not finishing college. She was only partially satisfied when I made sure that each of my five children received a college degree.

My mother never stopped believing that education was more important than athletics.

And as usual, she was right.

CHAPTER 4

I learned something important about baseball during spring training with the Giants in Phoenix in 1953. I learned that I still had a lot to learn about baseball.

When Leo Durocher first signed me with the Giants, I got him to promise that I could go to spring training the following season. This was unusual for a brand-new player. Ordinarily you would go straight to the minor leagues, most often at the lowest level, and then work your way up. Somehow I had the idea that I could go to spring training, show them what I could do, and then immediately start playing in the bigs.

I'm not sure why Leo even agreed to let me participate in spring training. Maybe he wanted to knock me down a peg. Or maybe he just liked having me around.

Whatever the reason, when I flew out to Phoenix that spring I was in for a big-time wake-up call.

I had never experienced that level of play before—the speed, the agility, the sheer strength. Even the minor league players who were there could run rings around me. And the guys already on the Giants' roster were like beings from another universe.

There were guys like Monte Irvin, a future Hall of Famer who had been a standout in both the Negro Leagues and with the Giants, and Hank Thompson, another Negro League alumnus. There was Bobby Thomson, who had hit the "Shot Heard Round the World" to win the pennant for the Giants in 1951; Don Mueller, who batted over .300 in three consecutive seasons and was known as "Mandrake the Magician" for his hitting skills. There was Alvin Dark, "the Swamp Fox," at shortstop, and catcher Wes Westrum, who played 902 games for the Giants behind the plate, and James "Dusty" Rhodes, one of the all-time great clutch hitters in the game.

And then there was me—Bill "Leo's Little Bobo" White.

The other guys called me that because I was Durocher's pet project, the kid whom for some reason Durocher liked and seemed to be grooming for bigger things. Most of them were nice to me— my roommate, Monte Irvin, was an especially good guy—but it was obvious they thought I wasn't ready.

And I wasn't.

Although Durocher liked me, it didn't mean that he was easy on me. Just the opposite. He was constantly on me to work harder, work harder, work harder. During infield practice, he'd come out and start hitting fungoes to me, blistering grounders that would hit my shins as often as they'd land in my glove. I remember him calling out to the other coaches, in that loud, rough, rocks-inside-a-tin-can voice of his, "I'll betcha five bucks I can hit him in the right leg this time," or "Ten bucks says I can hit him in the left leg." And often enough he did.

I played in only two games in spring training that year. One was an exhibition game against a visiting Japanese team whose pitchers specialized in breaking balls—and I struck out every time. In the other game, I did some pinch-hitting, but my fielding skills still weren't up to even spring training levels.

I had realized early on in spring training that any thoughts I had of going directly to the majors were naive. In fact, I was already contracted to play Class B ball in the Giants organization. Originally I was slated to play for their Class B team in Pennsylvania, which would have been perfect, since it was close to home. But then the Giants shifted the contract first to Knoxville, Tennessee, and later to Danville, Virginia. I'd be playing first base for the Danville Leafs at a salary of $250 a month.

I didn't know anything about Virginia or what the attitudes about race were down there. But before I went there, something happened in Phoenix that was a depressing harbinger of things to come.

Leo Durocher knew a lot of movie stars and other celebrities, and they would often come out to Phoenix for spring training. (During the off season, he had sometimes shared a house in Los Angeles with actor George Raft.) Sometimes Leo would even let some of his actor friends suit up and take the field to toss the ball around with the players.

One day a tall, good-looking guy was on the field, and we started talking. He said his name was Jeff. I hadn't recognized him, but it turned out that *Jeff* was Jeff Chandler, a pretty big movie star at the time. Although Chandler was known for Westerns, he was actually a Jewish guy from Brooklyn. We started hanging out together on the field, and at one point Jeff mentioned that he had been in a movie called *Broken Arrow,* in which he played the Apache Indian chief Cochise.

Later that evening I was passing by a movie theater in Phoenix and saw on its marquee, BROKEN ARROW, STARRING JEFF CHANDLER. So I went up to the ticket booth with my money in hand—a movie ticket cost about 35 cents back then—and the girl in the booth gave me a funny look. She left and came back with the theater manager, who told me, "I'm sorry, we don't have a balcony here."

And I thought, *So what?* I told him didn't want to sit in the balcony anyway. I just wanted a ticket to see the movie.

Finally I realized that in most movie theaters in Phoenix, as in many movie theaters across the country, blacks were restricted to balcony seats only—the movie theater equivalent of the "nose-bleed seats" high up in the stands at a major league ballpark. If there was no balcony, a black man couldn't come in.

It made me furious. I could hang out on the baseball field with the star of a big Hollywood movie, but I couldn't go into a theater to watch his film? I stalked off and went back to the team quarters at the old Adams Hotel in downtown Phoenix.

Later I angrily told my roommate, Monte Irvin, what had happened. Monte was older, in his midthirties, a veteran of the Negro Leagues before he followed Jackie Robinson into the majors and later into the Hall of Fame. He had seen a lot of what black ballplayers, and black people in general, had to suffer back then. He urged me to be patient.

"Listen, junebug," he said, "don't rock the boat. Someday all this is going to change."

Monte was right. Someday it would change.

But for me, before it got better it was going to get a whole lot worse.

CHAPTER 5

Nigger!"

The word drifted out from the stands and seemed to hang in the sultry Southern night air—or at least it did to me. Amid the rustle and hum of the crowd and the chatter of the players and the hiss of the stadium night lights, no one else even seemed to notice it. But I did.

Then it came again, louder.

"Hey, nigger! That's right, boy, I'm talking to you!"

Other voices took it up, some male, some female, even some voices of children.

"Nigger!"

"Coon!"

"Darkie!"

I glanced over at the people in the stands. Most of the men wore jeans or dirty overalls, while a few had on short-sleeved white shirts and skinny ties. The older women wore cheap faded floral-print dresses; the younger girls were in shorts. Of course, all of the faces were white. The black folks had to sit in the "colored" bleachers, far down the left field line. And all of the white faces looked angry.

I locked eyes with one guy sitting a few rows back, a middle-aged man in a checkered shirt, one stubbly cheek puffed out with a wad of chewing tobacco, a paper cup full of spit in his left hand. He didn't like my look. In the South in 1953, black men weren't supposed to look white men in the eye.

"You got a problem, nigger?" he called out.

Yeah, I had a problem.

No one had ever called me "nigger" before.

It was my first road game with the Danville Leafs, the Giants' Class B Carolina League farm team based in Danville, Virginia, a small tobacco and textile mill town just north of the North Carolina line. (Our team name was a reference not to trees but to tobacco. An earlier version of the Leafs was actually called the Tobacconists.) We were in a little town called Graham, North Carolina, playing another Class B team, the Burlington-Graham Pirates, part of the Pittsburgh organization.

And I was finding out what it meant to be a black ballplayer in the Jim Crow South.

I had just come off a long trip. After having finished spring training with the Giants in Phoenix, I had flown down to Melbourne, Florida, for spring training with the Leafs, and then took a team bus up to Danville. I hadn't known much about Virginia, in general, or Danville, in particular, when the Giants assigned me there. But before I got to Danville, I had happened to read an article in *Jet,* the African American magazine, about a seventy-six-year-old black farmer who had been arrested by a local sheriff near Danville for allegedly "eyeballing" a white woman from across a field.

Uh-oh, I thought. *Danville sure isn't going to be like Ohio.*

At the time Danville had about thirty-five thousand people,

almost half of whom were African American. But except for black women who worked in white women's homes or black men who worked in white men's farm fields or cotton mills, there was hardly any interaction between the races. Schools, churches, restaurants, hotels, buses—all were ruthlessly segregated by law.

The team found a room for me in the Holbrook-Ross district, the black section of town, in a boardinghouse run by a widow named Mrs. Wilson. I ate my meals there, or in the small restaurant that a man named Mr. Pringles ran in the basement of his house. (Actually, the soul food that Mr. Pringles served was probably better than anything I could have gotten in the white restaurants in town, even if I'd been allowed to eat in them.) Sometimes I'd sit in the restaurant and listen to black blues on the jukebox, or shoot pool over at the Harris pool hall. Sometimes I'd sit on the porch on warm summer nights and watch the moonshiners' souped-up cars drive by—early forerunners of NASCAR racers. In the afternoon I'd climb on the Main Street bus, take a seat in the back—that was the law—and ride down to the Leafs' stadium.

Like all the ballparks in the Carolina League, which covered eight small cities in Virginia and North Carolina, the Leafs' stadium wasn't much to look at. It was just a rickety, fifteen-hundred-seat wood structure with a threadbare field surrounded by a wooden wall plastered with ads for Coca-Cola and chewing tobacco and Stanback headache powders.

The stadium was the only place in Danville where I was allowed to interact with my white teammates. I didn't know where they lived, where they ate, what they did in their time off. On road trips, our bus driver would drop off the white players at their hotel and then drive me to some boardinghouse in the black section of whatever town we were in, and I wouldn't see my teammates again until we took the field. The result was that I didn't know anything about them—and most of them didn't seem to want to know much of anything about me.

For a black man in the South, minor league baseball was a lonely place to work.

I wasn't the first black player in the Carolina League. That distinction went to a man named Percy Miller Jr., a native of Danville who was the son of Percy Miller, a Negro League pitcher. Percy Jr. was signed by the Leafs in 1951, but played only nineteen games with the team, batting under .200. He never got another minor league contract.

So in 1953, I was the only black player on the Leafs and in the Carolina League altogether—which in Danville's black community made me something of a celebrity. When I walked to the bus stop in the afternoon and came home at night, people sitting on porches would call out encouragement: "You do it, Bill!" or "You show 'em, son!" And at home games, where black fans sat in the far left field section, separated from the white fans by a rope drawn up through the aisle, they would shout and cheer me on.

I was even asked to speak at the local black school, where I talked to the kids about the importance of education, and how they could be whatever they wanted to be. The kids seemed to enjoy it, although later one of the teachers told me, "We had a hard time understanding you 'cause you talked so fast!" Although I was black like them, to the black folks in Danville I was also a Northern Yankee, with the accent that went with it.

I didn't really understand it at the time, but to the black community in Danville I was a symbol of better things to come. This was before Rosa Parks and the Montgomery bus boycott, before the Freedom Riders, and long before the 1963 march in Danville when hundreds of black people marched to city hall to demand an end to segregation, only to be beaten with clubs by Danville police and city employees. It's not often recognized today, but in some ways, in the 1950s black baseball players in the Southern minor leagues—guys like Hank Aaron in Jacksonville, Florida, Curt Flood in North Carolina, and Willie McCovey, who followed me in Danville in 1956—were the point men in the fight for racial equality.

Unlike Dr. Martin Luther King Jr. and other civil rights leaders, we didn't change any laws; we were there to play baseball. But for the first time, we gave black people in the small towns and cities in the South the chance to *personally* witness black men competing with white men—and often as not, beating them. They could read about Jackie Robinson and the few other black players in the major leagues, or hear about them on the radio, but they could actually *see* us. And we forced a lot of Southern racists to see us, too.

Of course, the major league organizations didn't send us into the Southern minors to make social changes. They sent us there to hone our baseball skills, and because black players were a good draw for black baseball fans—and black people's money was just as good as white people's money.

Still, decades later a lot of black people would remember the first time they went to the local ballpark and saw a black man standing on equal footing with white men—on the field anyway. Not too long ago, I was talking about those days with an old friend, Leon Harris. In those Danville years, he lived across the street from me. "Bill, every time you walked out on that field we puffed our chests out because we had so much pride in what you were doing," Leon told me. "Back then there wasn't much that black people in Danville could rally around. But back then, you were our Obama."

That was nice of Leon to say. But I never thought of myself that way. In the early summer of 1953, I was just trying to deal with being called a "nigger."

Of course I had heard the word before; no one in America hadn't heard it said. And even back home in Warren, I'm sure there were times when people said it behind my back. But it was a word that was never allowed in our house. And no one had ever looked me in the eye and said it.

When I played home games in Danville, I didn't hear much racist talk. As a lot of minor league black players in the South noticed, the white fans were generally respectful, or at least subdued, toward the black players on their home teams. The attitude seemed to be that a black guy playing for their team was "our nigger" and not to be abused.

But it was different on the road—as I was now finding out in that first game against the Pirates in Graham, North Carolina, when the first "nigger" drifted out from the stands.

At first, except for that one quick glance into the stands, I tried to ignore the shouting. In fact, as I've said, it seemed ridiculous to me. Here I was—smart, well educated, a college student with top grades, and at $250 a month I probably was making more money than most of the people in the crowd. And yet these rednecked, stubbly-faced, gap-toothed, tobacco-stained crackers were looking down on me? I almost had to laugh—almost.

But as the game went on, it got worse. It was "What are you doing here, nigger?" when I went to the batter's box and "Look at the stupid nigger" when I took the field. Then the slurs turned to threats: "You'll be lucky if your black ass makes it out of here alive."

Ironically, among my teammates it was the Southern guys who seemed most embarrassed by the crowd. One of them, Charlie Allen, an outfielder from North Carolina, told me in a soft Southern drawl, "Don't let it get to ya, Bill." But the Northern guys on the team didn't react at all. Maybe they just couldn't believe it, or maybe they didn't care. Not even the team manager, a big Pennsylvania Polish guy named Andy Gilbert, bothered to give me any support.

When Jackie Robinson broke the color line in the majors in 1947, he was twenty-eight years old and had been carefully prepared for what he would have to face. Earlier, then Dodgers general manager Branch Rickey famously said that one reason he picked Jackie to be the first black man in the majors wasn't because Jackie was afraid to fight back, but because he had "guts enough not to."

But in 1953, I was nineteen years old and completely unprepared for what was happening. As the shouts and slurs went on, my impulse was to climb into the stands and start kicking some cracker ass. But I knew I couldn't.

So I did something else. In the middle of the eighth inning, as I jogged off the field, I raised my left hand and gave the crowd along the first base line the finger, the digital version of *Screw you!*

I was never sorry that I did it—the rednecks calling me "nigger" deserved that and worse—but in retrospect I realized that it probably was a foolish thing to do. This was, after all, the Deep South, at a time when black men had been murdered for less. Lynchings in the South were still very real. Just two years later, a fourteen-year-old black kid from Chicago named Emmett Till would be murdered by white men in Mississippi for allegedly whistling at a white woman.

A momentary silence fell over the people in the stands as they saw my upraised finger. It was as if they couldn't believe what they were seeing. Black men simply did not do that sort of thing in North Carolina in 1953. But then a wild and angry roar erupted, and shouts of "You see what that nigger did?" The slurs and the catcalls took on even greater volume.

When the game was over—we won—and my teammates and I were heading into the clubhouse, a middle-aged fat woman in a frumpy dress walked up, poked her finger in my shoulder, and said, "Boy, you got some nerve being disrespectful to all these people."

I couldn't believe it. Disrespectful? These people are out there calling me "nigger" and "coon" and this woman thinks I'm the one being disrespectful?

I didn't say anything, but Bob Knight, an outfielder from New Orleans, pushed her hand away and said, "Leave him alone. He's better than all of you."

Then things got worse. While we were showering and dressing, our combination bus driver and trainer, a guy named Harry, came in and told us there was a big crowd gathered outside between the clubhouse and the waiting bus—and they weren't happy. They wanted to get the "nigger" who had flipped them off.

Looking back on it, I probably should have been scared. But I don't frighten easily. I never have. The funny thing was that as I looked around at my white teammates, they were the ones who looked worried—especially the Southern guys. I think they knew better than the rest of us what an angry white mob could do.

Given the lack of support I'd gotten from most of my teammates when the racial slurs were being thrown at me, I wouldn't have been too surprised if some of them had offered to hand me over to the mob in exchange for safe passage to the bus. After all, they weren't my friends. Separated by law and custom in everything except baseball—in lodging, eating, socializing—we'd never had a chance to become friends.

But instead, someone suggested that we arm ourselves with our bats and if necessary fight our way through the crowd.

Which is what we did. Bats held high, we marched out of the clubhouse as a group—for once, as a true team—and headed for the bus.

Seeing us that way, twenty young men in excellent physical condition, wielding Louisville Sluggers that could bust a man's skull like a walnut, the mob fell silent and parted to let us through. Like bullies everywhere, none of the paunchy old rednecks and slack-jawed teenagers in the front ranks wanted to take us on if there was a chance they might get hurt.

We finally got to the bus and climbed aboard, and Harry quickly cranked the old crate to life. But as we pulled away, the crowd, emboldened now that we were safely on the bus, started throwing rocks. We could hear the stones hitting the back of the bus as we got the hell out of Graham.

That was the only time I had to face an angry mob in the Carolina League. Although nobody on the team ever spoke to me about it, I didn't give anyone the finger again. And even on our next road trip to Graham, the crowd seemed to have forgotten about it.

But the "nigger" shouts and taunts continued.

Some towns were worse than others—and for some reason, the town of Winston-Salem, North Carolina, was the worst of all. I remember once I was in the on-deck circle at the field and I heard someone calling out my name: "Hey Bill! Bill White!" I figured it was someone who knew me, so I looked over and there was a white guy sitting in a box seat, neatly dressed in a white shirt and tie. He looked back and shouted, "Hey Bill White. What are you looking at, nigger?"

It pissed me off, and as usual, I took my anger out on the ball, drilling a home run over the right field wall. Then at my next at-bat, I heard the same guy yell, "Well, Bill White, after that home run I guess I'll have to call you 'Mister Nigger.'" And the people in the crowd around him all laughed and started shouting, "Mister Nigger! Mister Nigger! Mister Nigger!"

(A few years later, I visited Winston-Salem for an exhibition game with the Willie Mays Major League Negro-American All-Stars Tour, an all-black team of major league players, and a young reporter from the local newspaper asked me how I'd liked playing in Winston-Salem during my Carolina League days. I don't sugarcoat things, for reporters or anybody else. "Worst town I ever played in," I told him.)

Thinking back on it, the five months I spent playing in the Carolina League was probably the worst time of my life, a time of loneliness and frustration and rage. Willie Mays always said that playing ball in the South was a lot harder for black players from the North than it was for black players who had grown up in the South, because the Northern guys weren't used to the way things were. I think that was partly true. But I also think that Northern black players like me in some ways were treated even worse than most Southern black players, because unlike them we had never had to learn how to hide our rage and frustration. It showed in our faces, and to white Southern racist eyes that made us seem "uppity," and thus deserving of even more abuse.

There was one good side to the anger I felt. It helped me focus on punishing the ball. That season I batted .298 and hit twenty home runs, second highest on the team.

Still, at the end of the season, as I headed back to Hiram College, I never wanted to see the South again.

For the 1954 season, I was promoted to the Sioux City Soos, the Giants' Class A team in the Western League. I figured it had to be better than playing in the Deep South, and mostly it was. Although sometimes it was tough on the road—including the time I wasn't allowed to eat at that burger joint outside Wichita—most of the time I stayed in the same cut-rate hotels as my white teammates, ate in the same restaurants, and even socialized with them after the games. For the first time in professional baseball, I felt like I was truly an accepted member of the team.

Another reason I looked forward to playing with the Soos was because at the start of the season they had another black player on the team, a guy named Marshall Bridges. Bridges, who was from Jackson, Mississippi, was a few years older than me and had played with the Memphis Red Sox of the Negro Leagues. We were assigned as roommates and immediately hit it off.

Unfortunately, within weeks Bridges was sent down to another team. (He eventually became a pitcher for the St. Louis Cardinals and won a World Series ring as a key relief pitcher for the New York Yankees in 1962.) And once again, I was the only black player on my team.

After that, the Soos' management tried to hook me up with a Hispanic roommate. Apparently they thought, *Well, White's a colored guy, and Hispanics are sort of colored guys, so they'll probably get along.*

The only problem with that was that Hispanic players didn't think of themselves as "colored guys." In the complicated racial atmosphere of the time, most Hispanic players thought they were socially above the black players, and worried that if they hung out with the black players they'd also be treated like the black players.

For example, my first roommate with the Soos was a guy named Ramon Conde, a third baseman from Puerto Rico. Ramon didn't speak very much English, but it was pretty clear that he was uncomfortable being around me. On our first night in a room together, Ramon wouldn't let me turn out the lights. I don't know if he was afraid of the dark or afraid of me, but we had to lie there all night with a naked sixty-watt bulb blazing over our heads. Ramon quickly asked for another roommate. (He made it briefly to the majors, playing fourteen games for the Chicago White Sox in 1962, and going to bat nineteen times without a hit.)

Next, I roomed with Dave Garcia, the Soos manager. As I said, Dave, who later managed the Cleveland Indians and the California Angels, was a good guy who sympathized with the problems I was facing as a black player in the slowly integrating minor leagues.

"Bill," Dave told me once, "you're on your way to being a great, great player. When you make it to the majors, you can put all this crap behind you."

I hoped he was right. But the crap wasn't over with yet.

I did well with the Soos that year, hitting .319 with thirty home runs. I went back to Hiram for another term, and then the Giants told me I'd been assigned to their Class AA affiliate team in the Texas League, the Dallas Eagles.

Although it was a step up in the farm system, from A to AA, my first reaction was "No way." No way was I ever, ever going to play in a Southern minor league again. I told them I would quit first—and I meant it.

But then the Eagles owner, a wealthy oil man named Dick Burnett, called and started telling me what a progressive city Dallas was, with a large and vibrant black community, and how much the local fans loved the team's players—the black ones included. Finally I relented.

Burnett was partly right. The Eagles—whose Dallas forerunners included such teams as the Steers, the Rebels, even the Hams and the Submarines—were extremely popular in Dallas. Although their home field was a ten-thousand-seat stadium in the Oak Park section of town, a few years earlier the Eagles had attracted more than fifty thousand fans to a special game at the Cotton Bowl, the second largest attendance ever for a minor league game.

And yes, the white fans in Dallas were respectful to their own black players, me included. But it was that "our niggers" syndrome at work. When black players from opposing teams took the field, many of the white Dallas fans were just as racially vile and insulting as any rednecks in Carolina. And when the Eagles went on the road to places like Beaumont, Texas, or Shreveport, Louisiana, I was bombarded with "nigger," "darkie," "spade," and "coon."

(Once during a game in Shreveport, there was a white guy loudly calling me a "nigger" as he walked up and down the aisles hawking copies of *The Sporting News*. After the game, this same guy walked into the clubhouse and actually tried to sell me a copy of the magazine—as if he hadn't been calling me names just minutes before. I jumped up, fists clenched, and shouted, "Get the hell out of here, you asshole!" The guy went pale and ran out of there like his pants were on fire, and the entire team, me included, started laughing. It was something I noticed again and again. People would cheerfully call somebody a "nigger" from the safety of the stands, but face-to-face they usually didn't have the guts.)

It was all slightly more bearable because, for the first time in my professional baseball career, I had company. There were three other black players on the Eagles: Ozzie Virgil Sr., the third baseman, a former marine who later became the first man from the Dominican Republic to play in the major leagues; a pitcher from Cuba named Roque "Rocky" Contreras; and Jim Tugerson, a pitcher who had played in the Negro Leagues.

Jim "Schoolboy" Tugerson symbolizes the professional barriers that black players faced in those days. Jim was a big guy, six foot four and almost two hundred pounds, with a powerful sidearm fastball that could brush batters back from both sides of the plate. A World War II veteran, he had pitched for the Indianapolis Clowns of the Negro American League—his roommate was Hank Aaron—and later signed with the Arkansas Hot Springs Bathers, the first black player in the all-white Cotton States League. His brother, Leander, signed with the Bathers as well.

But the Cotton States League wouldn't let them play. The league owners kicked the Bathers out of the league for signing black players, and Jim moved on to the Knoxville Smokies, where he won a phenomenal twenty-nine games in the 1953 season. He was moved up to Dallas the next year, but by that time he was thirty-one years old and his pitching ability was starting to fade. Although he played five seasons with Dallas, he never made it to the majors, and he finally wound up as a police officer in Florida.

I often think about black players like Jim, guys who easily could have made it in the majors if they'd been born a few years later, or if the racial barriers in baseball had been broken a few years earlier. There were far too many of them.

Jim gave me some advice that season with the Eagles that helped me go on, not only that season but throughout my baseball career.

"Stay focused on the game," Jim would constantly tell me. "Don't react to those racist rednecks in the crowd calling you names. They're trying to sidetrack you, take your mind off the game. Don't let 'em."

It was good advice, from someone who had been there, and I took it. I still heard the racial slurs coming from the stands, but I never again let myself show any reaction to them. I didn't give the bastards the satisfaction.

I did well in Dallas that season, batting .295 with twenty-two home runs. After the season, the Giants asked me to play winter baseball in Puerto Rico, where major league prospects could hone their skills. It wasn't an easy decision for me. The pay was good, about $5,000, and I knew the higher level of play would be good for my baseball career. But it meant that I would have to forgo my college education—temporarily, I thought at the time.

Winter ball was a great experience, allowing me to play with major leaguers like Don Zimmer, Roberto Clemente, and Ruben Gomez. For the 1956 season, I was moved up to the Giants' AAA team in Minneapolis, the Millers—the level just below the majors.

My three seasons in the minors had made me a much better ballplayer, far removed from the green kid who had showed up at Giants spring training in 1953. I had worked hard, not only in the games but in endless practice sessions, instilling the muscle memory that lets a ballplayer instantly react to every small nuance of every situation, in the batter's box or on the field. I was young, strong, confident, and I knew I was ready for the big leagues. All I had to do was wait for The Call.

In the spring of 1956, it came.

CHAPTER 6

May 7, 1956, was a warm evening in Busch Stadium in St. Louis. The New York Giants were in a three-game series against the Cardinals.

And for the first time in the major leagues, I was in the batter's box.

I'd gotten the call in my hotel room at three o'clock that morning, while I was in Indianapolis on a road trip with the Minneapolis Millers. The voice on the phone sounded a lot like Eddie Stanky, the manager of my team. Stanky was a former major league second baseman and manager who'd been fired by the Cardinals the year before and was now marking time by managing the AAA Millers.

"Congratulations, Bill," the voice said. "You're going to the Giants. Get yourself ready."

I didn't believe it. I was still half asleep, and middle-of-the-night practical jokes were common in baseball.

"Come on, it's late," I said into the phone. "Stop playing around."

"No, Bill, it's true," the voice said—and now I realized that it really was Eddie. "You're going to St. Louis to join the Giants. Your flight leaves this morning."

Getting called up to the Giants wasn't entirely unexpected. At spring training that season, I had thought I had a shot at making the roster, but the Giants already had a first baseman, Gail Harris, who had done pretty well in the previous season. But now in early 1956 he was struggling, hitting just .132 in his first dozen games. The Giants needed a replacement.

I was pleased at being called up, but not overly excited or nervous. That wasn't my nature, and besides, there wasn't time. I had a flight to catch.

I made the flight, barely, but my equipment bag didn't. When I got to St. Louis, the team had a Giants uniform ready for me—I was number 45—but the equipment manager had to find a pair of spikes. I thought I was going to have to make my major league debut in spikes that I hadn't broken in yet, but just before the game started my gear bag caught up with me.

Now it was the top of the second inning, my first time at bat. Cardinals pitcher Ben Flowers, who had a mean curveball, got a couple of strikes on me, along with two balls, one of them a high inside fastball, a "brushback" designed to see if he could rattle me—which it didn't. On his fifth pitch, he threw a curveball that just nicked the outside corner of the plate.

Damn it, I thought. *Strike three.* I was just turning to walk back to the dugout when I heard umpire Lee Ballanfant call out, "Ball three!"

So I had another chance. With a full count and me being a brand-new rookie, I figured Flowers wouldn't risk another breaking ball, that he would try to challenge me with a fastball. And he did, throwing a heater right down the middle of the plate.

There's a physical sensation when you connect with a ball in just the right way, a kinetic charge that travels through the bat and into your arms and then all the way down to your spikes. As you complete your swing, you know that ball is going out of the park.

That's what happened with that fastball. It soared over the twenty-five-foot wire fence that extended above the eleven-foot concrete wall in right field and hit the roof that covered the right field stands.

In my first major league at-bat, I had hit a home run.

That doesn't happen very often. In the first sixty years of the major leagues, out of thousands of players, I was only the thirtieth player to do it. (In all, between 1895 and 2010, only a little over a hundred players have hit homers in their first major league at-bats.) But as I rounded the bases, it never occurred to me to be particularly excited. I had hit plenty of home runs so far during my baseball career, and as far as I was concerned this was just another one. The fact that it was in a major league ballpark, in front of thousands of people, really didn't have an impact on me.

People sometimes ask me how it felt to take the field for the first time in a major leaguer's uniform. Playing in the majors is the dream of millions of American kids, so people expect you to talk about how excited you were, how in awe you were of the other players, how it felt like a dream come true. They're surprised when I tell them that for me, that first game in the big leagues was just another day at work—and that first home run was nothing special.

I don't mean to disappoint them. But it all has to do with the way I felt about baseball at the time.

Back then especially, ballplayers were supposed to talk about how much they loved the game, what a privilege it was to play. And maybe that was partly true. Maybe some of the great players loved playing the game, guys like Willie Mays and Stan Musial and Ernie Banks and a few others. Maybe that was why they were such great players.

Some players would even say things like, "I'd play for free if they weren't paying me." But to me that was just pure nonsense. We were professionals. Baseball was our job. And for the vast majority of players, in my opinion, love of the game had nothing to do with it.

It certainly didn't with me. At the start, baseball had been a way to get money for college, and then it became a way to make a living. Baseball was my *business*.

The team owners and front office management guys I worked for certainly looked at it that way. I realized early on that to them any individual player was just a piece of meat. They would keep you on as long as you were useful, but the minute you weren't, you'd be gone—and it wouldn't matter what you had done in the past, or if you had a sick child at home, or if you were broke and had nowhere to go. Business was business, and while baseball owners may have loved owning baseball teams, most of them didn't love baseball players.

And of course they would pay you as little as they could get away with. I started that 1956 season on the Giants team with a contract for $4,200, but after a month or so Giants owner Horace Stoneham, who was notoriously cheap with his players, bumped me up another $1,500. I thought I was getting a raise for a job well done. Only later did I realize that my initial contract had inaccurately listed me as a "provisional" player so the Giants could avoid paying me the league minimum salary. The $1,500 "raise" only brought me up to the league minimum that I should have been getting in the first place. They did stuff like that all the time.

So yeah, I respected many of the guys I played with and worked with in baseball. And I respected the game.

But I didn't love baseball. Because I knew that baseball would never love me back.

That approach occasionally caused me trouble with owners and front office types. Some of them thought I was cold and arrogant;

I was told that on occasion the word *uppity* was used, although never to my face.

But I also think that not loving baseball, not sentimentalizing it, actually made me a better player. Being analytical, and emotionally detached, I was never nervous in the batter's box or on the field. I gave it 100 percent effort, and if I didn't get some kind of emotional high when I did well, on the flip side I wasn't emotionally battered when I failed. That's important in a game in which even the best hitters will fail in the batter's box 70 percent of the time.

So as I rounded the bases after that first home run in Busch Stadium, I wasn't overcome with joy. I was just thinking about what I had to do next.

I did well in that first game. In my next at-bat, I smacked a double that missed going over the right field wall by a couple of inches, and later I singled. When the game was over—unfortunately, the Cardinals beat us, 6–3—I had three hits in four at-bats.

After the game, in the locker room, Willie Mays came over and put his hand on my shoulder.

"That was a good start," Willie said. "You're going to be all right."

That was the extent of the celebrating of my first game in the majors. I didn't hear anything at all from my mother or the rest of my family that night.

They still weren't sure that baseball was a proper job for a grown man to have.

Nineteen fifty-six turned out to be a good year for me. It reaffirmed what I already knew: I could play in the major leagues.

Of course, like any rookie, I had to prove myself not only to my teammates but also to my opponents. Baseball was a much rougher, more physical game back then, with less concern about players getting hurt. The guys you were playing against had plenty of opportunities to test what kind of a player you were, and what kind of a man. That testing could take place on the field, where a runner might slide in with spikes high, or barrel straight at you to try to drive you off the bag too early, or spike you if that didn't work. And testing inevitably took place in the batter's box. The first time you faced a pitcher, any pitcher, you could be sure he would try to intimidate you, throwing a fastball high and inside and, ideally, dropping your ass in the dirt. It was worth a wasted pitch to him to see if he could scare you, make you think more about getting hit than getting *a* hit.

I guess it would have been the rational thing to be afraid of getting tagged with a beanball, especially back then, when hardly any of us wore batting helmets. An average major league fastball travels at about 130 feet per second, which is only about one-sixth the speed of a .45-caliber pistol bullet—but then a bullet doesn't weigh a third of a pound. Although only one major league player has been killed by a beanball (that in 1920), a guy could still get seriously hurt by a pitch. For example, Don Zimmer, my old teammate in winter ball in Puerto Rico, took a fastball to the temple in the minor leagues in 1953 and was in a coma for two weeks; three years later in the majors, he took another beaning that broke his cheekbone.

I've always thought that while strength and good eyesight and quick reflexes are critical if you want to be a good hitter, the single most important element is fearlessness, the ability to stay focused and not to be intimidated in the batter's box. Obviously, a guy would never make it to the majors in the first place if he was afraid of getting hit, but even at that level some players were easier to intimidate than others.

I was never intimidated. And I was seldom hit by a pitch.

By the end of the season, my batting average wasn't what I wanted—just .256, partly because for some reason the team management tried to convert me from a pull hitter to hitting all over the field, a big mistake in a long center field park like the Polo Grounds.

But I still managed to drive in fifty-nine runs and hit twenty-two home runs—second to Willie Mays, who hit thirty-six.

Unfortunately, 1956 wasn't a good year for the Giants. Although they had swept the World Series against Cleveland in 1954, in just two years the team had fallen to second-tier status. We still had some great players, but some of the guys from the World Series team were getting older, some had been traded, and kids like me were taking their places. Leo Durocher had quit the year before to become a sportscaster, and while his replacement, Bill Rigney, a former Giants infielder, was a good enough guy, it just wasn't the same.

In addition, the fans weren't showing up. The neighborhood around the Polo Grounds in Upper Manhattan had gone seedy in recent years. Parking was scarce, and with the team dropping below .500, the gate for the season was way down. Only about six hundred thousand tickets were sold that year, the lowest gate in the National League, and only about half of what the Giants had drawn just two years earlier. At a time when good seats for a game at the Polo Grounds could be had for a couple of bucks, that didn't leave much money to run a ball club.

As a result, the old bathtub-shaped stadium, with its short right and left fields and impossibly long center field, was falling apart from lack of maintenance. And owner Horace Stoneham was already plotting to move the team west, originally to Minneapolis but then later settling on San Francisco, a move that eventually would see him vilified by angry New York fans and publicly confronted by weeping children begging him not to take the Giants away.

Despite the Giants' financial troubles, it was still the major leagues, which in terms of physical comforts was a huge step up from the minors. No more long hours of "ridin' the dog"—a Grey-hound bus—to road games. Although we took a train to games in Philadelphia, we flew everywhere else on a chartered Capital Airlines plane. The hotel accommodations were usually upscale, although in Chicago, St. Louis, Philadelphia, and Cincinnati the black players still couldn't stay in the same hotels as the whites, and had to be put up in the black sections of the city. It was insulting, but to tell you the truth, we really didn't mind it that much. We had a lot more fun at the restaurants and clubs in the black section, and since no white manager or coach was ever going to venture into the black area to check on us, we didn't have to worry about curfew.

It was a pretty good life, even on the road. And it was an especially good life for a young ballplayer in New York City.

The Giants had a guy named Frank Forbes who served as a kind of guardian and all-around fix-it man for the team's black players. A former basketball player with the New York Rens, later a boxing commissioner, promoter, and referee—he was the first African American to referee a world championship fight—Frank seemed to know everybody in New York. Once Frank gave me a decal to put on my 1955 Ford and told me, "As long as you have that, you can park anywhere you want in the city with no problems." I don't know what kind of fix Frank had put in, but I never got a parking ticket in New York.

When I first came on the team, Frank found an apartment for me on St. Nicholas Avenue in a black section of Manhattan that bordered Harlem and Washington Heights. Actually, it was just a room in an apartment occupied by a Pullman train porter named John Wideman and his wife, but it was comfortable enough, and convenient. I could walk to work at the Polo Grounds in ten minutes, and the nightlife in Harlem was close by.

Harlem was an exciting, vibrant place back then. The Red Rooster at the corner of Seventh Avenue and 138th Street was a favorite spot, the place to go if you liked Southern-fried chicken and collard greens. Joe Williams, Joe Louis, Sugar Ray Robinson, the comedian Nipsey Russell, Adam Clayton Powell, the first black congressman from New York, and so on—all of Harlem's elite went to the Red Rooster. Down the street was Small's Paradise, one of the most famous of the Harlem nightclubs, owned at that time by a New York radio DJ and music promoter, Tommy "Dr. Jive" Smalls. Small's was the place for black ballplayers to hang out. Whenever the Giants or the Dodgers or the Yankees had a home game, chances were you'd see Roy Campanella or Jim Gilliam or Don "Newk" Newcombe holding court in Small's.

And of course, there was Willie Mays.

I had first met Willie at spring training in Phoenix before the 1956 season. (Willie had been in the army when I'd gone to Giants spring training in 1953.) Although he was only a few years older than I was, he quickly became a mentor to me. Willie would invite me over to his house in the black section of town, and sometimes we'd hang out at the black American Legion Hall or the black Elks Lodge, shooting pool. When I came up to the Giants a few months later, Willie took me under his wing. At one point I even lived with Willie and his wife in the East Elmhurst section of Queens, known as the "black Beverly Hills" and home to such celebrities as Ella Fitzgerald and Louis Armstrong.

Willie was a bona fide superstar by then, throughout the nation and in New York City, but especially in Harlem. Friendly, personable, with a great smile, Willie was the kind of guy who lit up every room he ever walked into. He couldn't go anywhere in Harlem without photographers following him and famous people coming up to say hello. As for me, I was just the kid who happened to be with Willie Mays.

In fact, it was with Willie on the sidewalk outside of Small's Paradise that I first spoke with Jackie Robinson.

I guess you could say that I had met Jackie before then. I had "met" him on first base at Ebbets Field, four days after I'd been called up to the Giants as their first baseman, when Jackie got a walk. As he'd jogged up to first base, I had expected him to say something, maybe just a "How's it going?" But Jackie never said a word. He didn't even look in my direction. Jackie was 100 percent business.

Later that summer I "met" Jackie again when the Giants were playing the Dodgers at Roosevelt Stadium in Jersey City. (The Dodgers played seven games at the minor league stadium in 1956 and 1957 as part of an unsuccessful effort to get Brooklyn to replace Ebbets Field.) Jackie chopped a short grounder that our pitcher, Johnny Antonelli, had to hustle to field, and since Jackie was extremely fast from home to first, I had to go into full stretch to try to make the play. Meanwhile, I could see Jackie bearing down on me on the infield side of the line. Jackie wasn't particularly tall, just five eleven, but he was solid, and I could tell that all 195 speeding pounds of him was ready to step on me or knock me over to break up the play. The result was that I think I pulled off the bag just a little early, but the umpire called him out anyway. I was impressed with what an intense competitor Jackie was.

But the first time I ever spoke with Jackie was on the sidewalk in front of Small's. Jackie came up to say hello to Willie, and after they talked a bit he finally noticed me and stuck out his hand.

"Hey, kid. How you doing?" he said. And the best I could manage was "Hi."

Years later, when I was involved in a bitter controversy over segregation in spring training, Jackie went out of his way to offer me his support, which I deeply appreciated. Jackie was not the greatest baseball player ever, but he was a great man.

Willie Mays was both.

There were a lot of guys in baseball who could do one thing well—hit for percentages, hit for power, run, throw, field. But Willie could do them all, and do most of them better than anybody else. He had a career batting average of .302, had 3,283 hits and 660 career home runs, was an All-Star every year from 1954 to 1973—and was voted Most Valuable Player in two of those All-Star Games—won twelve Gold Glove Awards, and was twice the National League MVP. As far as I'm concerned, he was the best all-around baseball player who ever lived.

His athletic ability was amazing. But more important than that, he had a brilliant mind.

Everybody talks about Willie's over-the-shoulder catch on Vic Wertz in the 1954 World Series against Cleveland—they call it, simply, "The Catch"—but to me that's only because it was a big game and it was on television. The greatest catch I ever saw Willie make was years later, in a regular-season game, Giants versus the Cardinals, when a Cardinals batter hit a shallow pop-up and the Giants' young second baseman misjudged it, and Willie came charging in from center field to make a diving snag on the ball just before it hit the infield dirt.

It wasn't just the physical ability to make that play that was so amazing, or the speed and the agility it required. More important was the way Willie had been able to read the players and the situation, to predict what the batter would do with a particular pitch, to see from the tilt of the second baseman's head and the shape of his shoulders that he had lost the ball, and then to instantly respond. It was his lightning mind as much as his lightning body that made him such a great ballplayer.

So for me to be able to hang out with Willie Mays, to be able to tap into that mind and that knowledge, was one of the greatest gifts a young ballplayer could have.

I remember riding to the stadium with Willie in his tan Cadillac while he gave me a primer on whatever pitcher we might be facing that day.

Joe Black of the Cincinnati Redlegs? (The Reds were briefly renamed the Redlegs in the mid-1950s so nobody would think they were communists.) Joe's basically a fastball pitcher, Willie would tell me. That's his out pitch, his money pitch. Quick slider, not much of a curve. Lew Burdette of the Milwaukee Braves? Always throws screwballs to lefties, but on a really big pitch he'll load the ball up and throw a spitter. Warren Spahn? Curveballs and sliders to a lefty, never a screwball. Our Small's Paradise buddy, Don Newcombe of the Dodgers? Might come in with a slider, a curveball every once in a while, but his out pitch is a fastball. But if you see Newk stick his tongue out the corner of his mouth, he's going to throw a change-up.

And it wasn't just pitchers. Willie knew the subtle signals a certain runner would give off before he tried to steal, the way a certain first baseman held his glove just before a pick-off. He knew which umpires were low-ball umpires and high-ball umpires and which umpires had a wide plate. It seemed like he knew everything—and he was right on the money every time.

Willie Mays would have been a hell of a manager after his long playing career ended. It's a tragedy that because of Major League Baseball's stubborn resistance to hiring black managers and executives, he was never given the chance.

At the end of the 1956 season, I thought my future was all planned out for me. I would play winter ball in Puerto Rico, which paid decent money, and the following season I'd come back and play first base for the Giants. I was even planning to get married to my high school sweetheart, Mildred, while I was in Puerto Rico.

But then I got drafted—not by the NFL or the NBA, but by the USA. The United States Army.

Military service was a fact of life for most young American men back then—professional athletes included. Willie Mays had been drafted in 1952, during the Korean War, and served in the stateside army. Hank Thompson had been an army machine gunner in the Battle of the Bulge, and Monte Irvin had been an army engineer.

Joe DiMaggio had been an air force sergeant in the war, and Ted Williams was a fighter pilot in both World War II and Korea. Jackie Robinson had been an army lieutenant in World War II, and, long before Rosa Parks, he caused controversy when he refused to sit in the back of a bus at Fort Hood in Texas.

The point is that back then, when your country called, you answered—whether you really wanted to or not. It was harder to get a deferment then, and unlike in a later time, draft dodgers faced heavy criticism from the press and public, especially if they were professional athletes or celebrities. Even Elvis Presley went without any public complaint when he was drafted in 1958.

There were two ways I could fulfill my military obligation. The Giants' general manager, Chub Feeney, wanted me to go into a reserve program, where I would do six months' training and then go to reserve meetings once a month for the next five and a half years. That would have let me continue to play for the Giants, but it also meant I could be called up to active duty at any time. The other way was to do my two years' active service and get it over with.

I decided to get it over with. I said good-bye to my winter baseball teammates in Puerto Rico. *"Yo voy trabajar para Tio Sam,"* I told them—which I think meant "I'm going to work for Uncle Sam"—and took a two-year hiatus from big league baseball.

The army sent me to basic training at Fort Knox, Kentucky, and because I scored high on aptitude tests they made me a supply clerk. In classic army tradition, once the supply sergeant got me up to speed, he basically turned the supply room over to me and retired to the NCO Club (Non-Commissioned Officers Club).

Supply was a good job in the army. It was like running a small business, and since the various unit commanders were always in need of supplies, they were always nice to me even though I was just a lowly private first class. The job also gave me plenty of time to play baseball.

As you might expect, the commanding officer was eager to have a pro ballplayer on his Fort Knox team, and because it would be a break from the supply room, I agreed to play. We traveled by bus from Alabama to Missouri to Illinois, playing other military bases' teams. It was fun—until an incident in Missouri reminded me of how little the country had progressed since those days when I was in the minor leagues.

We had just finished a game at Fort Leonard Wood and had stopped to eat at a restaurant outside the base. There were twenty of us, all in uniform, but when we sat down at a table a waitress came up to me and said, "We don't serve coloreds."

Somehow this was even worse than being refused service as a civilian, or being forced to stay in separate hotels in some cities when I was on the road with the Giants. Here I was, wearing my country's uniform, nine years after President Truman desegregated the military, just a few years after black soldiers had been fighting and dying in Korea, and I still couldn't eat a burger in some dive restaurant in Missouri?

It made me furious. I got up and stalked out, and so did Lee Butz, a semi-pro player who is still one of my closest friends. A couple of the other white players left the restaurant, too, and we all wound up not eating. But the rest of my army teammates stayed in the restaurant and ate.

That pissed me off. I decided then and there that I would finish up the season with the Fort Knox team, but I would never play with them again.

And I didn't. We ended the season with an All-Army tournament at Fort Knox that featured some really fine ballplayers. For example, the Fort Carson team included future American League All-Star Leon Wagner, future Giants slugger Willie Kirkland, and a guy named Charley Pride, a former Negro Leagues player and future country-western star. Afterward, there was a lot of pressure on me to continue playing with the Fort Knox team, but I flat-out refused.

I didn't give up baseball completely, though. On weekends, I'd drive over to Lexington, Kentucky, and play semi-pro ball with a team sponsored by a restaurant called Frisch's Big Boy. It wasn't exactly the major leagues, but they paid me $50 a game, and I needed the money. My Giants salary had stopped when I went into the army. I was now a married man, and my army pay as a private first class was only $90 a month before deductions. With a double-header on a Saturday, I could make more in one weekend with Frisch's Big Boy than I made in a month in the army.

(Even the semi-pro league wasn't entirely free of racial restrictions. This was, after all, Kentucky. In order to mollify the white fans, and to keep black players from dominating the league, the teams were allowed to have only five black players on the roster and never more than three on the field at the same time.)

I finally finished my army service after twenty-one months at Fort Knox. The army gave you a three-month "early out" if you had a civilian job waiting for you, which I assumed I did. I assumed the job waiting for me was the first-string slot playing first base for the New York Giants.

But as it turned out, I was wrong.

After I had left for the army, the Brooklyn Dodgers made a move that shocked New York and baseball fans in general. In December 1956, they had traded Jackie Robinson to their archrival New York Giants for $35,000 cash and pitcher Dick Littlefield. The Giants were planning to play Jackie at my old position, first base.

Jackie was still a superstar, but he was thirty-seven years old then and already showing signs of the diabetes that would eventually kill him at the too-young age of fifty-three. Less than a month later, he announced that he would refuse the trade, and instead took a position as vice president of the New York–based Chock Full o'Nuts coffee company.

But by the time I reported back to the Giants in the last month of the 1958 season—the Giants' first season in San Francisco—there was a new kid in town.

Orlando Cepeda, a native of Puerto Rico, was twenty-one years old and had been called up to the Giants at the start of the season to play first. By the time I got back, he was well on his way to being named Rookie of the Year, with a season average of .312, twenty-five home runs, and ninety-six RBIs—second only to Willie Mays in stats. Meanwhile, waiting in the wings for the Giants was minor league first baseman Willie McCovey, who was having a great season. Both Cepeda and McCovey were future Hall of Famers—and I had gone from a starter and being a big part of the Giants' future to being low man on a three-man totem pole.

I played in only twenty-six games that last month of the '58 season, mostly as a pinch hitter and in the outfield—and I'm the first to admit I was a terrible outfielder. I couldn't judge fly balls, I couldn't throw, and I couldn't cover the ground.

I wasn't happy about my contract for the upcoming 1959 season, either. I wanted $12,000; the Giants offered $10,000. So when I reported to spring training in Phoenix for the 1959 season, and a reporter for the New York *Daily News* asked me how I thought I fit in with the team, I told him I didn't fit in at all.

"You've got a first baseman [Cepeda] who's tearing up the ball and another first baseman [McCovey] who's had a hell of a season in the minors," I said. "I think the Giants should trade me."

My logic was sound. If I stayed with the Giants, I wouldn't play very much, which would make my stats go down, which would make me less valuable to the team, which would mean I'd get less money. Those were just the hard facts.

The comment about wanting to be traded made Chub Feeney furious. Back then ballplayers, and perhaps especially black ballplayers, weren't just supposed to be happy playing for a team; they were supposed to be *grateful*. And here I had basically told the Giants to go to hell.

It was that "uppity" thing again.

The Giants started playing me in the outfield during spring training, mostly so other teams could see me batting and maybe raise my value as a trade. Finally one day Feeney called me up to his hotel room and asked me to sit down.

"I found a place where you'll be able to play," he said. "You're going to St. Louis."

At the time, St. Louis was the worst city in the league for black players. We couldn't stay at white hotels there, and couldn't eat in the white restaurants. For black players on the road, it was a terrible environment.

But the more I thought about it, the more I realized that at least in St. Louis I'd have the chance to play. And after all, Busch Stadium was where I'd hit my first major league home run, a stadium that let a left-handed pull hitter like me post some big numbers. (The stadium's name had been changed from Sportsman's Park to Busch Stadium in 1953, after Anheuser-Busch bought the Cardinals.)

"Okay, St. Louis is fine with me," I finally told Feeney.

Willie Mays was unhappy when he heard about it. Professionally, he hated to lose a young player whose career he'd helped guide, and whom he thought had real potential to help the team. Personally, he had been my mentor and friend, the guy I had hung out with in Harlem, the big brother who had even let me stay with him and his wife in New York and San Francisco. Willie would miss me, and I would miss him.

On a professional level, though, I couldn't have been happier. On March 25, 1959, the Giants announced that they had traded me to the St. Louis Cardinals. Eventually it would turn out to be one of the best moves of my life.

CHAPTER 7

I'm tired of this bullshit, Joe," I said. "How much longer are we going to be treated like we're less than human beings? I think about this every day, and it gnaws away at my heart."

It was 1961, in the Cardinals clubhouse at spring training in St. Petersburg, Florida. *Joe* was Joe Reichler, a longtime sports reporter for the Associated Press, a guy with bushy black eyebrows and a nose for controversial stories. Like the rest of the reporters who covered baseball, Joe moved freely around the locker room—and when I saw him there I pulled him aside.

I was fed up. I had had it. I wasn't going to be quiet anymore about a major industry—Major League Baseball—that meekly allowed its employees to be harassed and insulted and treated with contempt while those same employees were helping to bring in millions of dollars for their employers.

And if speaking out cost me my job, screw it, I didn't care.

In 1961, I was about to start my third season with the St. Louis

Cardinals, and as a player I was hitting my stride—this after what I'll admit was a pretty shaky start.

When I started with the Cardinals in the 1959 season, they hadn't put me in my preferred position on first base—because of Stan Musial. Stan "The Man" was already an icon in St. Louis—he spent his entire twenty-two-season career with the Cardinals— and although he had been a great outfielder, he was getting older and couldn't chase down the flies as easily anymore. But you don't bench an icon, especially when he's still a great hitter. So they often played Stan on first and put me in the outfield.

Stan did fine at first base, but for me the outfield was a disaster. Again, I couldn't run, catch, or throw, at least not at the level the major leagues demanded. I simply wasn't a major league outfielder.

I remember one spring training game against the White Sox when Luis Aparicio, one of the great base runners of all time, was on second and a Sox hitter sent a long fly ball to deep center field. I had been playing shallow and had to run back to catch the fly— and after I caught it, my momentum kept me going a few more steps. By the time I stopped and turned around, Aparicio had tagged up and was well on his way to the plate; he beat my relay easily. It probably was one of the few times in major league history that a runner scored from second base on a sacrifice fly.

The other guys on the team would rib me about my outfielding skills, or lack of them. One time I walked into the clubhouse before a home game against the Dodgers and the other guys were all laughing because I had been penciled in to play center field. Not only did I have to play at my worst position in front of the home fans, but the game was going to be broadcast on national TV! I had three errors in that game, all of them beamed live across the nation.

My outfielding wasn't just embarrassing. It was actually dangerous—dangerous to me. Once I failed to correctly "read" the ground while running for a ball and plowed headfirst into the concrete wall at Busch Stadium. That put me in the hospital for three days. Another time I ran into the chain-link fence at Candlestick Park in San Francisco and had to walk around for a week with fence marks on my face.

But even worse than my fielding struggles was my hitting. Shortly after the 1959 season started, I was hitting just .190. Although my first home run in the major leagues had been at Busch Stadium, the right field in St. Louis was a lot longer than right field at the Polo Grounds. And since I had always been a fastball pull hitter, the opposing pitchers had learned how to pitch to me with curveballs and change-ups.

There's an old joke in baseball about the rookie who starts off his first major league season drilling fastball after fastball over the fence. Then a few weeks later he sends a telegram: "Dear Ma, I'll be home soon. They've started throwing curveballs."

I was worried that was going to be me.

Finally the Cardinals handed me over to first base coach Harry Walker, a former player and manager who was then also acting as the batting coach. Before then I had always resisted any efforts by coaches to change my batting style. I always figured that if what I was doing was working, why mess with it? But when you're batting .190, you don't resist.

Harry had been an excellent singles hitter in his playing days—in 1947, he had batted .363—and he was also a great teacher. He got me off my front foot, got me to lay back a little, taught me how to wait a little longer with my swing. It gave the pitcher more of an advantage on the inside but it took the outside of the plate away from him—and I found that I could not only pull for power to right field but also hit for percentages to left. By the time of the All-Star break, I was hitting .360, and I finished the season at .302. As far as I was concerned, Harry Walker had saved my major league career.

In 1959, I played in my first All-Star Game—a great honor for me, since back then All-Star players were voted on solely by the other players, coaches, and managers. In the 1960 season, I was finally playing mostly first base—Musial, who was almost forty, was increasingly having to sit out—and again I made the All-Star team. That year I went on to win my first Gold Glove Award, given to the most outstanding fielder in each position in each league.

The only downside was that the Cardinals weren't doing well. In 1959, St. Louis finished seventh in the league, and while the 1960 season was a little better, with the team finishing third, we weren't living up to our potential. In my opinion, a lot of that—not all of it, but a lot—had to do with our manager, Solly Hemus.

Solly had been an infielder for the Cardinals until he was traded to the Phillies in 1956. When he left, he wrote a gushy letter to Cardinals owner August "Gussie" Busch, saying how much he loved the Cardinals, how he hoped he could come back, et cetera. It must have worked, because at the start of '59 season Hemus was back with the Cardinals as a player-manager.

Hemus hadn't been a great player, but he was a hustler. The thing he was best at was taking hits at the plate—hits to himself, not on the ball. In one year alone, he was hit twenty times. He would even wear puffed out baggy uniforms to make it easier to get hit by a pitch and take a base. He was also good at drawing walks.

But as a manager, Solly was inexperienced. He was also the sort of guy who just rubbed people the wrong way—shouting, throwing tantrums, getting in people's faces, yelling excessively at umpires and opposing players.

For some reason, I never had a problem with him. But some

of the other players, especially Curt Flood and pitcher Bob Gibson, absolutely despised him, partly because he didn't play them as much as they would have liked, but also because they thought he was a racist. Flood later said that Hemus "acted as if I smelled bad." In one famous incident, Hemus was pinch-hitting in a game against Pittsburgh, and black pitcher Bennie Daniels kept brushing him back. Hemus finally took a hit on the leg, and as he jogged to first he allegedly called Daniels a "black bastard." After that Daniels always called Hemus "Little Faubus," a reference to Arkansas governor Orval Faubus, who tried to block school desegregation in Little Rock in 1957.

Hemus was finally fired as manager in mid-1961, and was succeeded by Johnny Keane, a great manager and a great guy, under whom the Cardinals would dramatically improve. With Keane in charge, I would also have my best years ever as a player.

But before all that happened, there was trouble in St. Petersburg.

In the 1950s and early '60s, Florida was the spring training capital of baseball. Although the Giants, Cubs, Indians, and Red Sox trained in Arizona, the other major league clubs had spring training in Florida.

Generally speaking, the white ballplayers loved it there. And why not? Until the Dodgers and Giants moved to California, all the major league teams were in the North and Midwest—and who wouldn't gladly trade the snow and slush of February–March in Pittsburgh or Milwaukee for the swaying palm trees and balmy breezes of Florida? They could bring their wives and kids along, and stay in a nice hotel or rented home; in their off time they could relax on the beach, take in the nightlife, eat at nice restaurants, and just enjoy themselves.

But for the vast majority of the black major league players—by

1960, there were by one count fifty-seven of us—Florida was a much different experience.

As I've said, things weren't perfect for black players in Arizona, either. You never knew when you'd run into a situation like I ran into in Phoenix when the theater manager wouldn't let me into that Jeff Chandler movie. Still, in Arizona the Giants' black players stayed at the Adams Hotel along with the white players.

Even in my now home city of St. Louis, life for a black player was sometimes difficult, but not unbearable.

Although it was situated in the Midwest, St. Louis was actually a very Southern-style city. (Busch Stadium, back when it had been Sportsman's Park, had been the last major league stadium to abandon segregated seating for blacks.) My first year there I rented a small home for myself and my wife and two daughters in the black section of town, but later I bought a nine-hundred-square-foot home in the suburb of Rock Hill, the first black family on the block. When we moved in my neighbor, a white man, refused to speak to me. (Later we became so close that when I was away on road trips, he would mow my lawn for me.) But black players in St. Louis knew there were restaurants and hotels and other places where they weren't welcome.

While the racism in places like Arizona and Missouri was mostly covert, in Florida it was constant, inescapable, and all-pervasive—and it was codified in the state law. "Colored" bathrooms, "colored" drinking fountains, "colored" restaurants, "colored" taxicabs, "colored" seating sections at all the spring training ballparks, and on and on. If you were a black man and it didn't say COLORED on it, you'd best not go in. For black ballplayers, especially those from the North, it was like suddenly being transported to apartheid South Africa.

And to their shame, for the most part the major league clubs went along with it. Even owners and front office types who were appalled by the segregationist policies averted their eyes. For example, Cardinals general manager Bing Devine was one of the best, most decent men I've ever known, a man without a prejudiced bone in his body. And yet even he, when confronted with the racial prejudice and segregation in Florida, said publicly, "We [the teams] don't make the rules."

I'd had a long history of trouble with Florida spring training. In 1953, after spring training with the Giants in Phoenix, I'd been sent to Melbourne, Florida, a small town on the Atlantic coast southeast of Orlando, for spring training with my new Class B team, the Danville Leafs. The Giants organization used a training facility there that included baseball fields and old military barracks used for housing—one set of barracks for the white players, another for the few black players then in the minors. In their off time the white players could go anywhere, but the blacks were restricted to the black section of town.

One night some other black players and I were having dinner and hanging out at a black restaurant/club when we realized it was late, and we had to get back to the training complex. There weren't any cabs, so we decided to walk the three miles back. We didn't get far before a police car with a flashing "cherry top" pulled up next to us.

"What're you boys doin' out so late?" the cop asked us. I told him we were baseball players for the Giants organization and we hadn't been able to get a cab back to the training facility. The cop shook his head and said in a typical Southern drawl, "Y'all better hurry up and get back there then. An' make sure you don't ever do this again, ya heah?"

It turns out there was a rule that said blacks weren't allowed on the streets outside their neighborhoods after 11 PM. It was sort of like those signs posted in some Deep South towns that said, NIG-GER, DON'T LET THE SUN SET ON YOU IN THIS TOWN.

In 1959, when I first reported to Cardinals' training camp in St. Petersburg, things in Florida hadn't gotten any better. I had to catch a "black" taxi at the airport—black cabs had black drivers, white cabs had white drivers—to take me to the team hotel, a surprisingly seedy place near the water. (Shortly thereafter the team moved to the elegant Vinoy Park Hotel.) When I carried my bags into the lobby and told the desk clerk I was Bill White with the Cardinals, and asked for my room, he looked at me as if I had dropped in from another planet.

There's no room for you here, the guy said. He said I had to stay with the "other" players—that is, the black players. He gave me an address and called a cab that took me to a house in the black section of town where a widow, Mrs. Williams, rented rooms to black ballplayers.

As I was unpacking, Bob Gibson and Dick Ricketts, two Cardinals pitchers who had just come up to the majors, stopped in to say hello.

"So this is the way it is here?" I said. "Black players can't stay in the team hotels?"

Bob shrugged. "Welcome to St. Petersburg," he said.

A sense of camaraderie among the black players, a sense of shared experience, began to evolve. On non-game days we'd practice in the mornings and then have the rest of the day free. The team gave the black players their own car to get to the training facility, so most afternoons we'd load our gear in the car and go fishing.

We also had a pickup basketball team that was a killer. After two undistinguished seasons with the Hiram College Division III basketball team, my only contribution was to knock the hell out of opposing guards and get the ball to the real basketball players— Bob Gibson, Dick Ricketts, and George Crowe.

Our real star was Ricketts, a six-foot-seven All-American

basketball star out of Duquesne who had been the number one NBA draft pick in 1955 and had played pro basketball for three years. Dick playing basketball was a beautiful thing to see.

But Bob was outstanding as well. He had played basketball at Creighton University in Nebraska and before joining the Cardinals had played for a year with the Harlem Globetrotters. Gibson's nickname to fans and sportswriters was "Hoot," after Western star Hoot Gibson, but I always called him "Hoops." Bob, a future Hall of Famer, was my closest friend on the Cardinals.

A funny thing about Gibson was that he wore thick, Coke-bottle-style eyeglasses when he played basketball, and even then it seemed like he was squinting when he made a shot. But he never wore glasses when he pitched, so most players didn't know he wore them at all. Once I took Bob to visit Willie Mays in San Francisco, and at first Willie didn't recognize him.

"Is that you, Bob Gibson?" Willie said when he answered the door. "You wear thick glasses like that? I'll be damned!"

Although Bob had a reputation as the meanest pitcher in baseball—Dick Allen once said he would "knock you down and then meet you at the plate to see if you wanted to make something out of it"—Bob wasn't really baseball's primary "headhunter," a pitcher who routinely threw beanballs. He actually hit fewer batters than Don Drysdale. But he never hesitated to brush back a batter. I often wonder what those batters would have thought if they'd known that the guy throwing a ninety-mile-per-hour high inside fastball at them could hardly see. It probably would have scared the hell out of them, which is what every pitcher wants.

(Although he was one of my best friends, Bob even hit me once. After I went to the Philadelphia Phillies, Bob warned me before a game that he wasn't going to let me dive in on him and pull the ball. I did it anyway, and when I leaned in at my next at-bat Bob drilled me in the elbow. "I warned you, you son-of-a-bitch," he screamed as I jogged to first base. Then we laughed about it over dinner that night. And Bob never changed. Years later, at an old-timers' exhibition game in 1993, the fifty-seven-year-old Gibson threw a high inside brushback pitch at forty-seven-year-old Reggie Jackson and almost hit him—at an old-timers' game!)

One day in February 1961, Curt Flood and I drove up to Miami from Homestead, where we were working on special drills, and went to the Sir John Hotel in the Overtown section, an area earlier known as "Colored Town," where a lot of black celebrities stayed and performed—Count Basie, Ella Fitzgerald, Nat King Cole. We were standing in front of the hotel when a guy we knew came up and said he wanted to introduce us to a friend of his. The friend was a tall, good-looking black kid named Cassius Clay—later, of course, Muhammad Ali.

An Olympic gold medalist in 1960, Ali had just turned heavyweight professional and was in Miami for a fight. He told Curt and me he was going to a Nation of Islam meeting at a mosque across the street and invited us to go along. After being searched for weapons at the door, we went in and sat down and listened as a speaker talked about separating black people from the "white devils" and how black Muslims wanted to inflict mayhem on their enemies—which meant just about everybody who wasn't black, and some who were. After about ten minutes, Curt looked at me and I looked at Curt and then we got up and left. Ali left with us. I wanted to support anyone who was fighting against the oppression of black people, but the Nation's philosophy really wasn't my kind of thing. And while I've never been a heavy drinker, the Muslim group's prohibition on its members drinking alcohol would have been a problem. One of the perks of playing for a baseball team owned by a brewing company was that I got all the free beer I wanted. At one point, I had thirty-eight cases of Budweiser stacked up in my garage in St. Louis.

Ali got me a ringside seat for his fight against a guy named Donnie Fleeman. In typical Ali fashion, he had boasted to me that Fleeman would never lay a glove on him—and in typical Ali fashion, he was right. Fleeman didn't lay a glove on Ali, but Ali laid glove after glove on Fleeman—so much so that by the time he knocked Fleeman out in the seventh round, I had flecks of Fleeman's blood all over my clothes. I never went to another professional fight.

Fishing, basketball, hanging out together—there were some good things about spring training in Florida, some good memories. But as time went on, the resentments over the way black players were treated built up.

Although the segregation of black players was the biggest problem, there were other irritants—such as the way the team promoted white players for product advertising gigs but not black players.

I remember once I was in the locker room when Jim Toomey, a chubby guy who was the Cardinals' PR man, and who acted as a liaison for advertisers, came in and asked, "Who smokes? Who smokes? I've got some easy money for anyone who wants to do a cigarette ad."

I didn't smoke, and never would, but my friend Curt Flood did. (Excessively so, and eventually it would kill him; he died of throat cancer in 1997.) I thought maybe I could send a little extra money Curt's way.

"Talk to Flood," I told Toomey. "I bet he'd be happy to do it."

Toomey looked at me as if I were crazy. Curt Flood? He's *black*! Toomey finally signed Ken Boyer for the ad. (Ken died of lung cancer when he was only fifty-one.)

Again, it wasn't the worst thing black players experienced. But privately they grumbled. Black players smoked. Black players used shaving cream. Black players used deodorant. So why couldn't the team steer some advertising money their way?

As so often happens, the final straw for me wasn't in itself any big deal. If it hadn't been for all the other indignities—the segregated housing, the COLORED signs, the way black players had to take sandwiches on the bus during road trips because "white" restaurants wouldn't serve us—it probably never would have become the major issue that it did.

It all started with an invitation to breakfast at a yacht club.

One morning in early March 1961, I was in the Cardinals clubhouse in St. Petersburg when I saw an announcement posted on the bulletin board. It said that the St. Petersburg Chamber of Commerce's annual "Salute to Baseball" breakfast was being held at the St. Petersburg Yacht Club, and it included a list of Cardinals players who were invited.

Not one of the players listed was black.

That was bad enough. Then I saw that the list included a couple of rookies who had never swung a bat in the majors. The idea that the local bigwigs wanted to honor unproven players while ignoring proven players because of the color of their skin rankled me.

No, it more than rankled me. Combined with all the other crap that black players had to take, it made me furious.

I had always been leery of reporters who covered baseball, especially on anything to do with race. I knew they had their own agendas, and anything I said could be twisted or taken out of context. For example, a year earlier a white reporter who was writing an article called "The Private World of the Negro Ballplayer" had wanted me to reveal the alleged "secrets" of black ballplayers, everything from how they felt about whites to the slang words they used. I liked the reporter personally, but I wouldn't talk to him about it.

(Strangely enough, black baseball player slang was an issue for some white players and executives; I guess they thought it was some kind of secret code. At one point, National League president Warren Giles got upset that black ballplayers were using a certain word on the field. To avoid shocking his female secretary, he had her type up a memo to be posted in all the team clubhouses that said, "Any player using the word _____ will be fined $300." Then he told all the team managers to take a pen and write the word "motherfucker" in the blank space. After that some players started calling each other "You dirty three-hundred-dollar word!")

Anyway, after I saw that invitation, and despite being wary of the press, I spotted Associated Press sports reporter Joe Reichler and called him over and told him about it.

I told him the truth. I told him how I felt about the segregated accommodations and other indignities. I asked him when we were going to start being treated like human beings.

"How much longer must we accept this without saying a word on our own behalf?" I said. "I think about this every minute of the day. I'm a member of the ball club, but I can't stay at the same hotel with the white players. These players are my friends, yet I can't go swimming with them. I can't even go to the movies with them. Driving on the highways, I've got to be on the lookout for a Negro restaurant to eat because they won't let me in where the white folks eat. But the filling stations on the road have no compunction about selling me gas. The greenback knows no color.

"These things go on every day and yet they advise us to take it easy, we're making progress, don't push it too fast, it will come. How much longer are we to wait? When will we be made to feel like humans? When will they throw away those signs that read FOR WHITES ONLY, or FOR COLORED ONLY?

"As long as those things continue to go on, I'd rather not train here. I'd rather train somewhere else, like Puerto Rico or the Dominican Republic or Arizona."

Joe was a sympathetic guy, but I didn't know what he would do with what I'd said. It turned out that later that day he sent a story out over the wires, with all of those comments, and with my name on them.

Joe's story wasn't the first press coverage concerning resentment among black players about the conditions in Florida. Later I learned that a couple of months previous, a veteran black reporter named Wendell Smith had written some articles about the inequities between white and black players in spring training in Florida for the *Chicago American*. Smith deserves a lot of credit for that.

Smith's article was based entirely on unnamed sources—and for good reason. Black ballplayers rightly feared that if they spoke out by name, they might be sent down to the minors or even cut from their major league organizations. Black baseball players, like blacks everywhere, weren't supposed to "rock the boat."

At about the same time, Dr. Ralph Wimbish, a physician and president of the St. Petersburg NAACP, and Dr. Robert Swain, a dentist and NAACP member, jumped into the controversy.

The two men had long been involved in desegregation efforts in St. Petersburg. Just a few months earlier, they had helped organize "sit-ins" at segregated lunch counters in the city, eventually forcing them to end their segregation policies—part of a wave of such protests that swept across the Deep South in late 1960. Dr. Wimbish's home in St. Petersburg had also been a gathering place for many black ballplayers during spring training, a place to relax and enjoy a barbecue and swim in the pool—a welcome opportunity, since virtually all pools in St. Petersburg were off limits to blacks. Some players even stayed in his home, and he helped out the major league teams by finding rooms for black players.

After Smith's article appeared, Wimbish announced at a press conference that he would no longer help any teams keep their black players living separately from the white players—even though this would cost him money, since as a major property owner in the black district he often rented housing to black baseball players. He and Dr. Swain called for desegregation throughout spring training.

The point here is that a lot of good people worked hard, often at considerable risk, to improve conditions for black players in St. Petersburg and throughout Florida. No single person is responsible for desegregating baseball spring training.

But as far as I know I was the first active black major league ballplayer to speak out in the press, by name, at length, against the unfair treatment black players were experiencing in Florida spring training, not only in hotel accommodations but in every aspect of life. And the reason I was willing to do that was simple, the same principle that had guided me throughout my baseball career—I wasn't afraid of losing my job. I was twenty-seven years old, had completed two years of college, and was making a decent salary— about $20,000 in 1961. I didn't have enough money to retire, but I was confident that if my baseball career was derailed by what I'd said, I could do something else—maybe even finish college and go on to medical school.

Joe Reichler's story ran in newspapers across the country. Broadcast sports reporters, on the other hand, ignored it—with one exception. The exception was an odd-looking lawyer-turned-broadcaster named Howard Cosell, who had a show called *Speaking of Sports* on the ABC radio network and was sympathetic to the black players' frustrations. Later other black ballplayers started speaking up as well. But what really made it a hot issue as far as the Cardinals management was concerned was beer.

One of the papers that picked up Reichler's story was a black newspaper in East St. Louis, across the Mississippi River in Illinois. An editorial in the paper suggested that if this was the way the Anheuser-Busch company, which had bought the Cardinals in 1953, treated its black ballplayers, then maybe black people should boycott the company's beer.

This was now serious. Morality and social conscience may in some cases cause large companies to eventually take action, but nothing gets them moving faster than a threat to the bottom line.

Within days of my comments being published, with talk of a Budweiser beer boycott in the air in the black community, I got a visit in St. Petersburg from my old minor league manager Eddie Stanky, who was working in the Cardinals' front office. When he walked into the clubhouse, everybody wondered what Eddie was doing there, but I knew immediately.

Eddie invited me to go fishing, and that afternoon on a little outboard motorboat on Tampa Bay, Eddie got down to business.

"I know you have some concerns about this housing issue, Bill," he said. "But this is bringing a lot of heat on the company [Anheuser-Busch] and the team. We really need you to back off. Can't you just concentrate on baseball for now, and leave politics out of it?"

I had always liked Eddie, and still did. But I wasn't going to back down.

"You know I have a lot of respect for you," I told him. "But no, I'm not going to back off, not on this issue. What's going on in St. Petersburg is wrong, and as long as black players in spring training are made to feel inferior, I'm going to speak up."

I think Eddie understood. And though he couldn't say so publicly, I think he actually respected what I was doing.

I also got a visit from a guy named Roscoe McCrary, a reporter for *The St. Louis Argus,* a black newspaper in which Anheuser-Busch advertised heavily. Roscoe said he wanted to do a story on me, but I could tell from the softball tone of his questions that he wanted me to downplay complaints about conditions for black ballplayers in St. Petersburg.

"Listen, Roscoe," I said, "this is not a good place for us to have spring training. If you try to soften up what's going on down here just to help a big advertiser, you'll be doing all of us a disservice. If you do that, I won't be happy—and believe me, I'll let people in St. Louis know that you're trying to sugarcoat this."

Roscoe got the message. His subsequent story wasn't as hard hitting as I would have liked, but he didn't sugarcoat what I said.

And finally I got a visit from one of the big guns, Al Fleishman, head of the Fleishman-Hillard public relations agency, which represented the brewery company. But as it turned out, Al's message wasn't exactly the one the company wanted.

"They wanted me to tell you to cool down," Al told me. "But the hell with that. The last thing you want to do now that you've got their attention is to cool down. You need to keep pressure on their ass."

Al was a good guy, and like a lot of Jewish Americans, he had no patience with racial and ethnic bigotry. It probably didn't help Al's mood that many hotels in St. Petersburg excluded not only blacks but also Jews.

Meanwhile, fearful of losing the millions of dollars that spring training brought into the local economy, the St. Petersburg Chamber of Commerce backed down. Insisting that it had all been an unfortunate mistake, they invited me and another black player, Elston Howard of the Yankees, to the Salute to Baseball breakfast at the yacht club.

The Yankees ordered Elston to attend, and Dr. Wimbish and others urged me to go as well. But I knew the chamber and the yacht club weren't advocating full integration. The club still wouldn't let NAACP member Dr. Swain dock his boat there. I wanted to let them know that I had a choice—and my choice was not to go.

I hadn't wanted to eat with those bigots anyway. All I had really wanted, what all the black players wanted, was simply the opportunity to say no.

The end result of all this was that while Cardinals management initially tried to downplay the race issue, eventually the public pressure was too great, not only on the Cardinals but on all the teams. The Cardinals finally demanded that the Vinoy Park Hotel open itself to black players.

The hotel refused, so in order to help keep spring training in St. Petersburg, a local businessman bought a beachfront motel called the Outrigger and made it available to all Cardinals players and their families, black and white. As a show of solidarity, players who usually stayed in private beachfront homes, like Stan Musial and Ken Boyer, also moved into the Outrigger.

So by the start of spring training in 1962, all of the Cardinals were living under the same roof and eating at the same on-site restaurant. For the first time, black players felt comfortable bringing their families to spring training. Our kids went to integrated events organized by the players' wives. Black players and white players and their families were even swimming in the same pool. All this integration was so unheard of in Florida that people would drive by the motel all day just to gawk and stare.

The whole controversy helped black players realize that they had power—or at least some public leverage. When Southern cities like Houston and Atlanta were trying to get major league teams, Milwaukee Braves center fielder Billy Bruton and I got the Major League Baseball Players Association to vote unanimously not to play in any city that required black and white players to use separate living facilities.

Of course, ending separate living arrangements for baseball players in Florida didn't end segregation altogether. Over the next few years, and especially after passage of the 1964 federal Civil Rights Act that banned discrimination in public facilities, Dr. Wimbish would often recruit me and other black players while we were in St. Petersburg for spring training to help break the now illegal, but still very real, color barrier in local restaurants.

Dr. Wimbish would stop by the Outrigger and pick up Bob Gibson and me and say, "Tonight we're going to integrate this restaurant," or "Tonight we're going to this 'whites-only' club." We'd walk in and order a drink or some food, and while we got a lot of looks, no one ever gave us any trouble. We always dressed nicely, spoke in quiet tones, and in general acted respectably. Later Bob said it was like having dinner with a new girlfriend's parents night after night; you always had to be on your best behavior.

I've always been proud of what I did back then, that I had spoken up. Once again, no one person ever single-handedly defeats widespread social injustice; that takes millions of hands. Still, the spring training controversy focused a lot of attention on me.

And of all the messages of support I received, there is one that stands out. It came in the form of a letter from a man I had never gotten to know very well, but one whom I deeply admired, a man who had suffered greatly in the cause of equality. Today that letter remains one of my most cherished possessions.

"Dear Bill," the letter said. "I just wanted you to know that I appreciate everything that you've done for black baseball players. Keep up the fight."

The letter was signed, "Jackie Robinson."

Chapter 8

It's funny how dramatically your life can turn on a chance meeting or an offhand remark. I didn't realize it at the time—you never do—but my life turned late one summer morning in 1961, when I started needling Harry Caray.

Harry was then a sportscaster on St. Louis radio station KMOX, but he was more than that. He was a local icon. A rumpled guy with thick, oversize glasses, he had been covering the Cardinals and calling their games for fifteen years, starting with WIL-AM, where Harry loudly touted not only the Cards but also his sponsor, Griesedieck beer—pronounced, to everyone's amusement, *greasy-dick*. He moved to KMOX after Anheuser-Busch bought the Cards in 1953—so long Griesedieck, hello Bud—and was later teamed up with Jack Buck, another broadcasting icon. Long before he became nationally famous as the voice of the Chicago White Sox and then the Cubs, Harry had already staked out his trademark exclamation—"Holy cow!"—which he used whenever the Cardinals made a big play. (Harry always claimed that he trained himself to say that so he wouldn't use a career-ending on-air expletive like "Holy shit!" For the same reason, New York Yankees broadcaster Phil Rizzuto used the same expression; there were arguments over who had used it first.)

In any event, on that summer day in Busch Stadium, Harry was in the dugout, with a microphone in one hand and one of those giant tape recorders they had back then hanging by a leather strap from his shoulder, doing some pre-game interviews with Cardinals players. Harry was wildly popular with the fans, but he wasn't particularly well liked by a lot of Cardinals players. While he was a big supporter of the team—he had a reputation as a "homer," a broadcaster who actively rooted for the home team during broadcasts—he could be pretty caustic about individual players. Harry once said of me on the air, "Bill White couldn't hit a curveball with a canoe paddle."

That didn't really bother me, especially since it was pretty much true, but Harry seemed to think that playing baseball was easy.

So that day I decided to needle him a little bit.

"Hey Harry! You think baseball's easy? That looks like a pretty easy job you've got!"

Harry turned and looked at me, his eyes like hard little BBs through the Coke-bottle-bottom glasses. He was annoyed.

"If you think what I do is so easy, you should put that bat down and try it sometime," he said. "It's not as easy as you think."

Harry was right, of course. Broadcasting, like baseball, isn't easy. It's just that the best guys in each profession make it look like it is.

By this time some of the other players in the dugout were watching, and I didn't want to back down in front of them.

"You know, I think I'd like to give it a shot." I was half joking when I said it, maybe three-quarters joking. I'd never even thought of doing any broadcasting work. I didn't think Harry would take me up on it—but he did.

"Okay," he said, "we'll make a tape and I'll give it to Hyland."

Bob Hyland, the son of a former Cardinals team physician, was a CBS regional vice president, general manager of KMOX, and one of the most powerful media executives in the country. Although KMOX was St. Louis–based, it was a fifty-thousand-watt "clear channel" that, depending on atmospherics and the time of day, could be picked up across the nation. At the time, KMOX was beginning its groundbreaking shift from music to an all-talk format, the forerunner of the dominant genre today.

I probably would have forgotten about the whole broadcasting idea except that a few days later Harry grabbed me and had me start asking questions into his microphone: "Well, Harry, how long have you been in broadcasting?" and so on. My style was amateurish, but Harry edited the tapes to where I sounded at least coherent.

Later he gave the tape to Hyland, who liked working with ballplayers; he had given former Cardinal Joe Garagiola his start in the broadcasting business. I guess Hyland liked my voice, because less than a week later he called me and set up a meeting at the station.

Hyland asked me what I wanted to do at the station, and I had to tell him I didn't know. Hyland said he was going to show me the entire operation, from top to bottom, so I could decide what, if anything, appealed to me.

So for the next few months I would go to the station and watch, listen, and try to learn. I sat in the control room with the engineers, producers, and directors, seeing how a radio broadcast was put together. I reviewed tapes in the archives and sat in on Hyland's organizational meetings. I even went out with the station salesmen on advertising sales calls. I did everything at the station except sweep the floor.

I also got to watch some of the greats in action—Caray, Garagiola, and Jack Buck, the third man in the Cardinals broadcast booth.

All three are now in the broadcasting section of the Baseball Hall of Fame.

The station started paying me $100 a week to do fill-in jobs; once they even put me in as a DJ on one of the station's remaining music segments, spinning Pat Boone and Frank Sinatra and Doris Day records. Thankfully, that only lasted a month. Sometimes I would fill in for Jack Buck on his sports show, and other times I would cover some local sports. Once they sent me out to cover a soccer game at St. Louis University, even though all I knew about soccer was that if you kicked the ball into the net you got a point. It seemed to me the soccer players wasted a lot of time running back and forth on the field for a game that would end with a score of 1–0.

By 1965 I had enough experience to get my own show—*The Bill White Show*—a five-minute segment that aired on Saturday afternoons before Cardinals home games. I would put on my uniform, interview another player or manager, and then go out and play the game.

My early efforts weren't exactly a ticket to broadcasting stardom. I remember once the New York Mets were playing the Cardinals at Busch Stadium with Yogi Berra on the roster. Yogi, who had been born and raised in St. Louis in the Italian section of town known as The Hill, had been fired as the Yankees manager the year before and was now working as a coach for the Mets.

I saw Yogi before the game and asked for an interview, figuring it was a natural. Not only was he a St. Louis native, but he was one of the most colorful and most quoted guys in baseball. "This is like déjà vu all over again." "Baseball is 90 percent mental; the other half is physical." "You can observe a lot just by watching." The list of "Yogi-isms" went on and on. I never thought Yogi actually said half the things that were attributed to him, and apparently neither did he; he was once quoted as saying, "I never really said all the things I said." But I thought it would be an entertaining interview.

At first Yogi didn't want to do it, but then I promised him one of the transistor radios that KMOX handed out for promotional purposes and to guests on shows. They were just cheap, poorly made radios, but Yogi wanted one.

(Back then a lot of players, me included, collected stuff like that. Whenever you'd make a promotional appearance or do a radio or TV interview they'd give you something, usually a sample of their sponsor's product—razor blades, cigarettes, a case of shaving cream, whatever—and if you didn't want it you'd trade the stuff with other players. I had so much of that stuff that I filled up an empty locker next to mine and put up a sign that said BILL WHITE'S TRADING POST.)

Anyway, after Yogi agreed to the interview I got a sound engineer and set up near the batting cage near the stands behind home plate. The interview with Yogi went something like this:

"So, Yogi, is it good to be back in your hometown?"

"Yes."

"Are you happy you left the Yankees for the Mets?"

"No."

"Do you think we're going to have a good game today?"

"Yes."

It went on, seemingly forever, with nothing but yes and no answers. Finally I wrapped it up.

"Well, thanks for talking to us today, Yogi."

"Sure. Now where's that radio you promised me?"

It was my fault, not Yogi's, that it was so bad. I was still too inexperienced to phrase questions in a way that forced the interviewee to give expanded answers.

Harry Caray had been right. Broadcasting was a lot harder than it looked.

Eventually I would get better. But in the meantime I had other things to think about.

Because while I was experimenting with broadcasting, I was also playing the best baseball of my life.

Early in the 1962 season, I was playing first base when the batter popped a foul ball toward the stands along the first base line. I dove for it, and although I made the out I managed to hurt my left shoulder. It hurt like hell, but I stayed in the game, and fortunately I didn't have to make any long cutoff throws.

The shoulder was still hurting the next day when Johnny Keane, in his first full season as a manager after replacing Solly Hemus, came over and sat down next to me.

"Listen, Bill, I don't want to see you diving for balls ever again," he said in that soft, quiet voice of his. "You're too important to this team, and I don't want you to get hurt. I want you to be able to play 162 games every year."

I could hardly believe what I was hearing. I was used to playing for managers like Durocher or Solly Hemus, guys who wanted you to dive for every ball, to run into walls if you had to, and who would yell and scream at you for not hustling. And now Johnny Keane was telling me that my future with the team was more important than any single play?

That was the way Johnny was. And although in the end baseball did not treat him well, he was the best manager, and one of the best men, I ever knew.

Johnny had never played in the majors. A shortstop in the minors, he'd been injured by a beanball early in his playing career, and later went into managing various minor league teams for the Cardinals. In 1959, at the age of forty-seven, and after more than three decades with the Cardinals organization, he finally was hired on as a Cardinals coach.

Johnny was loyal up and loyal down. While the rest of us would bitch to him about Hemus, Johnny would just sit there, a cigarette between his lips, saying nothing. Even though I'm sure he felt the same way we did, his sense of honor wouldn't permit him to bad-mouth the man he worked for. And he expected the same from us. The only time I ever saw Johnny angry, the only time he ever raised his voice, was several years later, when he felt some members of the team were undermining him behind his back. He lined us all up. He didn't scream. As a deeply religious man who had once considered the priesthood, he didn't cuss, either. Johnny simply told us what we had done wrong and insisted that we not do it again.

That made an impression on me. I realized that the slightly elevated voice of a quiet man had far more impact than the loudest shriek of a chronic screamer. And the best players and managers were the quiet players and managers.

After Hemus was fired in the middle of the 1961 season—at that point we had thirty-three wins and forty-one losses, and were fourteen and a half games out of first place—and Johnny was named the new manager, the team immediately took off. Although we ended the season fifth in the National League, under Johnny our win–loss record for the post-Hemus remainder of the 1961 season was 47–33. Because of Johnny, we were all looking forward to next year.

One of the things Johnny started doing immediately was to put Curt Flood in every game. Flood, who had languished under Hemus, became one of the best all-around players in the game, batting near or above .300 for five years running and winning seven straight Gold Glove Awards.

Johnny also brought out the best in Bob Gibson. Bob had struggled under Hemus, who publicly questioned not only his pitching ability but even his intelligence, and refused to put him into the regular rotation. On his first day as manager, Johnny told Bob he'd have the ball every fourth game, and in his first full season Bob went on to strike out more than two hundred batters and make the All-Star team. Without Johnny Keane, Bob might never have had the chance to become one of the greatest pitchers of all time.

Johnny was good for me, too. Maybe it was an omen, but the day before Johnny was named manager, during the first game of a two-game series against the Dodgers at the Coliseum in Los Angeles—Dodger Stadium wasn't built yet—I hit three home runs. It was the only time in my career I had three home runs in a game. I wound up batting .286 that year, with ninety RBIs, was selected for the All-Stars, and won another Gold Glove.

That continued into the 1962 season, when I batted a career-high .324, with 102 RBIs, and into '63 as well, when I hit career-highs of twenty-seven home runs and 109 RBIs, with Gold Glove Awards in both years. Also in 1963, I played in all 162 regular-season games, for the only time in my entire career.

So I was feeling good about myself and, more important, about my team. We had gotten closer without the stresses of the Hemus days, and we were confident in ourselves. Most of us felt that we were supported not only on the field but off it as well.

For me, at no time was that more apparent than when I tried to buy a house.

As I mentioned earlier, I'd been living with my family in a small, nine-hundred-square-foot house in the St. Louis suburb of Rock Hill. But my wife and I now had three children—Edna, Debbie, and Tommy—with another on the way, so in late 1963 we decided we needed a bigger house. My real estate agent said he'd found one he thought I would like, a new, three-bedroom, single-story brick home on a nice cul-de-sac in a new development in Des Peres, about twenty miles outside St. Louis. I looked at the house, liked it, and made an offer of $40,000.

The builder initially accepted the bid—until he found out I was black. At that point he withdrew the contract, saying he planned to build more homes on the cul-de-sac and that having a black family in one of them might make it hard to sell the others.

Nothing personal, he said through my agent. It was just a business decision. I guess the guy actually thought that would make me feel better.

In truth, I was ready to let it pass. But what I hadn't figured on was that members of the Cardinals family would find out that some developer didn't think their star first baseman was good enough to live in one of his houses.

Soon after the builder canceled the contract, Jack Buck, who with Harry Caray was the voice of the Cardinals for KMOX, invited me out to his home in an upscale area of Clayton, Missouri. He wanted to help me buy a home in his neighborhood—but frankly, I couldn't afford it. Back then, top broadcasters made more than most baseball players.

Then Al Fleishman, Anheuser-Busch's PR chief, the same guy who had backed me during the spring training controversy, came and spoke to me. He was angry.

"Bill, do you want that house in Des Peres?"

"Yes I want the house. I need a bigger place."

"Leave it to me and Bing," Al said.

It turned out that general manager Bing Devine was also ticked off about the situation. I don't know what kind of pressure Bing and Al and Jack exerted behind the scenes, but they were influential men in St. Louis and the surrounding area. A few weeks later, I was signing a contract for the Des Peres home. Bob Hyland, the KMOX general manager, had the entire property landscaped as a housewarming gift, and Johnny Keane had a big pine tree planted in my yard.

Of course, I hadn't set out to integrate the neighborhood; I just wanted to buy a house. It just so happened that I was able to break another color barrier.

And I wasn't the only ballplayer to do so. For example, after the Giants moved to San Francisco, Willie Mays and his wife were initially denied the right to buy a home in one of the nicer neighborhoods in the city. But they persisted, and after public pressure grew they got the home they wanted. In late 1964, my teammate Curt Flood also was refused entry into a white neighborhood in the Oakland suburb of Alamo, but finally moved in after getting a court order.

Both incidents attracted widespread publicity. And they raised the question: How could Americans cheer for a man and call him a hero on the ball field or the gridiron or the basketball court, and then refuse to let him move in next door?

The answer was that they couldn't. Although for some reason the major civil rights organizations didn't make much use of sports figures in the battle for equal rights, throughout the 1960s black sports figures across the country were desegregating previously all-white neighborhoods—usually quietly, sometimes publicly. They had the money and the contacts and the celebrity status to win those fights, and once they broke the barriers it paved the way for other black people to live where they wanted.

In any event, there weren't any serious problems when my family and I moved into the Des Peres neighborhood. The builder who had first refused to sell the house to me lived a couple of doors down, and for as long as we lived there he refused to speak to me—but I didn't care. At first the local police thought there would be trouble—not from me but from people who didn't want the neighborhood to be integrated. I would see patrol cars passing by often, and sometimes a police car would stop outside my home.

Finally I went out to the parked patrol car and told the officer it wasn't necessary.

"I don't expect any trouble," I said. "But if there is I'm going to handle it."

And I would have. I had taken up waterfowl and upland bird hunting with Cardinals outfielder Charlie James, and I had several shotguns in my house. If anyone had threatened the safety of my family, I wouldn't have hesitated to use them.

(One of the shotguns was a beautiful over-and-under Browning that I'd gotten during a promotional appearance at a St. Louis sporting goods store. The store had offered me either $100 or the shotgun, and I took the shotgun. It was a good choice. The hundred bucks would have been quickly spent, but I still have that beautiful shotgun.)

But no shotguns were necessary. My two daughters, Edna, seven, and Debbie, six, were enrolled in elementary school, and although they were the first black students to attend the school they didn't have any trouble with teachers or their fellow students. Prejudice has to be taught, and at that age their fellow students were too young to learn it. And except for the sullen builder, my neighbors in Des Peres were great. We enjoyed living there, and I was always grateful for the help I got from the Cardinals family.

It was a good feeling knowing that the team I played for, players and management alike, had my back.

As a team we felt confident going into the 1964 season.

Curt Flood was our anchor in the outfield. Bob Gibson had won eighteen games and struck out 204 batters the year before. Our infield, with Ken Boyer at third, Dick Groat at shortstop, Julian Javier at second, and me at first, was in many people's opinion the best in baseball. We had a manager, Johnny Keane, whom we liked and respected.

And we clicked as a team. During spring training we socialized together; our wives and kids all knew one another; we helped one another. There were no superstars on the field—Stan Musial had retired at the end of the '63 season after a remarkable twenty-two-year career—and no bitter jealousies, just nine guys who knew one another and what they had to do. There's no way to quantify the spirit that a group of men share, but in baseball, as in the military, that spirit can sometimes make the difference between victory and defeat. And our team spirit was sky-high.

True, our '63 season had been disappointing in the end. By mid-September, we had won nineteen of our last twenty games and were just one game behind the Dodgers in the pennant race—until the Dodgers swept us in a three-game series and we finished the season six games back in second place.

Despite that, we felt strong when the '64 season began.

The feeling didn't last. In June we were in eighth place, and management was desperate. Bing Devine and Johnny Keane traded with the Cubs for Lou Brock, giving up some of our best pitchers in the process. Lou would soon become an outstanding ballplayer, but at the time of the trade he was struggling. We all thought that Bing was crazy.

It was about this time that a reporter asked me what was wrong with the team, and my response was, *"I'm* what's wrong with the team." I went on to explain that when your third, fourth, or fifth hitters weren't hitting well—which I wasn't—it threw the entire team out of balance.

For some reason a number of sportswriters made a big deal out of that quote, of the fact that I was blaming myself for the team's problems. They started describing me as a modest, self-effacing kind of player—by implication different from so many of the whining, excuse-making players in the game.

I wasn't modest, though, then or ever. When I was doing well I said so, and I was never afraid to demand the compensation and consideration that I thought good performance deserved. But if you want people to believe it when you say you're doing good, you'd damn well better be willing to admit it when you're doing badly. All I was doing was being honest.

In any event, by August we were still in fifth place, nine games behind the Phillies. So Cardinals owner Gussie Busch, who really didn't know much about baseball, fired Bing Devine as general manager—this just a year after Bing had been named the major league Executive of the Year by *The Sporting News*—and replaced him with Bob Howsam. (Bing took it hard; he later said, "If you weren't a grown man you might cry.") Eddie Stanky quit, and the rumor was that Johnny Keane would be the next to go, supposedly to be replaced by none other than Leo Durocher.

Right after Bing left, we were suddenly on fire. From that point on, we won twenty-nine games and lost only fourteen. The once struggling Brock batted .348 and stole thirty-three bases. Ken Boyer on third base wound up hitting twenty-four homers and 119 RBIs, the best in the league, and went on to become the National League MVP. Pitcher Ray Sadecki won twenty games, while Bob Gibson won nineteen and struck out 245 batters. I wound up hitting .303 for the season, with twenty-one home runs and 102 RBIs—72 of them in the second half of the season.

Lou Brock was one reason for that. I usually batted behind Brock, so if he walked or got a base hit it was a big advantage for me or for any other batter who followed him. With a guy that fast on first, no pitcher wanted to risk a breaking pitch that his catcher might have trouble catching or have to dig out of the dirt—by which time Lou would be well on his way to another stolen base. So whenever Lou was on base, I could look forward to a steady diet of fastballs—and I could hit fastballs.

The upshot was that in two months we went from fifth place to first in the National League, finally beating out the Philadelphia

Phillies for the pennant by one game. Then it was on to the World Series against the vaunted New York Yankees.

In 1964, the Yankees weren't just a baseball team; they were a dynasty. That year marked their fifth straight World Series, their twenty-ninth in the past forty-four years. They had superstars like Mickey Mantle and Roger Maris and Whitey Ford.

But dynasties fade. Just three years earlier, in 1961, Maris and Mantle had starred in the famous pursuit of Babe Ruth's 1927 season home run record, with Maris finally breaking it with sixty-one homers and an injured Mantle not far behind with fifty-four. (That was when baseball commissioner Ford Frick announced that because Ruth's record had been set during a 154-game season, and Maris was playing a 162-game season, there would be two distinct home run records on the books—Ruth's and Maris's. That ruling was later rescinded. It's a persistent baseball myth that Maris's record ever had an asterisk next to it.)

No question, the Yankees had been a great team. But by 1964, Mantle was thirty-two years old and plagued with injuries, and while he could still turn in a respectable slugging performance, his thirty-five homers that year didn't compare to his earlier performances. Maris was just thirty, but his twenty-six home runs in the 1964 regular season were a shadow of his former glory. Ford, meanwhile, was thirty-five, and while he'd had a 17–6 season in 1964, it didn't compare to his career best 25–4 a few years earlier.

And besides, we knew these guys. We had shared the same field in St. Petersburg before the Yankees had moved to Fort Lauderdale, and even after they moved we played them often in spring training. We knew their weaknesses as well as their strengths. To be frank, we also thought of them as a bunch of prima donnas, stars who just went through the motions in spring training and even in the regular season. By contrast, Johnny Keane made certain that we were in shape and ready to play by the end of spring training, and that we stayed that way throughout the regular season.

"We beat these guys so many times in spring training," Johnny told us before the series. "There's no reason we can't go out and beat them now."

There was another reason why, in my opinion, we were better than the Yankees. It wasn't discussed much at the time, but to me it seemed apparent. It was well known that George Weiss, the Yankees' general manager from 1947 to 1960, had a problem with black ballplayers. The Yankees didn't bring up their first black player, Elston Howard, until 1955, eight years after Jackie Robinson broke the color barrier with the Dodgers. Even then, Yankees management worried about having "too many Negroes" on the team. The result was that by 1964, the team had lost out on many of the most promising young black players, guys who could have filled the gaps as the older white stars began to fade.

Despite all that, the series was close and hard fought. We took the first game in St. Louis; the Yanks took the second. In New York, the Yanks took Game 3 but we took Games 4 and 5, with Ken Boyer hitting a grand slam in Game 4 and Bob Gibson striking out thirteen batters in Game 5. Back in St. Louis, the Yankees won Game 6 to tie the series 3–3.

It was an exciting series. But for me it was also the worst hitting performance of my entire baseball career. In the first six games I had one hit in twenty-three at-bats.

The problem was that I had fallen back into my old habit of trying to pull every ball, and the Yankees responded by pitching me outside. I was hitting a lot of easy grounders and pop-ups. Finally after Game 5, I called my old batting guru Harry Walker, who had been managing a Cardinals minor league club and was now at his off-season home in Leeds, Alabama. He gave me the same advice he gave me before: Lay back a little, wait for the ball, hit it straight away instead of trying to pull every pitch.

It worked, and I redeemed myself somewhat in Game 7 in St. Louis. I got two hits, and we jumped on the Yankees early, getting a 6–0 lead. But Bob Gibson was the star of the game. He'd already pitched two games, and he was exhausted after just two days' rest. But Johnny kept him in, and although Mantle hit a three-run homer in the sixth and the Yankees got two more homers in the ninth, Bob held on.

As I've said before, I was never an emotional ballplayer. But standing on first base in the top of the ninth, with the score 7–5 and two outs, watching Cardinals second baseman Dal Maxvill catch a pop fly by Yankee Bobby Richardson for the final out—and with Roger Maris waiting on deck for the Yankees—was the biggest thrill of my baseball career. For the first time since 1946, my team, the St. Louis Cardinals, had won the World Series.

There was pandemonium. Fans rushed the field while we all rushed one another, hugging and shouting and jumping up and down. The celebration surged into the locker room, where the champagne—and of course the Budweiser—flowed.

We didn't realize it at the time, but the drama wasn't over.

The team planned a victory celebration that night at Stan & Biggie's, the St. Louis restaurant that Musial owned with local businessman Julius "Biggie" Garagnani. But I had a previous commitment. A month earlier, when the Cardinals were six and a half games out of first place, the Webster Groves Christian Church had asked me to be the featured speaker at a banquet on October 15. At the time, I never dreamed that we'd be in the World Series, and that we'd win the championship on the same day as the banquet.

But a commitment is a commitment. While my teammates headed to Stan & Biggie's, I drove to the church, where the banquet organizers were frankly surprised to see me. But they were happy to have me, and when I finished the event I drove over to Stan & Biggie's.

My teammates had a big head start on me with the champagne and other booze. I won't say I was the only sober guy in the room, but I was one of the few. Maybe that's why when Bob Howsam got up to give a little speech, I actually heard what he said—and I didn't like it one bit.

Howsam, who had replaced Bing Devine as general manager in August, was a heavy fellow who spoke with a pronounced lisp. He and his brother had founded the Denver Broncos football team and also owned the Denver Bears minor league baseball team. He must have known something about baseball, because later he led the Cincinnati Reds to success as "the Big Red Machine."

But hardly any of us liked the guy. As far as most of us on the Cardinals were concerned, it was Bing Devine, not Bob Howsam, who had made our World Series victory possible, not least of all by bringing in Lou Brock.

So when Howsam stood up that night in Stan & Biggie's and told the crowd, "I just want to point out that this turnaround didn't happen until I took over the team," I went into a slow burn.

Team captain Ken Boyer stood up next and said a few words, and then I followed him.

"This is a great, great day for the city of St. Louis and a great, great day for the Cardinals," I said. "We won this title for Bing Devine. Bing put this all together. And Bing is the reason we're all here."

Howsam didn't say anything. I knew he must have hated hearing that—but I didn't care.

The drama continued the next day at a post-series press conference. Gussie Busch and Howsam showed up intending to announce that Johnny Keane had been hired for another season as manager.

But Johnny, who despised Howsam and had been deeply hurt by the leaked reports earlier in the season that Durocher would be replacing him, had a surprise for them. He took the microphone and announced that he was quitting the Cardinals and handed Howsam and Busch his letter of resignation. I wasn't there, but I was told that Busch and Howsam looked as if Johnny had just kicked them in the teeth—which in effect he had.

(Johnny went on to take over as manager of the Yankees, replacing Yogi Berra, who was fired after we beat them in the World Series. Unfortunately, Johnny and the Yankees weren't a good matchup. I always thought that Johnny tried to apply a National League hard-work ethic to an American League team of complacent, aging superstars and was resented for it. He was fired during the 1966 season. Early the next year, my friend Johnny Keane died of a heart attack at age fifty-five.)

The drama continued. Before Johnny resigned, we had had a team meeting to figure out our World Series winnings, which were based on gate receipts at the first four games. A player's full share came to $8,900—before taxes. After Uncle Sam took his cut, I wound up with $4,900. That probably sounds laughable today. Forty-two years later, when the Cardinals won the 2006 World Series, with broadcasting revenues included, each player's share was $362,000.

At the same team meeting, we discussed how to distribute the thirty-eight authorized World Series rings. We all agreed that Bing Devine should get one, even if we had to pay for it ourselves. Despite having been fired in August, Bing was again named *Sporting News* Executive of the Year for the 1964 season. I had to tell Howsam about the ring—and that burned him up.

So the Cardinals 1964 championship season ended with bad blood between players and management. And that continued into the 1965 season.

Howsam named Red Schoendienst as manager, and in future years Red would do well. But in 1965 our once tight team collapsed. A lot of guys were banged up, me included, and our stats showed it. I went from 102 RBIs in '64 to just 73 in '65, and batted .289. Ken Boyer dropped from 119 RBIs the year before to just 75 in '65. And so on. We just weren't effective as a team anymore.

And most of us had no respect for Bob Howsam. He just didn't seem to know how to act in the big leagues. For example, in 1964 the Cardinals had paid me $47,000, second only to Ken Boyer. I always waited until the Anheuser-Busch annual profit statements came out after the first of the year before I started negotiating my next contract—and in 1964 the company had record profits. So in January 1965, I asked for what I felt was a fair raise.

I deserved it. But Howsam hemmed and hawed and then claimed he couldn't give me a raise because he had to spend $30,000 to smooth out center field in Busch Stadium and there was no money left for player raises. It was nonsense, the sort of bush league stuff that Howsam tried to pull on young players who were eager to play and didn't know the score. It wasn't the sort of argument you made to a veteran player—and I told him so. He finally came through with another $10,000, but it rankled me.

(Howsam had a weird thing about the appearance of the stadium. In the 1965 season, he put out an edict forbidding Cardinals players from stepping out of the on-deck circle and tromping on the grass between the base line and the stands. He said it killed the grass around the batter's on-deck circle and made the field look bad. The problem was that by stepping out of the circle and bending down to tie a shoelace or something, we could sometimes see the catcher's signals to the pitcher. If we could spot the catcher's signals we'd be able to alert our batter as to what the pitch was going to be. "Let's go, Kenny!" would mean a fastball was on the way, while not saying anything would mean a breaking ball. It was part of the "All is fair in love and baseball" game. But Howsam either didn't understand that or cared more about how the grass looked than about winning games.) In the end, the Cardinals finished the 1965 season in seventh place, second to last. And Howsam decided to clean house.

In mid-October, Howsam traded Ken Boyer to the Mets. A week later I was goose hunting near Sumner, Missouri, with my former teammate Charlie James, and on the ride back to St. Louis we had the car radio tuned to KMOX. Suddenly we heard the announcer say, "The Cardinals have made a major deal, sending Bill White, Dick Groat, and Bob Uecker to the Philadelphia Phillies..."

I wasn't that surprised. Although I had won my sixth Gold Glove for the '65 season, and batted .289, it hadn't been the best year for me or the team. Besides, trades are a fundamental part of baseball. I didn't take being traded personally.

Still, going to another team and another city is a major change for a player, and even more so for his family. So most general managers made it a point to give the player being traded a heads-up before it was officially announced, so that he could prepare himself and his family.

I had been out of contact while hunting—this of course was long before cell phones—so I thought maybe management had tried to reach me at home. When I got back home I asked my wife if the Cardinals' front office had called.

No one had called.

It was the sort of petty, unclassy behavior I had come to expect from Howsam. But the next day it got worse. In the *St. Louis Globe-Democrat,* Howsam was quoted as saying that one reason I'd been traded was because "Bill White is older than he says he is." Howsam told the *Globe-Democrat* that I was actually thirty-seven, not thirty-one.

And that made me furious.

It's true that some baseball players tried to pass themselves off as younger than they were. With baseball players, like cars, your "model year" made a big difference in your value; a 1959 Cadillac was worth a lot less than a 1965 Cadillac. It's also true that fudging on age was more prevalent among black players, especially former Negro League players from the rural South where birth records weren't as meticulous as in other places. I couldn't blame the black players for that. Denied access to the majors for so long, it was understandable that they would try to string out their playing years.

But I had a birth certificate, high school and college records, military records, any of which could have established my age if anyone wanted to check. Howsam hadn't bothered. He just flat-out lied, presumably to get back at me for supporting Bing Devine. It was the most vicious, contemptible thing that anyone in baseball management had ever done to me.

The next day, I stormed down to the Cardinals' office. Ada Ireland, the receptionist outside Howsam's office, saw the look on my face and knew exactly what the problem was.

"Go in there and get him!" she said—and I did. I walked into Howsam's office without knocking and lit into him.

"I've been traded before, no big deal," I said. "But what gives you the right to say I lied about my age?"

Howsam actually looked afraid.

"The trainer told me you were older."

"Bullshit. Bob [Bauman, the trainer] would never say that."

"Harry Walker told me that, too."

That was even more ridiculous.

"More bullshit," I said. "You're lying. Harry and I are like brothers. He would never say that. You're trying to hurt my career with these lies."

It went like that for a while, and finally a cowed Bob Howsam promised not to make any more references to my age. I stormed out, not shutting the door behind me.

As it happened, years later I would settle the score with him.

I played three seasons as first baseman for the Phillies. It was a lot different from playing in St. Louis.

The Phillies were the longest-running same-city franchise in sports. They had started there in 1883 and while they'd had a few good years, in the late 1950s and early 1960s they consistently ranked at or near the bottom of the National League; in 1961 they lost twenty-three straight games. Their 1964 team had had a shot, with the Phillies six and a half games in front until they suddenly collapsed—it was called "the Philly Phold"—and wound up losing the pennant to the Cardinals by one game.

The Philadelphia fans were unforgiving of failure. I remember playing the Phillies in Connie Mack Stadium in 1961, a season in which the Phillies would finish forty-six games back, and while the fans were tough on us (the visiting team from St. Louis) they were even tougher on their home team. It was a small park, with the fans close, and when the Phillies took the field they were pelted with shouts of "Bums!" "Losers!" and worse. The fans' mood had not improved by the time I got there in 1966, even though we had a pretty good team that year.

People often ask me what it's like for major league ballplayers to be on the field while people in the stands are booing them. I can't speak for other players, but it never bothered me a bit. In fact, after the verbal abuse I'd taken as a minor league player in the South, merely being called a "bum" by an opposing team's fans was almost like a promotion.

Sometimes I even got a kick out of it. I remember when I was with the Cardinals, whenever we'd have a road game in San Francisco there was an elderly Chinese gentleman with white hair and a cane who would come to the park early to watch us warm up. I would hear the *tap, tap, tap* of his cane as he walked down to the rail, and then he would call out, "Bill White, you horseshit! You horseshit Bill White!" I don't know why he singled me out. Maybe he remembered that I'd briefly been a San Francisco Giant before I had publicly asked to be traded, and he thought I was a traitor or something. But it happened before every game we had at Candlestick. "Bill White, you horseshit!"

Then one day I heard the *tap, tap, tap* of his cane and I heard him call out, "Hey Bill White! Gimme a ball!" I figured, *Hey, no hard feelings,* so I picked up a ball and tossed it to him. He looked at the ball, and then he looked at me and said, "Thanks, Bill White! But you still horseshit!"

I busted up laughing. That was just the way fans were. You couldn't take it personally. In fact, when the old gentleman died a year later I missed him.

Still, the Philadelphia fans were tougher than most. Oddly enough, I don't remember them ever singling me out for booing, even when I made a mistake. I like to think it was because they knew I was giving the team 100 percent, that I would never, as we said in baseball, go out there and "jake it"—that is, just go through the motions.

But if the Philadelphia fans were tough on their team, the local media were even worse. In St. Louis we had taken occasional shots from Harry Caray, but in general the St. Louis media loved their Cardinals. They ate with us, drank with us, hung out with us. But reporters in the City of Brotherly Love didn't show a lot of love for their team.

Still, I liked the area, and so did my family when they joined me there. Eventually we built a nice home on five acres of land in a community called Chalfont in Bucks County, about sixty miles outside Philadelphia. It was a good place to raise our kids, who now numbered five; my son Steve had been born in 1964, and Mike was born in Doylestown, Pennsylvania, in 1969. The public schools were good and there were a number of outstanding colleges in the area.

True, in the late 1960s some communities in the area still tried to bar blacks from buying homes, but we never had any problems. That may have been partly because I was a major league ballplayer—African American athletes, entertainers, and other "celebrities" were often treated better than, say, African American bankers or lawyers—but also because our neighbors realized that we were no different from anybody else. We wanted a nice home, a nice yard, a safe environment for our children.

Most of our kids' friends were from white families, but that never made any difference. Our kids were too young to remember or understand the bitter civil rights struggles of the '50s and '60s, and I never told them about the indignities I'd encountered in my early days as a ballplayer. I thought if I told them about what I'd gone through, they might expect to be treated the same way, and I didn't want that. I didn't want them to feel like they were somehow different from any other Americans.

In any event, I knew that I would probably stay in Pennsylvania when my playing career ended.

And I also knew that would be coming soon.

Someone once calculated that the average career of a major league baseball player was 5.6 years—and even after subtracting my two years in the army, by the beginning of the 1966 season I was already beyond that, with nine seasons in the majors. I was thirty-two years old, which is late middle age by baseball standards, and I was already dealing with injuries to my left shoulder. I knew I was closer to the end of my career than I was to the beginning.

In my first season with the Phillies I batted a respectable .276, had 103 RBIs, and was awarded my seventh—and last—Gold Glove.

But after the season, just before Christmas, I was playing racquet-ball at the Jewish Community Center in St. Louis when I tore my right Achilles tendon.

Given the medical treatments available at the time, Achilles tendon injuries were often career enders. I had an operation and spent a month in a cast, but then I went to spring training and tore the damn thing again. The docs told me I shouldn't play again until August, but I felt an obligation to play before that. That was a mistake. In the 1967 season, I played in only 110 games, often as a pinch hitter, and had only thirty-three RBIs. By 1968, with the tendon injury still hampering my play, I was down to .239. I simply wasn't playing up to my own expectations. I felt I was embarrassing myself and the team.

I decided it was time to go.

I had planned to retire at the end of the '68 season, but Phillies general manager John Quinn asked me to stay another year. He thought that my ankle problems would clear up and I could still be useful to the team. I finally said I would, but I told John they could cut my $64,000 salary down to $54,000.

That's right. I offered to take a pay cut. That may sound crazy— and I guess it was. But as I said earlier, I had never been afraid to demand more money when I was playing well, so it was only right that I got less money when I was playing badly.

In the meantime, though, Bing Devine had been rehired as the Cardinals' general manager, and he wanted me to come back to St. Louis for the '69 season. His plan was for me to play one more year and then go into managing, starting with running the Cardinals' AAA club in Tulsa.

At first I said no to the proposed trade, but Bing was persuasive. So I left my family in Pennsylvania and went back to St. Louis.

I had a dismal year. I played in only forty-nine games, mostly as a pinch hitter. I batted just .211, with only four RBIs and not a single home run.

And finally it was over. At the end of the 1969 season, I played my last game in the major leagues. When an announcement appeared on the scoreboard saying that Bill White was retiring, I didn't notice many cheers, or many boos, either. I wasn't surprised. I had been gone from the Cardinals for three years, and there were a lot of newer, younger players for the fans to root for. They were respectful to me, but my time was past.

That's the way baseball is. Sooner or later, the cheering stops.

Now, I know what people expect. They expect me to say that as I left the clubhouse for the last time as a major league player that I felt an ache in my heart, or that tears welled up in my eyes, or that as I walked away I stopped and took a long, mournful look back.

But no. Being a baseball player had been a big part of my life, and for the most part I had had a good run.

But I wasn't sad to leave playing baseball behind.

I had other plans.

CHAPTER 9

One day in late 1970, I was at a luncheon in Philadelphia when I ran into Howard Cosell. And once again, through a chance meeting, my life took another turn.

I had known Howard Cosell before he *was* Howard Cosell. When I first met him at spring training in Florida in the late 1950s, he was far from being a nationally known figure. Instead he was just this strange, aggressive guy who'd come up and stick his little tape recorder in your face and start bombarding you with rapid-fire questions for his five-minute radio show, *Speaking of Sports*.

A lot of players I knew avoided him and wouldn't give him interviews—at least not until he got famous. They were used to reporters who only wanted to ask about baseball, homers who would lob them softball questions that wouldn't annoy either the players themselves or the fans back home who supported them. But Howard wasn't like that. He wanted controversy. And besides, Howard didn't hand out cheap transistor radios or boxes of razor blades or cartons of cigarettes or any of the other crap that baseball players liked to get in exchange for radio or TV interviews. So why should they waste time with the guy?

But I respected Howard, especially after he took up the cause of racial segregation in baseball spring training in 1961. Howard was the only broadcaster to push the story. And in fact throughout his career, Howard was publicly identified as a crusader against racism in sports.

Anyway, the luncheon at the Sheraton Hotel in Philadelphia was being put on by the National Football League—NFL commissioner Pete Rozelle was there—and the banquet room was filled with local sportswriters and broadcasters and some of the more prominent local Eagles season ticket holders. Howard was the scheduled entertainment.

But before lunch began, as everybody was milling around, Howard saw me and came over to say hello. We chatted for a while, and he said he'd seen some of the sports reports I'd been doing for a local Philadelphia TV station. Then Howard told me he was going to cover a fight in Italy in a few weeks, and he wanted me to come along and work the event with him.

"Howard, I don't know anything about boxing."

"That's all right," he said. "If you listen to my critics, neither do I."

That was a joke, of course. By this time, Howard was nationally known for his boxing coverage, most notably his coverage of the career of Muhammad Ali.

Howard persisted, and while I was flattered by the offer, in the end I turned him down. Although I often watched boxing on TV, I hadn't been to a fight since Ali spattered me with Donnie Fleeman's blood in Miami in 1961. I just didn't think that I was ready for such a high-profile assignment in a sport I had never covered.

Howard was nice about it. I think he understood.

But as it turned out, Howard's interest in me didn't end there.

                    *   *   *

By the time I had that chance meeting with Howard Cosell, I had already had years of broadcasting experience—in virtually every sport except boxing.

When the Cardinals traded me to Philadelphia after the 1965 season, I gave up my radio reporting for KMOX in St. Louis. And when I got to Philadelphia, I had no intention of taking up broadcasting again. I wanted to concentrate on playing baseball.

But I hadn't figured on Lew Klein.

Lew Klein was executive producer at the local Philadelphia TV station WFIL (now WPVI), an ABC affiliate owned by Walter Annenberg. A true broadcast pioneer, Lew had helped develop everything from college educational programs to *Romper Room* to a Philadelphia-based teen music and dance show called *Bandstand,* with a young host named Dick Clark; later it became better known as *American Bandstand*.

When Lew heard I'd been traded to the Phillies after the 1965 season, he called me in St. Louis and asked if I wanted to do some TV sports work in Philadelphia when I got there.

I was noncommittal. Although I'd been interviewed on TV numerous times, I'd never done TV work as a broadcaster; I wasn't sure I'd have the time to learn how to work in a new medium. But I agreed to meet Lew at the upcoming annual Sports Writers Banquet in Philadelphia in January. At the luncheon, Lew took me aside and told me he wanted me to work for WFIL-TV. But I had been thinking it over and I told him no.

I had good reasons. I knew how tough the Philadelphia sports media were on players. I could imagine what they'd do to me if as a brand-new and relatively well-paid Phillie—I was making $64,000 a year—I immediately took a job with local TV and then slumped on the baseball field. The sportswriters and the fans would murder me, saying I was more interested in seeing my face on TV than in my batting average. Besides, my family was happy in St. Louis, and I planned to spend the off season back there.

But Lew, being Lew, was insistent. Finally I told him that no matter what I wanted, I was sure Phillies manager Gene Mauch and general manager John Quinn would never approve.

So Lew pulled a fast one on me.

"If they [Mauch and Quinn] agree to it, will you?" Lew asked me. I told him, yeah, if it was okay with Gene and John I would seriously consider it.

Having never spent much time in Philadelphia, what I didn't know was that both Mauch and Quinn already had their own five-minute sports shows on WFIL—and that Lew had already pressed them to let me have a show as well. So later, when I casually mentioned Lew's offer to them, their immediate response was, "That's a great idea!"

I was boxed in. Later Lew Klein prepared a three-year contract with the station for me, and I told him I would sign it on one condition: Lew would have to call my wife and kids in St. Louis and tell them they had to move to Pennsylvania. Although they later came to love the Philadelphia area, moving is always hard on a family with young children. Lew agreed to make the call—and being a persuasive guy, he got my wife to agree to the deal.

So even as I was getting used to a new town and a new team, I was back in broadcasting.

Lew and the other top people at WFIL were supportive of me, but I knew I had a lot to learn about television. I was still a ballplayer who was broadcasting, not a broadcaster who was also playing baseball. I had a tendency to look down at my script, to avoid speaking directly to the camera. And my diction was that of the ball field, not the broadcast booth; for example, I routinely dropped my g's, saying "goin'" instead of "going," and so on.

To help me improve, twice a week the station sent me up to

New York to meet with a voice coach named Lilyan Wilder, who during her career would help a host of TV personalities and politicians hone their skills, including Oprah Winfrey, Maria Shriver, Jessica Savitch, and NBA star Oscar Robertson.

(Although Lilyan helped teach me how to say things, she couldn't teach me what to say—and what not to. After years of trash-talking with other players on the ball field, I was terrified that when I actually went live on the air I would accidentally use profanity—drop an F-bomb, or even a mother F-bomb—without even thinking about it. I wasn't a natural cusser, but in baseball, as in the military, cussing was simply part of the life. I sometimes got around that by imagining that my churchgoing grandmother was standing next to me while I was on the air—and only once in more than two decades of radio and television broadcasting did I actually slip in that regard. While I was calling a Yankees game, there was a bobbled ball that I lost sight of and for some reason I said, "Where's the goddamn ball?" Fortunately this was before the days of instant digital playback, and while I'm sure some viewers might have thought, *Did he just say what I thought he said?* there was no way to prove it. The station didn't get a single complaint.)

I started off at WFIL during the baseball season doing a five-minute pre-game show. The slot had previously been occupied by Phillies first baseman Dick Stuart, a good hitter but a notoriously spotty fielder. Variously known to sportswriters as "the Man with the Iron Glove" and "Dr. Strangeglove," to this day he holds the season record for errors by a first baseman (twenty-nine). When Dick was traded to the Mets after the 1965 season, I took over both his position with the Phillies and his slot at WFIL; *The Dick Stuart Show* became *The Bill White Show.*

The show itself was pretty easy. All I had to do was answer baseball questions sent in by viewers. The show was taped, and I got to choose the questions, so fortunately I never had to deal with questions like "That guy Mauch is a lousy manager, why don't they get rid of him?"

The show was sponsored by Coca-Cola and by the Philadelphia-based Tasty Baking Company, maker of Tastykake packaged cakes and pies. Only after I started the show did I learn that some years earlier, in 1960, a group of black ministers had organized a boycott of Tastykake products because of racial discrimination within the company. The boycott ended when Tasty management agreed to hire more blacks and desegregate locker and washrooms at their plants, but when I started my show there were still some complaints about limited hiring of blacks in the company. That was troubling to me. If it was true, I didn't see how I could continue to promote their products, whatever the impact on my budding TV career. So I initiated a meeting with company executives, who assured me they were working hard to correct the problem—and in fact, by the 1970s Tasty Baking had become a leader in black employment and community support programs.

After the 1966 baseball season ended, I started working full-time as a sports reporter for WFIL, at a salary of about $35,000 a year—which combined with my baseball salary gave me a pretty good annual income. I worked under longtime WFIL sports director and anchor Les Keiter, and basically covered the stories that Les either didn't want or didn't have time to do.

Eventually I covered almost every sport. Big Five college basketball games, Ivy League college football, college gymnastics, horse racing, professional tennis. I even covered the Cowtown Rodeo in New Jersey. If I didn't know anything about the sport involved—I certainly didn't know much about rodeo—I always made sure to have an expert with me to try to avoid making a fool of myself. I often wondered how I got away with it, but I did.

Still, there were occasional slipups. For example, although

another Philadelphia station held broadcast rights for the Philadelphia Flyers NHL hockey team, they would occasionally contract with us to cover out-of-town games. Once I flew out to the West Coast to do play-by-play for a Flyers game, and while I knew a little bit about hockey—I had season tickets to the Flyers games—after so many years in baseball I couldn't break myself of the habit of calling the puck a "ball." Luckily the game was being taped for later replay, not broadcast live, so when I took the tape back to Philadelphia the engineers had to dub me in saying "puck" every time I had actually said "ball."

Another time the station wanted me to do a televised spot with the Flyers, so they dressed me up in a goalie uniform and parked me in front of the net during a practice session. The players thought that was great fun. I didn't have a mask, or a cup for that matter, so the players had been instructed to keep their goal shots below knee level so that I wouldn't ruin the promo by getting hit in the teeth— or worse, even lower—by a hundred-mile-an-hour puck. But one of the Flyers must have forgotten because he shot the puck straight at my head. Fortunately, while I may not have been a hockey player, I was still a first baseman; I gloved that puck like a pro.

All in all I enjoyed being a television sports broadcaster—and with a lot of help, I was getting better at it.

Then, as I said earlier, before the 1969 baseball season I got traded back to the Cardinals, with Cards general manager Bing Devine hoping that I would stay on with the club as manager of their Tulsa AAA team. But by this time my family was settled in the Philadelphia area, and I just couldn't see myself managing a minor league team until the Cardinals' front office saw fit to bring me up. I turned the managing job down.

WFIL management was nice enough to keep my Philadelphia job open for me during that final year with the Cardinals, and when the Cardinals played in Philadelphia I would do specials for

With my friend, the late
Bart Giamatti, when Bart
was commissioner of Major
League Baseball

With George Stein-
brenner and Dr. Bobby
Brown, the former
Yankee great and
American League
president

With President
George H. W. Bush

With my friend
and former
teammate,
Willie Mays

With Fay Vincent, Monte Irvin, Buck O'Neil, and, in front, Roy Campanella, Buck Leonard, and Ray Dandridge in Cooperstown, New York (White is top row, far right)

With Hank Aaron

With Phil Rizzuto and Yankee broadcaster Mel Allen

With tennis great Arthur Ashe and Arthur White (no relation), at a Jackie Robinson Dinner

My first home run at Busch Stadium on my first at-bat in the big leagues

With Yankee catching great
Elston Howard

With Peter O'Malley
and Chub Feeney

Making the put-out on Billy Bruton of the Milwaukee Braves

With Donn
Clendenon

With Johnny Keane
and Julian Javier

On the air at KMOX
Radio (circa 1960)

At Danville,
Virgina, in 1953

With my children:
(from l to r) Debbie,
Tom, Steve, Bill,
Edna, Mike

Edna M. Young, my
mother

A photo of me fishing on
Kodiak Island, Alaska

My high school
basketball team
(White is bottom
row, far left)

My high school football team (White is top row, second from the left)

Ready for some
glove work at
first base

Eager to hit with
the Cardinals

At Jackie Robinson's gravesite

the station. After I retired from baseball after the 1969 season, I
went back to WFIL as their 6 PM and 11 PM sports anchor, part of
the "Action News Team" concept that was just being developed.
I like to think that I played a small role in helping WFIL go from
last place to first in Philadelphia TV news ratings. Later I was also
named the station sports director.

In short, by 1970 I had a good job and a nice home in Philadelphia. At age thirty-six, I was looking forward to a long career as a
Philadelphia broadcaster.

And then I ran into Howard Cosell at that luncheon.

Howard was a friend of Mike Burke, the president of the New York
Yankees, which were owned by CBS. Shortly after I saw Howard
at the luncheon in Philadelphia, Burke mentioned to Howard that
the Yankees were looking for a new broadcaster to help call the
Yankees games.

At the time, the Yankees were slowly climbing out of the worst
slump in the team's history. After the Cardinals beat them in the
World Series in 1964, the Yankees finished the next season in
the bottom half of the American League for the first time in four
decades. The year after that, in 1966, they finished dead last—
something they hadn't done since 1912. By 1970, they were improv-
ing somewhat, finishing second in the AL East, but it would be
several more years before they again became serious contenders.

Of course, all their biggest stars were gone—Mantle, Maris,
Ford, and on and on. And their fans had left them, too. In one infamous home game against the White Sox in September 1966, with
the Yankees in last place, Yankee Stadium reported a paid attendance of just 413—this in a stadium with 67,000 seats. The New
York *Daily News* ran a photo of Mike Burke, attending his first
game as Yankees president, sitting alone in the deserted stands—
and he was yawning.

There was trouble in the Yankees broadcast booth as well. Mel Allen, the legendary "Voice of the New York Yankees," with his trademark "Hello-o-o-o-o every-*body*!" had been unceremoniously fired in late 1964. The explanation was that his major sponsor, Ballantine beer, was losing sales and blamed Mel for it. Although for years Mel had shamelessly plugged them on the air—when a Yankee hit a home run, Mel would sing out, "There goes another Ballantine Blast!"—Ballantine executives had decided that he was talking too much and was boring on the air. Although major sponsors couldn't technically fire a broadcaster, they exerted a lot of influence. First Mel was passed over to cover the 1964 World Series—the first Yankees World Series he'd missed in almost two decades—and then a couple of months later he was given the boot.

Red Barber, who had broadcast Yankees games with Allen since 1954—not always happily—was also fired, in 1966. Unemotional on the air, Red was the exact opposite of a homer, who rooted for the home team. To the frustration of the Yankees owners, he called the games from a neutral point of view. Red also had an annoying habit of correcting on-air the grammatical mistakes of his cobroadcasters, especially Phil Rizzuto, the former Yankees shortstop who had joined the broadcast team in 1957. Red hadn't increased his popularity with the owners when he unsuccessfully demanded that the cameras scan the meager crowd at the aforementioned 1966 game against the White Sox, and then went on and on about the poor attendance—again, this while president Mike Burke was sitting in the stands. Burke fired him a week later.

The Yankees tried various fixes in the broadcast booth. In 1963, they brought in Jerry Coleman, a former Yankees second baseman. Jerry was nicknamed "the Colonel," because he was one; he had flown combat missions in World War II and Korea as a marine aviator and was a lieutenant colonel in the reserves. Coleman was later replaced by a guy named Bob Gamere, who was a former announcer for Holy Cross football games. Gamere lasted just one season.

In 1965, the Yankees had brought in Joe Garagiola, the former Cardinals catcher who had called games for KMOX radio in St. Louis. Joe was colorful, with a great on-air personality, but he was destined for bigger things with the network and left after a couple of seasons. Joe was replaced in 1968 by Frank Messer, a traditional play-by-play announcer. Rizzuto called him "Old Reliable"—and he was exactly that. But even though Frank was a great traditional broadcaster, he didn't light a fire among the fans.

The bottom line was that by 1970 the Yankees were struggling on the field, at the ticket booths, and on the air. They needed something to make headlines, fire up the fans, put some spark into the team's image.

So when Mike Burke mentioned to Howard Cosell that the Yankees were looking for a new broadcaster, Howard told him that he had heard me calling a basketball game in Philadelphia and had been impressed.

It was later reported that the Yankees looked at a field of two hundred candidates for the broadcasting job, although I don't know if that's true. All I know is that late in 1970, Burke called and invited me to a meeting in New York.

I had just signed a three-year contract as sports director for WFIL in Philadelphia, and I was happy in the job. And as it turned out, since I was an unproven commodity, the Yankees were actually offering less money than I was making at WFIL.

But I couldn't turn down the invitation. The Yankees may have had their troubles, but they were still the big time. And New York City was the center of the broadcasting world.

So I took the train up to the city and met with Burke and his right-hand man, Howard Berk, in the thirty-fifth-floor conference room at "Black Rock," the CBS headquarters. We talked for ninety minutes while Burke and Berk sized me up. Howard Cosell later told me that the two executives liked my voice and relaxed style, and thought I would click with Messer and Rizzuto in the broadcast booth. Although I'd never called baseball play-by-play before, they thought I could do the job.

Nobody mentioned it at the time, but there was another reason the Yankees were interested in me—I was black. There had never been a full-time black play-by-play announcer in the major leagues, and the Yankees knew that hiring me would create some buzz.

In any event, a few weeks after the meeting, the Yankees offered me the job.

(It's a little confusing, but while the Yankees picked me for the job, none of the Yankees broadcasters worked directly for the Yankees. The team contracted out its game coverage to New York independent TV station WPIX, channel 11, which in turn sold the radio broadcast rights to WMCA AM-570. But although WPIX signed my paychecks, the Yankees retained the right to decide who broadcast their games.)

It was a big break for me, and I was always grateful to Howard Cosell for helping to make it happen. But sadly, things didn't turn out well between us.

I can hardly even remember how it started. But apparently years later one of my broadcast teammates made an on-air remark that Howard thought was disparaging to the ABC-TV network—and I had laughed about it on the air. Howard was always fiercely loyal to ABC, and I guess he took it personally. The next few times I saw him at games or other functions I would say hello to him and he would completely ignore me, just walk on by without a word. At first I didn't think much of it—Howard was always kind of moody and strange—but after a few times I called him on it.

"Howard, is there a problem? Why are you ignoring me?"

"You denigrated my company," Howard said. (He always called ABC "my company.")

I honestly didn't know what he was talking about. And after he explained it, I still didn't understand what the problem was. Maybe he was expecting an apology, but I didn't think I owed him one.

"So is this the way you want it to be?" I said. "Just ignoring each other?"

"Yes," Howard said.

So that was how it was. We never spoke again.

Howard became a sad figure toward the end. During his career, he made far more enemies than friends—and as he did with me, he often turned on people for little or no reason. He was drinking heavily, pouring down vodka like water, and he became increasingly isolated. I would see him sometimes in stadium press rooms, sitting alone—no one wanted to sit with him—and ranting to himself.

In one bizarre episode, I was broadcasting a Yankees game when I noticed Howard coming into the broadcast booth. I didn't think anything of it, but then Howard, apparently drunk, slipped up behind me, reached his hand around, and without saying a word poked me in the larynx with his finger! I gagged a little, quickly cut the mike, then jumped up and shouted "You son-of-a-bitch, what the hell are you doing?" But by that time Howard had already fled out the door.

Like I said. Bizarre.

When Howard died in 1995, I was asked to say a eulogy at his funeral. I was still grateful to Howard for the help he had given me, but this was a funeral, and I knew they wanted me to stand up there and talk about what a good guy and a good friend Howard had been.

I couldn't. I had to pass.

I just couldn't bring myself to lie.

*   *   *

As expected, the announcement that the Yankees had hired former first baseman Bill White as a full-time broadcaster generated
headlines—for what I thought was the wrong reason. High up in
every story, in the lead or the second paragraph, the writers always
noted that I was the first black full-time announcer in Major League
Baseball history.

I wasn't naive. I knew that the words *first* and *black* were what
made a small story a bigger story. But I had never emphasized my
being black during my broadcast career—and now not just the
sportswriters but Yankees management were, in my opinion, over-
emphasizing it. In virtually every statement about my hiring, Yankees president Mike Burke said something along the lines of, "I
think Bill's going to be good. I think he'll be a fast learner. And
being black is a plus."

That last line bothered me. If I failed at the job, I didn't want it
to seem that I had failed black people in general, or that a failure
on my part meant black people couldn't do the job. I didn't intend
to fail, but if for some reason I did, I didn't want it to be symbolic
of anything.

So a couple of weeks after I was hired, when Mike Burke took
me out to dinner at Pearl's Chinese restaurant, I brought it up.

"Do we have to keep pointing out that I'm black?" I asked him.
"I think everybody already knows that—and if they don't, they'll
figure it out the minute they see me on television. Why keep making an issue out of it?"

Burke was a smart, articulate, interesting guy. A former college
football player, he had served with the OSS (Office of Strategic Services, the forerunner of the CIA) in World War II and had
parachuted into occupied France. A former executive director of
Ringling Bros. circus, as an executive at CBS he had talked the network into buying the Yankees and then was named president of

the club. He told me straight out that his repeated references to my race had a serious purpose.

"We have a stadium not too far from Harlem," he said. "I want those black kids growing up in Harlem to realize that when they grow up they can do what you're doing."

I thought Mike was being sincere. I also thought he was a smart businessman. So I let it go.

In the meantime, I was determined to be the best major league broadcaster that I could be—of any color.

I first called Jack Buck, who was still calling games for the Cardinals in St. Louis, and set up a meeting. A week later, I walked into the Stadium Club at Busch Stadium and found Jack sitting with Dan Kelly, another KMOX radio man who was one of the best hockey broadcasters in the business. Our "lunch" meeting lasted for six hours as those two fine broadcasters held a seminar on how to do play-by-play. I took notes and taped every word, and then went over it again and again.

After that I called Vin Scully, the great Dodgers broadcaster, and asked for some tapes to study; he was glad to help. The Yankees also sent me tapes of their TV broadcasts, which I watched with the sound off, recording myself calling the game as I watched. Then I sent the tapes to Lilyan Wilder for critiquing. Then I would do it all over again.

The point is that I worked hard to get ready. As with everything else I'd done in my life, I wasn't going to let myself fail for lack of preparation.

There wasn't much time. After taking the Yankees job, I had promised WFIL in Philadelphia that I would stay on as sports director and sports anchor until a replacement was found. (Although I was under contract with the station when I accepted the Yankees job, the station was in the process of being sold and didn't try to hold me to the contract.) Finally, on the day after my last day at

WFIL I got on a plane and flew to Miami, where the Yankees were playing a spring training game.

Marty Appel, the team's assistant PR director, picked me up at the airport and drove me to the stadium, where the game was already under way. It was there that I met for the very first time my new Yankees broadcast partners, Frank Messer and Phil Rizzuto.

I couldn't have known it at the time. But it was the start of a long and beautiful friendship.

CHAPTER 10

Spring training 1971, New York Yankees versus the Baltimore Orioles at the old Miami Stadium. It was the bottom of the ninth, score tied, Orioles at bat, two outs, and the Orioles' Chico Salmon was stepping up to the plate.

I was just seconds away from a disastrous debut as a play-by-play announcer for the New York Yankees.

And it was all because Phil Rizzuto wanted to play golf with Joe DiMaggio.

I actually wasn't supposed to be doing play-by-play at all. Given my lack of play-by-play experience—I had done color commentary for basketball and hockey at WFIL, but never play-by-play—the Yankees had decided that for my first few months in the broadcast booth, I would do background and color commentary. So when Marty Appel brought me to the booth that day, the plan was for me to watch Phil and Frank Messer for a while and then join Phil for the last three innings to be introduced to the Yankees' radio audience as the new broadcaster.

It seemed like a good way to ease me in. This was, after all, just an exhibition game, and it was being broadcast back in New York only on radio, not on WPIX-TV. A spring training game against the Mets or maybe the archfoe Boston Red Sox might rate a TV broadcast back home, but not a routine spring training game against Baltimore.

But what a lot of people don't realize—I didn't quite realize it, either, at the time—is that calling a baseball game on radio is a lot harder than calling a game on TV. The reason is simple: On TV, the camera does most of your work for you. On radio, your audience knows only what you tell them.

Anyway, it went well at first. I sat in the back of the booth for a few innings and watched Rizzuto and Messer work.

As I said, I'd never met either of them before—which wasn't unusual. Messer had always been a broadcaster, and Rizzuto had left the game as a player just as I was starting in the big leagues.

But it was immediately clear to me that Messer was a consummate professional broadcaster—low-key, knowledgeable, absolutely competent at everything he did. Rizzuto, meanwhile, was—well, he was Phil Rizzuto.

By that time, 1971, Phil was in his fifteenth season as a Yankees broadcaster, this after thirteen years as the Yankees' shortstop— and he was a certified New York City icon, what one writer described as "every Yankee fan's favorite daffy uncle." He was already famous for calling people "huckleberries" and for his signature expression, "Holy cow!"

(People used to argue about whether Rizzuto had stolen "Holy cow!" from St. Louis's Harry Caray. Harry had been in broadcasting longer than Phil, and had probably used it before Phil did. But it was an old expression, dating back at least to the early twentieth century. In any event, it was Phil who made it most famous.)

Frankly I hadn't heard many of Phil's broadcasts before then;

I had always been more of a National League guy, and so I hadn't watched many Yankees games. But as I've mentioned, I'd done some research. I had called around to ask about Phil "Scooter" Rizzuto.

One of the people I called was Larry Doby, the second black major league player (he joined the Cleveland Indians eleven weeks after Jackie Robinson joined the Dodgers in 1947) and the first black player in the American League. Another was Elston Howard, the first black player with the Yankees. Both said the same thing:

"Scooter? Great guy."

Although he never got nearly the attention that Jackie Robinson received, Larry Doby had suffered many of the same indignities that Jackie had, including being snubbed by many of his team-mates. But Larry said that even though they were on opposing teams, Rizzuto had gone out of his way to make him feel welcome, shaking his hand when some of his own teammates wouldn't. Ellie Howard said that Rizzuto did the same when he joined the Yan-kees as their first black player in 1955.

Of course, I would have to make up my own mind about Phil. But the initial reports I got gave me a good feeling.

And while Phil and Frank couldn't have been more different—Frank six foot two and big-shouldered, with a clear, deep-timbred voice, Phil barely five foot six at the tallest time of his day, with a high-pitched, nasally Brooklyn accent—they seemed to work well with each other.

So at the top of the sixth inning I sat down next to Phil at the microphones and he introduced me—something like, "Ladies and gentlemen, I'd like to introduce the newest member of our broad-cast team, Bill White, former star first baseman for the Cardinals and the Phillies."

We chatted a bit between action on the field, with Phil asking me about my sports reporting in Philadelphia and me throwing in some observations on the game. Frank Messer had left the booth to go down to the field.

Then, just as the aforementioned Chico Salmon was stepping up to the plate, there was a commotion in the back of the press box—a commotion in the form of Joe DiMaggio.

Even though DiMaggio had been retired from baseball for almost twenty years, he was still a star. Everywhere he went people gawked and shouted and waved—which is exactly what was happening as he walked past the press box at Miami Stadium. People were gawking and shouting and waving—Phil Rizzuto included.

"Holy cow!" Phil said on-air when he saw his old Yankees teammate. "There's the Yankee Clipper!" Then he leaned over to me and whispered, off-air, "Hey, White, take the mike, I gotta set up a golf game with DiMaggio." He took off his headphones and bolted out the door.

There were three firsts that occurred in that moment.

It was the first of thousands of times that I would personally hear Phil say "Holy cow!"

It was the first time Phil called me "White"—not Bill, just "White," last-naming me the same way he did with everybody he ever worked with. Although he would occasionally refer to me on the air as "Bill White," never in all the years we knew each other did Phil ever directly address me as "Bill."

And the final "first" was that it was the first time I had to call a Yankees game alone.

It wouldn't have been so bad if Chico Salmon, who had batted .250 the season before, had had the decency to strike out. Instead, he crushed a ball deep toward left field.

And as the ball sailed up and up toward the left field fence, all I could think to say was, "Uh-oh."

And after that, for a few terrible seconds, silence.

Remember, this was radio. On TV, viewers could have seen

what was happening, but on radio they were depending on me. So I should have said something like, *It's a hit, deep to left field, it's going, going...*

But I didn't. I just said "Uh-oh."

In fairness, as the ball cleared the fence I recovered somewhat.

"Ladies and gentlemen," I said, "there's a parking lot out there beyond left field, and that ball is in it. That's a home run and this game is over."

The words themselves weren't bad. But my delivery lacked any emotion, was almost monotone, without the audio drama and excitement that radio requires. My first time behind a Yankees microphone and I had fallen flat.

At that point Phil came rushing back in, grabbed the mike, and told the listeners to be sure to stay tuned for the post-game show with Frank Messer. After we signed off Phil couldn't have been nicer, telling me what a great job I'd done and so on.

It never even occurred to me to be mad at Phil for leaving me alone in the booth. I was already realizing that Phil was one of those guys you just couldn't be mad at. He was so open, so genuine, that you didn't just forgive him his trespasses—you laughed out loud about them.

Unfortunately, not everyone was as kind as Phil. Back in New York, Howard Berk, Yankees president Mike Burke's right-hand man, was listening to the game and heard me call the home run. He immediately called Miami Stadium and spoke to Bob Fishel, the Yankees' PR director.

"Bob, that was the worst call I ever heard!"

I made more mistakes along the way, but the Yankees management stood behind me. A few months after my debut Howard Berk invited me to lunch at 21, the popular restaurant near CBS headquarters, and had me sit down with Bob Fishel and Tom Villante, a former Yankees-batboy-turned-advertising-executive who later became Major League Baseball's executive director of marketing and broadcasting.

Villante was a sharp guy, and had good advice to offer. For example, he said I sometimes stumbled in my play-by-play by trying to give too many names—especially when they were names like "Swoboda" or "Stottlemyre." He suggested I make it simple, leaving the names out until the end: "There's a ground ball to shortstop, he picks it up, throws to first for the out—a nice play by Gene Michael."

Villante also advised me to constantly provide the score, especially on radio broadcasts, since listeners often tuned in and out. Keeping a three-minute egg timer with me in the booth would help remind me about that, he said.

But the most important advice Villante and the others gave me had to do with Phil Rizzuto. Since the Yankees were playing so badly—they finished the season twenty-one games back—the fans needed something else to concentrate on.

"Phil's an oddball and the Yankees are bad," Villante said. "If Phil does something outlandish, pounce on it. Don't fight him, feed off him. Have some fun with him."

And for the next eighteen years, that's exactly what I did.

Most people think of Phil Rizzuto as an eccentric character, not as a broadcast pioneer. But in fact he was one of baseball's early players-turned-broadcasters, helping to pave the way for guys like me.

Born in Brooklyn, the son of a streetcar motorman, Phil had signed with the Yankees in 1937. That he made it into baseball at all was something of a miracle. Earlier he had been rejected by the Dodgers, with manager Casey Stengel telling him that at five foot six and less than 150 pounds he was too small to play in the major leagues. Although he never said so, I don't think Phil ever forgave Stengel for telling him to "go get a shoe-shine box" and start shining shoes for a living instead of trying for a career in baseball.

Phil started out with the Yankees' Class D team in Virginia—the Bassett Furnituremakers—and later played AA ball in Kansas City. In 1941 he was called up as the Yankees shortstop and managed to hit .307 in his rookie season in New York. The following season, he was selected as an All-Star. He spent three years in the navy in World War II and then returned to the Yankees and became the cornerstone of their infield lineup. His best season was in 1950, when he batted .324, made countless brilliant defensive plays, and was voted the American League MVP.

Phil was crushed when in 1956 the Yankees unceremoniously released him—this at the hands of then Yankees manager Stengel, who had treated Phil so shabbily years earlier. Phil freely admitted that he cried when he left the stadium that day.

Still, at age thirty-eight, he had other options. For the past couple of years, Phil had occasionally worked his way into the broadcast booth and called an inning or two of Yankees games when he wasn't playing. And he was a golfing buddy with a lot of executives of the Ballantine beer company, then one of the Yankees broadcasts' major sponsors. The Ballantine guys strongly suggested that the Yankees find a full-time place for Rizzuto in the broadcast booth—and at the time, a suggestion from Ballantine was about the same thing as a direct order. In December 1956, the Yankees announced that Phil would join veteran professional broadcasters Mel Allen and Red Barber in the broadcast booth the following season.

Allen and Barber weren't particularly happy about it. Both of them had attended college—Allen even had a law degree—neither had ever played baseball, and they didn't like the idea of a former player invading their turf.

(Of course, Phil wasn't the first player-turned-broadcaster. There had been a few others, including former Cardinals pitcher Dizzy Dean, who started calling Cardinals games on radio in 1941. Dean was famous for butchering the English language, using *slud* as the past tense of *slide,* and signing off with phrases like "Don't fail to miss tomorrow's game!" Dean was kind of a country-boy version of Phil.)

At times Allen and Barber tried to embarrass Phil, even going so far as to correct his English on the air. For example, Phil would pronounce the word athletics as *atha-letics,* and Mel would say, "Phil, there's no second *a* in *athletics.*" With everybody listening!

Others weren't very supportive, either. Bill MacPhail, a former road secretary for the Yankees and then president of CBS Sports, told Phil, "You'll never make it. You talk through your nose, you've got a Brooklyn accent, your voice is too high, and you breathe at the wrong time."

And Howard Cosell, who himself was then just breaking into sports reporting, told Phil, "You'll never last. You look like George Burns and you sound like Groucho Marx."

Phil didn't think that sounding like Groucho Marx was such a bad thing. But the lack of faith hurt him, and he talked about quitting.

Then a funny thing happened. If the broadcasting pros looked down on him, the fans loved him. They didn't care if he took off on loopy digressions on the air, talking about the lasagna and the cannolis at an Italian restaurant he'd been to the night before, or sending out a happy birthday message to a fan while a fly ball was hanging in the air. They didn't care that he talked about his wife, Cora—he called her "my bride"—or that at times he hardly seemed to know what was happening on the field. They didn't care that he had a Brooklyn accent, and that he said "Holy cow!" in every other sentence, and that he said "atha-letics," and that he was an unabashed homer, openly rooting for the Yankees to win. They loved him for all of it.

Phil later explained his style this way: "First thing that comes in my head I say without really thinking about it. Of course, my wife has told me many times that everybody's got a little trapdoor in the back of their head, and you get an idea and it sits there, and then if you think it's all right to say it, the trapdoor opens and it comes out. And she says my trapdoor is constantly open."

That was Phil. His trapdoor was constantly open.

So the others came and went: Allen and Barber, Joe Garagiola, Jerry Coleman, Bob Gamere. But Phil remained. By the time I joined the Yankees broadcast team in 1971, Phil was a New York institution.

We couldn't have been more different, Phil and I. He was older, fifty-three at the time, and I was thirty-seven. He was the street-wise big-city kid, I was from a small town in the Midwest. He was a high school dropout, while I had been to college for a couple of years.

But we were both old baseball players, and we knew the game and the guys who played and managed it. And somehow, we just clicked. I can honestly say that in our eighteen years, spending hundreds of days together, and thousands of hours, we never once had a cross word, on or off the air.

And I think the viewers and listeners knew that, they could tell that it wasn't some phony broadcast thing where two guys who can't stand each other act like buddies on the air. With Phil and me it was real, and that's what made it work.

Phil was notorious for leaving games early. I'm told that when he first started in broadcasting he was much more conscientious, but by the time I got to the Yankees it was a running joke that Phil would leave a home game in the seventh or eighth inning to beat the traffic over the George Washington Bridge and back to his home in Hillside, New Jersey.

It got to the point that when the WPIX outside camera would

pan the New York skyline during a game and show the George Washington Bridge, whoever was calling the game would say, "And there goes Scooter, heading home to Cora!" Even the fans in the crowd were in on the joke. At a double-header they would hold up signs in the first seventh inning that said things like, HEY SCOOTER, DON'T FORGET THERE'S A SECOND GAME! Eventually someone spoofed Phil's work ethic by posting a sign on the cinder-block wall outside the broadcast booth that said, PHIL RIZZUTO'S OFFICE: OPEN 7–7:30 PM WEEKDAYS, 1–1:30 PM WEEKENDS.

I learned early on about how Phil operated. We were broadcasting a spring training game in Fort Lauderdale, but I had to get down to Miami to pick up my kids, who were flying in for a visit. Phil and Frank Messer told me no problem, I could leave after the sixth inning and they'd handle the rest of the game. So I drove down to Miami, picked up my kids, and drove back to the Yankees' team hotel in Fort Lauderdale—a process that took about four hours. When I walked into the hotel at about 1 AM, the desk clerk had the game on the radio. It was going into the sixteenth inning—and the only voice I could hear was Frank's.

The next day when I went to the stadium, poor Frank was sitting in the broadcast booth, still weary after almost single-handedly calling ten innings of baseball the night before.

"Hey Frank, what happened yesterday? Where was Phil?"

Frank shook his head.

"I don't know. In the seventh inning he asked me if I wanted a cup of coffee and I haven't seen him since."

Just at that moment, Phil walked in with a Styrofoam cup in his hand. He went up to Frank and said, "Hey Messer, here's that coffee I promised you!"

Frank and I looked at each other—and then we burst out laughing. If I'd been in Frank's place, and if it had been anyone but Phil, I would have jumped up and strangled the guy for leaving me in the lurch like that. But it was just Phil being Phil.

I found out later it wasn't the first time, or the last, that Phil had used the "you want a cup of coffee?" gambit to duck out of the broadcast booth. He would say he was going to get a cup of coffee, or go to the bathroom, or to talk to somebody in the hall—and then he'd be on the George Washington Bridge. Everybody knew that once Phil was out of the booth, he was gone.

Sometimes he wouldn't even use a pretense.

Phil was terrified of flying. He'd get on the plane, throw back a couple of straight vodkas—he called it "holy water"—and spend the entire flight with a blanket over his head. So whenever possible he would drive to road games in relatively nearby cities like Baltimore. Once we were doing a game against the Orioles and at the top of the ninth Yankees catcher Thurman Munson hit a shot that looked like a double, but Orioles left fielder Tommy Davis somehow tracked it down and made a beautiful lunging catch. Phil was doing the play-by-play, so he said, "Fly ball to left field, Davis makes the catch—White, tell everybody what happened."

So I turned to the replay monitor and watched the catch, explaining to the viewers the finer points of outfielding, and when I was finished I said, "Back to you, Phil."

Silence. I looked over and Phil was gone. He wanted to beat the stadium traffic and get home to Cora.

I can't think of anyone else, in any profession, who could have gotten away with that sort of thing for as long as Phil did. But again, you didn't just forgive Phil his trespasses, you laughed about them.

Phil was also notorious for his lack of preparation before games. He famously said, "Statistics bore me," an attitude that had infuriated veteran broadcasters like Red Barber. But Phil didn't care.

Once we were calling a game together, and when a batter got a hit off Catfish Hunter I said on the air that it was the seventh hit that season the batter had gotten off Catfish. This little factoid didn't require any special research or feat of memory on my part. It was right there in the press kit, the three- or four-page pre-game report that the Yankees prepared for every game to help the sportswriters and broadcasters pick up on interesting little facts and statistics. Before the game they would put stacks of press kits on a table in the hall to the press room and broadcast booth.

But Phil was amazed at my insight.

"White, how did you know that?" he said on-air.

"It's in the press kit, Phil."

"The what?"

"The press kit. They're over there by the door."

Phil looked confused. Then he said, "Oh. Well, I don't go that way."

Almost twenty years as a Yankees broadcaster. And Phil seemed genuinely amazed that there was this thing called a press kit.

The small but important housekeeping details of broadcasting always strained Phil's attention span. Once I came on to relieve Phil for the last three innings and asked him for his scorecard, the notes that indicated what had happened in the previous innings. The notes were in a form of shorthand: *6–3* meant "shortstop to first," a *K* meant a strikeout, and so on. But I noticed that on Phil's scorecard there were a number of notations that said *WW.*

"Hey, Phil, what does this *WW* mean?"

"Oh. That means I 'wasn't watching.' "

Phil's cheerful lack of preparation inevitably led to snafus. The story goes that once in the 1960s Phil was calling a Yankees double-header against Cleveland, and he kept going on and on about how much better the pitcher in the first game was than he had been in the past, how much more control he was showing—almost like he was different pitcher, Phil said. Finally in the fourth inning someone from WPIX called and told Phil that the reason the pitcher seemed like a different pitcher was because he *was* a different pitcher. Somehow Phil had confused the lineup for the first game with the lineup for the second game of the double-header.

Another time Phil and I were on the road for a series in Milwaukee. I had opened the first game's broadcast the day before, and Phil was supposed to open the second. As we were standing next to each other on camera, Phil looked at the teleprompter below the camera and started to read the script:

"Hi everybody, and welcome to Yankees baseball," Phil said. "I'm Bill White and . . . hey wait a minute!"

Apparently somebody had forgotten to change the teleprompter script from the day before. Fortunately, the opening was taped, not broadcast live, so Phil could do it over. But WPIX kept Phil's "I'm Bill White" tape and replayed it from time to time to kid Phil. Eventually it became a classic bit of baseball broadcasting lore.

But that was Phil. He read what was put in front of him.

I used that against him on one memorable occasion. Usually broadcasters wrote up their own batting lineup cards for a game, but Phil would never do that. Most of the time he had WPIX cameraman Duilio Costabile do it for him, which Duilio loved to do, because Phil would talk about Duilio on the air. But one day Duilio wasn't there, so I grabbed Phil's lineup card and started to write.

As the game began Phil took the card and started to read, on-air:

"We've got Phil White leading off and playing shortstop, Bob White is batting second and playing first, John White's in right and batting third, Jack White is . . . hey, wait a minute!"

And then Phil turned to me and screamed "White! What did you do to me?"

I didn't stop laughing till the third inning.

Phil was also amazingly open and public about his many fears and phobias. Most guys would try to keep stuff like that quiet—partly because they don't want to look like sissies, and partly because they don't want to give their buddies the opportunity to play jokes on them. But not Phil.

By the time I joined the broadcast team, every Yankee fan already knew about Phil's fear of thunder and lightning. A bolt of lightning would make him give out this high-pitched "Ooooooooh!" sound. It was so bad that once when Phil was interviewing Yankee Bobby Murcer on the field in Kansas City, a clap of thunder caused Phil to throw the microphone in the air and bolt for safety on live TV—after which Murcer bent down, picked up the mike, and said to the camera, "Folks, we'll be right back."

Of course, I wasn't about to show Phil any mercy on that score. During a home game in August 1974, I was standing outside the broadcast booth while Phil was doing his three innings on radio—and suddenly there was a clap of thunder. I started laughing, because I knew what was going to happen. Then the radio listeners got a chance to hear Phil in a quavering voice try to call a game while in the grip of mortal terror.

It went like this:

"Uh-oh, as they put the error sign up, a bolt of lightning! Now you hear the thunder right in back of the scoreboard. [The pitch is] outside—and that's where I'm heading in just a moment, only there's nobody to hand the microphone over to. Al Brown [the cameraman] can't do it because of the union rules...The crowd is starting to scatter now. There's the pitch, hit in the air to deep right center but moving to his left is Nettles, and Morris Nettles makes the catch, one out...Oooooh! You shoulda seen that bolt of lightning! Holy cow! The whole crowd saw it! If Bill White was any kind of a buddy he'd come over and grab this mike! You saw that lightning out there, I know you did. I wanna tell ya...Oooooooh, there was another bolt, and another clap of thunder. Holy cow! What a bolt of lightning!"

Finally I took pity on him and walked back to the microphone table to take over. And Phil, pale as a ghost, looked at me as if I had just saved him from certain death.

"Oh, Bill White, what a buddy you are!"

None of this was an act. Phil's fears and superstitions were the same on the air and off the air. I remember once on a road trip to Milwaukee we checked into a hotel, and as we got on the elevator I asked Phil what floor his room was on.

"Fourteenth floor," Phil said. "Boy, I'm glad they didn't put me on the thirteenth. That's bad luck!"

I couldn't help myself. I told Phil the hotel didn't have a floor that was numbered thirteen—most hotels at the time didn't—so the fourteenth floor was actually the thirteenth floor.

"If you don't believe me, count the floor buttons on the panel there."

So he did, putting his finger next to each one.

"One, two, three...six, seven, eight...ten, eleven, twelve, thirteen"—at *thirteen* his finger was next to the fourteenth-floor button.

Phil went white.

"Holy cow! Oh no! This is terrible!" He immediately took the elevator back down to the lobby and made the desk clerk change his floor.

Phil was also afraid of just about every form of animal life—and made no secret of it. It was a situation that guaranteed he'd be the butt of endless practical jokes.

Once before a game at Yankee Stadium, I was walking down Madison Avenue when I saw a street vendor selling big rubber spiders. He would throw the rubber spiders against a piece of cardboard, and then the spiders would kind of wiggle down to the ground.

So I bought one for five bucks. As I handed over the money the street vendor, obviously a Yankees fan, recognized me—and he knew immediately what I had in mind.

"I know what you're going to do with that," he said, laughing.

And he was right. At the game, Phil was in the radio broadcast booth, which was separated from the TV booth by a clear glass window. When I saw Phil looking my way I threw that rubber spider against the window and it started wiggling down, amazingly life-like. Phil screamed—"Oooooooh!"—and threw off his headphones and bolted for the door.

Another time I was in the broadcast booth when some uniformed inspectors from the city health department came by. The inspectors were always coming to the stadium, pretending to be checking on this or that, when really they just wanted to see the game for free. When Phil came in, he saw them standing outside the booth and asked me who they were.

"Health inspectors. Apparently there's a big rat infestation here in the booth."

"Oooooooh!" went Phil—and he called his three innings with his feet hiked all the way up on the chair.

But come to think of it, maybe Phil was right to be afraid of animals. In 1985, when the Yankees had a pre-game "Phil Rizzuto Appreciation Day" ceremony and retired his uniform, No. 10, they brought a live cow onto the field with a gold halo strapped to its head—the "Holy cow" thing. It was probably the closest Phil had been to an actual cow in his entire life—and the cow responded by stepping on Phil's foot and knocking him over.

"That big thing stepped right on my shoe and pushed me backward, like a karate move," Phil said later.

Phil loved the attention, loved having his "days"—and he had a lot of them. Once on-air I was doing a promo for yet another "Phil Rizzuto Appreciation Day" at Yankee Stadium, and I said to him, "Hey Phil, how many days have you had, anyway?" Most players, no matter how distinguished their careers, are lucky to get even one "appreciation day." And Phil smiled and said "Seven." I think he got another "day" or two after that.

Phil especially liked the gifts his "days" brought him. Once the Yankees gave Phil and Cora an all-expenses paid trip to Rome after he said on-air that he'd always wanted to go to Italy but never had. They gave him a Cadillac and everybody said it was so he could cross the George Washington Bridge in style. They gave him a big TV set, and the joke was that he could use it to watch the last three innings at home with Cora.

Like a lot of Depression-era kids, Phil had a thing about money. He could be incredibly generous, giving time and money to various charities in his New Jersey town and elsewhere. But he could also be incredibly cheap.

Once, on the air, Phil started telling me about how he and Cora had stopped at an Italian restaurant in Hoboken, and of course the owner recognized him and came over. The check was already on the table, and when the owner said not to worry, the check would be taken care of, Phil said, "Oh, okay, in that case, let me have another holy water"—which is to say, vodka. Then, as they were leaving the restaurant, Phil told me, he went to the cashier with the comped check and took out his AARP (American Association of Retired Persons) card and asked for the 10 percent senior citizen discount—in cash! I couldn't believe it. He got a meal on the arm and then wanted the restaurant to pay him!

Phil was always angling for free stuff. He'd talk on the air about a certain restaurant he'd been to, how good the food was—"They had this lasagna, it musta had fourteen layers in it!"—and the next day the restaurant would send a giant spread of lasagna or pizza or cannolis to the broadcast booth or to his home in New Jersey. Cannolis especially. Phil used to say that a day without those little Sicilian pastries was like a day without sunshine, and fans and restaurants gave them to him by the thousands, free.

It wasn't just free food, either. Once before a game I had stopped in Bloomingdale's to kill some time, and I found some men's cologne that I liked, made by Lagerfeld. I bought a bottle and put some on, and during the game broadcast Phil said, "White, what's that you got on? It smells good, where'd you get it?"

So I told him it was Lagerfeld and I got it at Bloomie's. And for the rest of the broadcast Phil kept saying, "Man oh man, White, I gotta tell ya, that sure smells good, I wish I had some of that."

I knew exactly what he was doing. The next day, sure enough, we got to the broadcast booth and there was a whole case of Lagerfeld waiting for him.

It wasn't that Phil was strapped for cash. I never knew how much Phil's contract was for—that was something you didn't ask about—but it must have been pretty generous. And Phil had outside gigs as well.

Most famously, in the early 1970s Phil started doing commercials for The Money Store, a small New Jersey–based lending company that specialized in home equity loans; they were sub-prime lenders before anyone had ever heard the phrase.

Phil's commercials started out simply enough: "Hello, I'm Phil Rizzuto for The Money Store," and then he'd give the pitch. Later on they had him sitting at a desk piled with tax forms and saying "Arrrrgh!" or talking to Santa Claus about great holiday deals. "One percent above prime?" Santa would say. The commercials were awful, but effective; the rapidly expanding company made millions thanks to Phil. In fact, the phrase "I'm Phil Rizzuto for The Money Store" so dominated the airwaves that a lot of people thought Phil actually *owned* The Money Store.

(I'm not criticizing Phil for the goofy commercials. I once did a TV advertising gig in which I allowed myself to be dressed up like Sherlock Holmes—pipe, funny hat, and all. The theme was that I was "investigating the best deals" and of course finding them in the sponsor's store.)

As if the commercials weren't ubiquitous enough, sometimes Phil would give The Money Store a free plug on the game broadcasts. The producers and TV executives hated it—nothing wounds a TV executive more deeply than giving away free advertising—but Phil kept doing it. Finally one day I gave him a jab.

"So, Phil, about these loans from The Money Store. Do they break your legs if you don't pay?"

Phil was shocked.

"White!" he screamed. "You can't say that!"

Phil's wife, Cora, was a strong, vivacious woman who'd been a knockout in her younger days and retained her good looks well into her senior years. She generally shunned the limelight, and didn't particularly like Phil's constant references to her on the air. She also tried to restrain his more outlandish behavior, with mixed success. On several occasions, she asked me to reach over and poke Phil in the shoulder if he started to say anything politically incorrect.

I could seldom do that—who could predict at any moment what Phil was going to say?—but sometimes I tried to cover for him. Once at a Yankees game in the early '80s Phil spotted former president Richard Nixon, who was a big baseball fan, sitting in the owner's box seat near the broadcast booth.

"Hey, White!" Phil said on-air. "Look over there—it's Tricky Dick!"

Of course, Nixon had been forced to resign in disgrace in 1974 after the Watergate scandal, but he was still a former president of the United States. I motioned to Phil to shut up and then I said,

"Yes, the honorable Richard Nixon, former president of the United States, is next door."

The funny thing was that the viewers and listeners didn't get mad at Phil for calling Nixon "Tricky Dick." They got mad at me for calling him "the honorable." I got the angry mail, not Phil.

But even if I could have restrained Phil, I couldn't always be there. One story involves Phil and Fran Healy, a former Yankees catcher who in the late 1970s sometimes worked with Phil calling Yankees games. They were in Seattle, and they and the team stayed in one of those tall, modern, cylindrically shaped hotels.

Healy (on-air): What did you do last night, Phil?
Rizzuto: Well, I didn't like the room I had.
Healy: Why?
Rizzuto: Well, it was a round room and I couldn't corner my wife.

"You shoulda seen the mail I got," Phil said in a later interview. "They all liked it, but the station didn't too much."

Phil even managed to get in trouble with, of all things, a rock-and-roll record. In 1976, the singer called Meat Loaf hired Phil to record a voice-over on a song he was doing. Phil showed up at the recording studio, got his paycheck—he wouldn't say how much—and read the script. It turned out the song was about a guy and a girl making out in a car, with the guy singing that they were going to go all the way. And then you heard Phil's voice break in over the music, like he was calling a game, and describing a runner "rounding first" and "try[ing] for second," and so on.

The song, called "Paradise by the Dashboard Light," went on to become a big hit. But Phil got some grief for it from priests and nuns and others who thought it glorified premarital sex. Phil always claimed that he didn't know what the song was about when

he did it, that Meat Loaf—"That huckleberry!" Phil called him—
had pulled a fast one on him. Phil said he just read what was put
in front of him, and I actually believed him. Remember, this is the
guy who read the words, "Hello, I'm Bill White..." But whether
Phil had known what was going on or not, he never gave Mr. Loaf a
refund on the paycheck.

Sometimes, I'll admit, I even tried to get Phil into trouble, just
for fun. Once Ken Griffey Sr. made an amazing leaping catch on a
ball to left field, after which a white player from the opposing team
failed to catch a similarly hit ball in the next inning. I jokingly said,
"Well, Phil, it looks as if he has the disease. What do you think?"

Of course, as Phil well knew, *the disease* referred to white athletes' supposed lack of jumping skills. But he wouldn't touch that
question. I don't think Phil had a prejudiced bone in his body, but
he was always afraid to talk about somebody's race. Or almost
always, anyway. There was one memorable time when he said of
a visiting team's lineup, "They've got so many Latin players we're
gonna have to get a Latin instructor up here."

And I wasn't above giving Phil a jab when he went on and on
about the Italian thing. Once he was talking on-air about a new
shortstop that Oakland had, an Italian American kid named Rob
Picciolo, and Phil said, "White, don't you just love those infielders
with names ending in vowels?"

"You mean like Shapiro and White?"

That stumped him for a second. Then he said, "White, you
huckleberry!"

There were a thousand Phil stories. There was the time Phil's
son, Philip Francis Rizzuto Jr., who was in his thirties at the time,
lost his job and Phil put out a call on-air to find "Little Scooter" a
new job—and by the time the game was over, Little Scooter had
nine job offers. There was the time WPIX showed a shot of the full
moon during a night game and Phil blurted out, "White! Look at

that moon! I think I can see Texas!" And then there were the many, many long, loopy digressions that came out of nowhere—like this one during a night game on the West Coast.

> *Rizzuto*: You won't believe it, White, but I did something I wanted to do my whole life, and finally today I got nerve enough to do it. I got a facial.
>
> *White*: You got a what? What could they do with that face?
>
> *Rizzuto*: I know, I know. It's not that it makes you beautiful, which is hard to do with me, but anyway, it feels good! It's no wonder the women do it! Ohhhh, I'm tellin' ya, they massage your face with oil, then cream, and ohhh, they rub your eyeballs...

A facial. They rub your eyeballs. This in the middle of a major league baseball game.

Of course, not everybody liked Phil's shtick. WPIX executives, especially the younger ones, would tear out their hair when Phil started going off on birthdays and cannolis and facials. Even Yankees executives who liked Phil would often roll their eyes.

But one thing that Yankees execs—and the fans—liked about Phil was his unabashed homerism, his unflagging rooting for the home team. Other broadcasters criticized it—it was, they thought, unprofessional—and when he did a national broadcast that opposing-team fans would see or hear, Phil tried to tone it down. But everybody knew that despite the shabby treatment of him at the end of his playing career, Phil was a Yankee to his core.

In fact, nothing better sums up the Yankees' relative position in Phil's universe than something he said at the close of a 3–0 win against the Orioles in August 1978. The news came over the wires that Pope Paul VI had just died, and Phil said this on-air:

"Well, that kind of puts the damper on even a Yankees win."

That was Phil.

There's no doubt in my mind that my association with Phil Rizzuto made my broadcasting career. In the fans' eyes and ears, we were the best show in town, the Rizzuto–White Show. Just as Tom Villante had suggested, I played off Phil—and not only did it make me more famous as a broadcaster than I probably had a right to be, it was fun. Phil made broadcasting fun.

I have only two regrets about that time. One was that while Frank Messer was always included as part of the Yankees broadcast team—some people called us "the Three Amigos"—Frank never really got the recognition he deserved.

That was partly because Frank was such a consummate professional. He genuinely liked Phil, and would play around with him on the air, but there was always a slight tone of disapproval in it—and I think the listeners picked up on that. Frank was also an emotional guy, prone to tears sometimes, and terribly insecure as a broadcaster, always thinking that he was on the verge of being fired. I would tell him that was crazy, that he was the rock, the guy everybody depended on—and it was the truth. But unlike Phil and me, Frank's insecurities made him reluctant to push the boundaries on the air, to turn himself into a memorable on-air personality.

I had tremendous respect for Frank, and tried to show him the deference that he deserved. Once on the Fourth of July in 1983, Yankees pitcher Dave Righetti was on the verge of pitching a no-hitter against the Red Sox, and although I was scheduled to call the last three innings I insisted that Frank as the senior man should call the ninth inning. Being able to call a no-hitter was a big deal for a broadcaster, because it would inevitably be played over and over again.

Which is what happened. Righetti was pitching against Wade Boggs in the ninth, two outs, when Frank made his most famous call:

"The kick, and the pitch—*he struck him out!* Righetti has pitched a no-hitter!...He strikes out Boggs for the final out of the ball game, and the Yankees pour onto the field to congratulate Dave Righetti!"

Frank, who died in 2001, said after that famous call that my giving him that final inning was a "class act." But it really wasn't. It was simply the respect due a great broadcaster, and a good man.

My only other regret about those days is that sometimes as a broadcaster I wasn't serious enough about baseball. In the early 1970s, when the Yankees were doing so badly on the field, it didn't matter so much—in fact, the broadcast booth banter between Phil and me helped keep up fan interest. But as the Yankees' fortunes improved, it was too late to stop the Rizzuto–White Show and concentrate on baseball; the fans expected the banter. It wasn't Phil's fault—Phil was just being Phil—but I should have known better.

Other than that, though, I have no regrets, and certainly no complaints. The years I spent with Phil were some of the best of my life.

I know I had never laughed as much as I did then. And I probably never will again.

Everything has to end. And so did my time with Phil.

By the late 1980s, the broadcast world was changing. The Yankees were shifting more games to cable TV, and my employer, WPIX-TV, no longer was involved in the Yankees radio broadcasts. In the early 1970s, Phil and I had covered all 162 season games on radio, TV, or both, but by the late 1980s we were covering only about 60 games a season, all for WPIX.

I finally left broadcasting in 1989 after being named president of the National League. At the time, a reporter asked me why I had taken the new job, and my answer was this:

"If you had worked eighteen years with Rizzuto, you wouldn't ask such a question."

I'm sure the fans who read that comment, and who had listened to Phil and me over the years, could hear the laughter behind it. I'm sure Phil could, too.

Phil stayed on with the Yankees, working with a variety of broadcasters: George Grande, Tom Seaver, Rick Cerrone, Bobby Murcer, and others. And in 1994 Phil was finally, at long last, voted into the Hall of Fame. (As a member of the Hall's Veterans Committee, of course I voted for him—not because he was my friend but because if any baseball player deserved it, Phil did.)

I was at Cooperstown for Phil's Hall of Fame induction ceremony—and as with just about everything connected with Phil, it was memorable. In typical Phil fashion, he got up and gave a long, rambling acceptance speech that went from his days as a kid in Brooklyn to the time he stuck his hand in a snow blower to trying to remember what they call that Southern food "that looks like oatmeal." (He meant grits.)

Through it all, as always, Phil laughed at himself.

"This is going nowhere," he said during the speech. "You see how I do this. I get sidetracked, then I don't know where I was going. See! I did it again!"

Phil initially quit the Yankees broadcasting booth in 1995 after WPIX made him call a game against the Red Sox instead of letting him attend the funeral of his Yankees teammate and friend Mickey Mantle in Dallas. As he watched the funeral on television during the game, Phil audibly broke down and left the booth early—and for once, nobody thought it was just because he wanted to beat the traffic over the George Washington Bridge. Later he was persuaded to come back for one more season, in 1996, but that was it. At age seventy-nine, after forty seasons as a Yankees broadcaster and thirteen seasons as a Yankees player, Phil retired—and naturally, they gave him yet another "Phil Rizzuto Day."

I didn't see Phil as often in those days as I would have liked. But I would meet him and Cora for dinner once in a while, and I'd see him at various baseball functions. We always stayed in touch.

In 2006, Phil was admitted to a rehab facility in West Orange, New Jersey, near his home, for treatment of a variety of ailments. I was seventy-two then, and retired, so I had time to visit him every couple of weeks. It was a good facility, clean and well kept, and they took good care of him there. Cora was a constant presence, as were Phil's children. Yogi Berra, Phil's best friend from the Yankees, also visited him every Wednesday.

Whoever was there, we always had a good time, talking about the old days and eating the Italian food—including the cannolis— that continued to be sent by well-wishers. But as time went on, it was clear that Phil was declining.

Once I came in for a visit and found Phil, wearing a nice sweater, sitting by the window, looking outside. It was his favorite spot, a place to catch the morning sun. I sat down in a chair next to him, and Phil tried to turn and say something, but by that time it was hard for him to talk. Instead he held up his hand, and I took it in mine.

For the next forty-five minutes we sat there, holding hands and saying nothing. I wondered if maybe having me next to him reminded him of the old days, if looking out that window reminded him of the broadcast booths in which we had sat together so many times.

Two old men, old baseball players, old friends, holding hands in a sunbeam. I didn't know whether to laugh or cry—but I'm pretty sure Phil would have wanted me to laugh.

Phil died not long after that, on August 13, 2007, at the age of eighty-nine. Tributes poured in from friends and fans, and later there was a memorial service for him at Yankee Stadium—the last ever "Phil Rizzuto Day." One by one people got up and spoke about him, and each time they finished I could feel people's eyes on me, waiting for me to stand up and say something. Sometimes I still wish I had.

But I couldn't. As I've said, I'm not an emotional man, but I knew that if I got up there and tried to talk about Phil, I wouldn't be able to get through it, I would break down. To be honest, I was afraid—because to me, breaking down in public was what lightning was to Phil.

Maybe no one else understood that. But I know Phil would have.

Still, as I think back on what Phil meant to me, how close we were, how much we respected each other for so many years, there's something I could say, a word I could use. It's a word that's thrown around way too casually these days, one that like most men of my generation I use sparingly, usually only with my children or other close family members. It's a word that I'll admit I have trouble saying.

But if, as Phil might put it, you catch me with the little trap-door in the back of my head in the open position, if you can corner me in a round room, then I have to say it.

I loved Phil Rizzuto.

CHAPTER 11

Hiram College, winter of 1953, just before I first reported to spring training for the New York Giants. I was playing center for the Hiram Terriers basketball team in an exhibition game against a team from Lockbourne Air Force Base, a Strategic Air Command base near Columbus, Ohio.

The air force guys were killing us.

That was only to be expected. Hiram had just four hundred students, only a little more than half of them men, which meant that the basketball talent pool was limited—so limited that at six feet, I was their best rebounder. The air force team, meanwhile, had thousands of young, physically fit guys from the base to draw on.

Still, we were trying to give it our best. At one point, I grabbed a rebound and started dribbling downcourt, with the air force players in pursuit. The Hiram gym was pretty small, so as I dribbled along the line I had to pass within inches of the guys on the air force bench, all of whom were standing up and shouting.

As I went by them, a big guy in a blue blazer, the air force team's coach, reached out from the sideline and grabbed me by the jersey, trying to pull me out of bounds or at least slow me down.

I shook off the guy's grasping hand pretty easily, and the ref didn't see it. I went on to make the basket, although it didn't change anything; we still wound up getting clobbered. But I remember wondering why in the world the air force coach would be so blatantly aggressive—aggressive to the point of actually cheating—when his team was winning by a large margin anyway?

Of course, it was a small incident. And I didn't think about it again until twenty years later, when the Yankees were having a luncheon for some season ticket holders at a popular Italian restaurant called Mama Leone's, in the Manhattan theater district.

Phil Rizzuto and I were there as the entertainment, doing our usual routine, and everybody seemed to have a good time. As the event ended and people started leaving, I saw George Steinbrenner, the new Yankees owner, standing at the front door, chatting with people as they went out.

I was hoping I could just walk by him. After the way Steinbrenner had treated Mike Burke, I didn't want to talk to the guy.

The previous year, in 1972, Burke, the Yankees president, had decided to try to buy the team from CBS. The Yankees hadn't been doing well. They were losing money, and somehow CBS ownership had never seemed like the right fit for the club. CBS, which had owned the team since 1964, was happy to let Mike buy the franchise—if he could find $10 million or so.

Mike was having trouble putting together the money, but then Gabe Paul, a veteran baseball executive with the Cleveland Indians, hooked Mike up with an investors group headed by a guy almost no one had heard of—a forty-two-year-old Cleveland shipping company owner named George Steinbrenner.

Steinbrenner had dabbled in sports franchise ownership before. In 1960, he bought the Cleveland Pipers in the old American

Basketball League—losing considerable money on the team when
the ABL folded—and in 1971 he had been part of a failed effort to
buy the Cleveland Indians. When Steinbrenner heard the Yankees
were up for sale he jumped at the chance, putting together a group
of "limited partners" that included Texas oilman Nelson Bunker
Hunt and then General Motors vice president John DeLorean.
Steinbrenner put up just $168,000 of his own money, but it was
enough to give him the largest individual interest. In January 1973,
CBS sold the Yankees to Steinbrenner's group for $10 million.

The problem was that Steinbrenner had repeatedly assured
Mike Burke that he, Burke, would continue to run the Yankees
as chief operating officer—but then as soon as the deal closed,
Steinbrenner started undermining Mike's authority. Steinbrenner
brought in Gabe Paul as Yankees president, and Steinbrenner
became increasingly outspoken about his disdain for Mike. Mike
finally decided that his position was untenable, and in April, just a
few months after the sale, he resigned. By the end of Steinbrenner's
first year, Yankees vice president Howard Berk, general manager
Lee MacPhail, manager Ralph Houk, and publicity chief Bob Fishel
had all left as well.

(Mike remained a limited partner in the team for a number
of years before cashing out. Most of the other limited partners
eventually got out as well. One of them, John McMullen, a marine
architect and shipping executive, later explained that "there is
nothing in life quite so limited as being a limited partner of George
Steinbrenner.")

I owed Mike Burke a lot. After my rocky first year with the
Yankees broadcasting crew, he could easily have not rehired me.
Instead he stuck with me, patiently helping me to become better at
my job. I hated to see him treated so callously.

And the more I heard about this guy Steinbrenner, the less I
liked what I was hearing. He had a growing reputation as a schemer

and a manipulator, a guy whose word couldn't be trusted. There were also stories beginning to circulate about the abusive way he treated his employees, from executives to low-level gofers—screaming and cursing at them, summarily firing them for little or no reason, publicly humiliating them.

The stories of these humiliations would pile up over the years. For example, Steinbrenner reportedly made one high-level team executive who had displeased him stand facing the wall during a meeting, like an errant four-year-old. Another story had it that when Steinbrenner found an unemptied garbage bag in Yankee Stadium, he made the executive responsible for stadium maintenance walk around all day carrying the garbage bag in his hand. And on and on.

True, there were also stories—much less publicized ones—about the many acts of kindness and charity that Steinbrenner performed over the years. He set up scholarships that helped put hundreds of kids through college, set up a foundation to help the families of slain police officers, supported and encouraged young black athletes in his native Cleveland. On a personal level he could often be caring and compassionate—although people close to him knew that could change at any moment.

In any event, the first few months after Steinbrenner had taken over the team I had simply ignored him. After all, it wasn't as if he was my boss. Again, technically I worked for WPIX-TV, not for George Steinbrenner.

So when we passed in the stadium hallways or on the field I would just nod and he would nod back. And that was what I was planning to do again when I saw him standing by the door at Mama Leone's after the season ticket holder luncheon.

But as I started to go out the door, Steinbrenner looked directly at me and said, "Hey!"

He was a big guy, not especially tall but broad-shouldered, with a big head—literally and figuratively—and one of those booming voices that fills a room. There was no way I could politely ignore him, so I looked his way.

"You don't remember me, do you?" he said.

I was certain that Steinbrenner and I had never met. Although, like me, Steinbrenner was from Ohio, he had grown up as the privileged scion of a wealthy shipping family, while I had grown up as a kid from the public housing projects. We hadn't exactly moved in the same social circles. But it soon became clear that Steinbrenner knew about my background.

"No, I don't remember you," I told him, somewhat coldly.

Steinbrenner laughed.

"Remember that basketball game you played for Hiram College against an air force team? In '53? You were dribbling down the sideline and someone grabbed you from the bench?"

It took me a few seconds. But finally it came back to me.

"Yeah, I remember a guy in a blue blazer who grabbed me."

Steinbrenner laughed again.

"I was the guy in the blue blazer!"

It was true. After graduating from Williams College in 1952, where he was a varsity hurdler on the track team and a halfback in football, Steinbrenner had joined the air force and been commissioned a second lieutenant. Assigned to Lockbourne AFB, he had been tasked with reviving the base's languishing athletics program—which he did with a vengeance, coaching baseball, basketball, football, and track. Even back then, coaches and players of the teams opposing him had been astonished at his competitiveness, his almost physical need to win at anything and everything, and the lengths to which he would go to do that—including, it seemed, grabbing an opposing player from a tiny liberal arts college as he dribbled down the sideline to make an essentially meaningless score in an essentially meaningless basketball game.

Now at Mama Leone's we both laughed over the memory—

Steinbrenner most of all. He wasn't at all apologetic about the long-ago incident, didn't try to say that he'd been caught up in the heat of the moment and had grabbed me on a momentary impulse. On the contrary, he seemed proud of it—and especially proud that he hadn't gotten caught. That was simply the way he played the game, any game.

I have to say that in our conversation that afternoon I found Steinbrenner to be charming, pleasant, personable. And maybe he sensed at our first meeting that I wouldn't take the kind of crap he was famous for dishing out, from him or anyone else. Maybe he was aware of my reputation in baseball as someone who treated other people with civility and expected the same in return.

Like all bullies, George Steinbrenner respected guys who stood up to him and refused to be intimidated—and so in the remaining sixteen years I had with the Yankees organization I was never subjected to the "Steinbrenner treatment."

That's not to say we didn't have differences; we did. But while Steinbrenner certainly would have had the power to force me out of the Yankees broadcast booth if he'd wanted to, he never tried to do it.

Meanwhile, Steinbrenner did what he set out to do—turn the Yankees into a winning team. In two decades under his stormy leadership, the Yankees won eleven league championships and seven World Series. The team he bought for $10 million in 1973 is worth more than a billion dollars today. If you measure a man solely by his results, and not by his methods, then despite his many, many flaws, Steinbrenner was a success. And for that he always had my respect.

But despite that, if at any time during the years that I worked with the Yankees I had somehow found myself in a basketball game, and George Steinbrenner had been sitting on the sidelines, and I was making a fast break for his team's basket, I know this:

I wouldn't have gotten too close to him.

*   *   *

When Steinbrenner first took over the Yankees ownership, he made a point of saying publicly that he would not be a hands-on owner, that he wouldn't be involved in the day-to-day operations of the team. If that was ever his intention, it lasted about a minute.

From almost the first day, Steinbrenner became perhaps the most hands-on owner in modern baseball history. From the hiring and firing of managers and general managers, to ordering changes in the batting lineup, to checking the Yankee Stadium restrooms for cleanliness, Steinbrenner had his hands in every facet of the Yankees organization. He changed managers twenty times in twenty-three seasons, and over three decades employed eleven general managers. He was a hands-on owner even when he was under orders to be hands-off.

I found that out in 1975, when Steinbrenner invited me to lunch at the Diamond Club in Shea Stadium, where the Yankees were playing while Yankee Stadium was being renovated. Steinbrenner was in the middle of a two-year suspension imposed by baseball commissioner Bowie Kuhn, this after Steinbrenner pleaded guilty in 1974 to felony charges involving illegal campaign contributions to Richard Nixon's 1972 presidential campaign. (Steinbrenner was later pardoned by President Ronald Reagan.) Under the terms of the suspension, Steinbrenner wasn't supposed to have anything to do with the management of the Yankees. But Steinbrenner didn't let a little thing like that get in his way.

I had no idea what the lunch invitation was about, but as I walked in and took a seat with Steinbrenner at a table overlooking the field, he got right to the point.

"Bill, I want you to be general manager of the Yankees."

I'm seldom at a loss for words. But at that moment, with this out-of-the-blue job offer hanging over the table, I was dumbstruck.

I quickly recovered. I didn't have to ponder or calculate or agonize. Although I was confident I could have done the job, I knew what my answer was. I said all the polite things—that I appreciated the offer, the chance to be a major league general manager, but that I was happy being a broadcaster. But the real reason I refused the job was this:

I knew I could never work for George Steinbrenner.

Again, I could respect Steinbrenner as a businessman. But I knew that the first time he got in my face, the first time he screamed at me, the first time he called me an idiot or a moron or an errand boy or any of the other invectives he directed at his employees, I might have decked him.

Steinbrenner took my refusal with good grace. In fact, I'm not even sure how serious the offer was. Steinbrenner had a habit of making offers to players and managers and then the next day, if not sooner, changing his mind.

Then Steinbrenner dropped another bombshell on me. He said, "You know, we're about to fire Bill Virdon."

I was surprised. Virdon, a former outfielder for the Cardinals and the Pirates who had also managed the Pittsburgh team for a year, had been hired by Steinbrenner as Yankees manager the year before. He had improved the team's standing in the 1974 season, finishing second in the American League East. True, he was a quiet, somewhat standoffish guy who wasn't particularly popular with the players, but Steinbrenner had known that when he hired him. So why fire him?

"He's too much of a stick on the bench," Steinbrenner explained. "He doesn't go out there and yell and scream. What I really want on the bench is someone with more fire."

After the lunch was over, I thought about going down to the clubhouse and warning Virdon, whom I'd known when he played for the Pirates. But finally I decided not to. It wouldn't have made any difference, and besides, Steinbrenner had a habit of leaking news of impending firings to third parties. I didn't want to be his bad news messenger. In fact, I found out later that Steinbrenner had already leaked the news about firing Virdon to several reporters.

A few days after our lunch at Shea Stadium, Virdon was out and Billy Martin was in—and the Yankees would never be the same.

The era the sportswriters dubbed "the Bronx Zoo"—the years of Martin and Reggie Jackson and Steinbrenner, of revolving-door managers and rowdy fans and screaming headlines in the tabloids—had officially begun.

George Steinbrenner's determination to control everything about the New York Yankees didn't end with the team itself. He not only wanted to control the Yankees, he wanted to control what was *said* about the Yankees—not just by sports reporters, who routinely found themselves frozen out when they displeased Steinbrenner, but also by broadcasters in the Yankees booth.

Steinbrenner had a red phone installed in the broadcast booth so he could always be sure to get through when he heard something he didn't like. When that red phone rang, everybody knew it was Steinbrenner—and that he was pissed off.

Like a lot of people, Steinbrenner loved Phil Rizzuto. Also like a lot of people, he was occasionally driven to distraction by Phil's stream-of-consciousness riffs.

For example, once Phil started talking on-air about a trip he and Cora had taken to Intercourse, Pennsylvania—and of course, with that name anything Phil said came off sounding like some sort of sexual double entendre. The FCC was a lot stricter about such things back then, so when Steinbrenner heard what Phil was saying, the red phone started ringing.

"We're going to be pulled off the goddamn airwaves!" Steinbrenner screamed at the producer, Arthur Adler. "Shut him up, will you?"

Still, Steinbrenner made no secret of the fact that he wanted homers broadcasting his Yankees' games—and Phil was a true homer, unable to hide his love of the Yankees and his joy when they won. I'm not criticizing Phil for that. That was simply the way he was, and it worked for him.

But I was another story.

Unlike Phil, I didn't have an emotional attachment to the Yankees, as a player or as a broadcaster. My job was to call the games as I saw them. If the Yankees played well I said so, and if they didn't, I said that, too. But Steinbrenner wanted something else.

"Why can't White be more like Rizzuto?" he would ask the broadcast producers. As diplomatically as possible—most of them were afraid of Steinbrenner's rages—they would explain that the broadcast needed straight play-by-play to balance Phil's homer-ish style. And in any event, they would say, "Nobody's going to change Bill White."

Still, the calls from Steinbrenner to the broadcast booth came in during almost every game. A production assistant whose job it was to monitor the red phone would take the calls and write down Steinbrenner's demands and then pass the notes to whoever was calling the game.

If an umpire blew a call to the Yankees' disadvantage, Steinbrenner would want us to rip the ump. If a Yankees player who was in Steinbrenner's doghouse bobbled a play, Steinbrenner would want us to question his playing abilities and value to the team. With managers especially, if the Yankees were doing badly Steinbrenner would want us to knock the manager's decisions on-air.

Sometimes he seemed to think that such on-air critiques would actually be a motivational exercise, driving the player or manager to do better. At other times Steinbrenner, who was notorious for using the news media to communicate his displeasure with a player or manager, apparently wanted to use us to validate his intentions to get rid of a guy.

But whatever his motives, I wouldn't go along.

The first few times I got the notes, I ignored them. Finally I told the young production assistant, "Tell the Skipper I'm not even going to read this note." Given Steinbrenner's temper, that probably wasn't fair to the production assistant.

(Most people who worked for Steinbrenner called him either "Mr. Steinbrenner" or "Boss"; he would get furious if an underling had the temerity to call him "George." I didn't call him any of those. Since he owned a shipping company, and sometimes wore a captain's hat, I always called him "Skipper.")

The notes from Steinbrenner kept coming, and I continued to ignore them. Then suddenly one day they stopped. When I asked the production assistant why, he said, "Mr. Steinbrenner is still calling in the notes. He just told me not to give them to you anymore."

That was fine with me.

Although the notes stopped, the meddling continued. At one point Steinbrenner, who hated the New York Mets, demanded that the Mets not even be mentioned on any Yankees broadcast. It was a nonsensical demand, because our viewers and listeners expected us to keep them informed of developments in other games. The broadcast producers successfully resisted that one—but it was an example of the dumb things Steinbrenner wanted us to do.

(In fairness, Steinbrenner wasn't the only one with dumb ideas. Our producers and directors were bright guys, but they made mistakes as well. Once I was handed some advertising copy to read on the air, and as I got into it I realized it was an ad for toilet paper. I finished the ad, but then I suggested to the producer that fans listening to a ball game really didn't want their announcer to go from calling a dramatic home run to praising the absorbent qualities of Super-Soft toilet paper. They agreed; we never had to do another toilet paper ad.)

I didn't take any of Steinbrenner's attempted meddling personally. And in fact, on only two occasions did Steinbrenner ever criticize me face-to-face or in the news media.

The first time was when I was assigned at the last minute to do some pre-game on-field interviews for the TV broadcast. I hadn't expected to be on camera that day—I was scheduled for the radio broadcast—so I did the interviews in blue jeans and a Western-style shirt. Steinbrenner saw me on the broadcast, then called and told me that Yankees broadcasters should always wear coats and ties on camera. I didn't argue, because I knew he was right.

The only other time that George Steinbrenner publicly criticized me was when Chris Chambliss hit the home run that won the Yankees the American League championship.

It was 1976, Billy Martin's first full season as Yankees manager and the first season back in Yankee Stadium after the two-year renovation project. With the pennant series against the Kansas City Royals tied 2–2, the fifty-seven thousand fans in Yankee Stadium were in a state of near hysteria.

At the bottom of the ninth, the game was tied 6–6. I was broadcasting the play-by-play for WMCA radio—and I was about to call what I thought was one of the most thrilling moments in baseball history.

After a delay for the groundskeepers to pick up some bottles thrown on the field by over-exuberant fans, Chris Chambliss, a great clutch hitter, stepped up to the plate. On the first pitch, Chambliss swung and I called this:

"It's deep to right field! It's going, it's going, that ball is gone! A home run for Chris Chambliss, and the New York Yankees are the 1976 American League champions!"

The only problem was that as the ball cleared the wall and Chambliss was rounding the bases, fans started rushing the field by the hundreds. They grabbed the bags at first and second and swarmed around Chambliss, trying to grab his batting helmet—he took it off and held it like a football as he ran—and at one point they caused him to stumble. Trying to make it to home plate, which was completely blocked by the mob, Chambliss wasn't able to touch the plate. Instead he ran into the Yankees dugout to get help.

I knew that, technically, under the rules, it wasn't a home run until Chambliss touched home. And that was the way I called it.

"Chambliss hasn't gotten to home plate yet... Fans are on the field... Chambliss still hasn't touched home plate... But the ball game—I think—is over, and the Yankees win by a score of 7–6."

Maybe it was the *I think* that got Steinbrenner going. As far as I could tell, I was the only one of the broadcasters covering the game—among others, Howard Cosell was on for ABC-TV and Phil for WPIX-TV—who immediately raised an on-air question about the untouched home plate.

As it turned out, Royals manager Whitey Herzog didn't protest the home run. And some time later, Chambliss, with a police escort, walked out of the dugout and officially touched home plate—or rather, he touched the dirt where home plate had been, the plate itself already having been dug up and carried off by the riotous fans. But when I talked about it on-air it had been a legitimate issue, one that could have prompted an official protest from the Royals.

Steinbrenner apparently didn't see it that way. I didn't hear him say it, but a reporter later told me that while Steinbrenner hadn't said anything about the *I think* comment, he did accuse me of being insufficiently excited on-air by the Yankees win. While everyone else was delirious with joy, I was calmly telling listeners what was happening on the field.

In short, I wasn't enough of a homer.

When the reporter asked me for my reaction to Steinbrenner's comments, my response was direct, earthy, and unprintable. The reporter got my drift.

I knew that I had made the right call in that famous game.

Strange things happen in baseball, and umpires can nullify a home run on a technicality. In fact, that was exactly what happened seven years later, in July 1983, in the infamous "pine tar incident."

I was calling that game, which once again pitted the Yankees against the Royals at Yankee Stadium. At the top of the ninth, with two outs, Royals slugger George Brett came to the plate and smashed a two-run homer, giving the Royals a 5–4 lead. But after Brett rounded the bases Billy Martin invoked an obscure rule that banned any substance on a bat from extending more than eighteen inches from the tip of the handle. In this case, it was grip-improving pine tar. Sure enough, when the umpires measured it, Brett's bat had twenty-four inches of pine tar.

It was a bush league protest. Pine tar doesn't help a hitter hit a home run; the only reason for the rule was to keep the balls from getting scuffed up with pine tar. Nevertheless, home plate umpire Tim McClelland called Brett out, nullifying the home run and giving the Yankees the game. Pandemonium erupted. A furious Brett stormed onto the field and was ejected from the game, and everyone was screaming at everyone else.

American League president Lee MacPhail later overruled the umpire, reinstating Brett's home run and ordering the remainder of the game to be played in August. Interestingly, at the start of that replay game Billy Martin lodged a new protest against Brett's earlier "pine tar" home run on the grounds that Brett hadn't touched all the bases—the same protest that Royals manager Whitey Herzog could have made against Chambliss's home run in the 1976 ALCS game. But Martin's protest was denied, and when the Yankees failed to score in the bottom of the ninth the Royals finally won 5–4.

Like I said. Strange things happen in baseball.

Major League Baseball players often have big egos. But I was constantly amazed at how sensitive they could be, how the smallest criticism, spoken or implied, could send them into a sulking blue funk.

Alfred Manuel "Billy" Martin Jr. was like that.

Martin had started his major league career in 1950 as a twenty-two-year-old second baseman for the Yankees, and went on to be named MVP of the 1953 World Series; he was an All-Star in 1956. A tough street kid from the San Francisco Bay Area, on the field he had a reputation for being a scrappy, aggressive player; off the field he had a well-deserved reputation as a drinker and a brawler.

That reputation was famously intensified in 1957, when Martin was celebrating his twenty-ninth birthday at the Copacabana nightclub in New York with Mickey Mantle, Yogi Berra, Hank Bauer, and some of their wives. Sammy Davis Jr. was headlining at the club, and when some drunken members of a local bowling club sitting at a nearby table started making remarks about Davis, calling him a "nigger" and so on, Martin, to his credit, took offense. Punches started flying, and when it was over one of the bowlers had a broken jaw. The fight generated enormous publicity in the tabloids, and Yankees general manager George Weiss blamed Martin for being a bad influence on the other players. A month later, Weiss traded him to Kansas City.

Martin was bounced around among various teams after that—Detroit, Cleveland, Cincinnati, Milwaukee, Minnesota. Later he became a manager, first with the Twins in 1969, then the Detroit Tigers from 1971 through 1973, and then the Texas Rangers. He was a good manager—the Tigers almost won the pennant in 1972, and Martin took the Rangers from last place to second place in 1974—but trouble always followed him.

He got in a drunken fight with one of his pitchers, Dave Boswell, outside a bar in Detroit. He publicly ordered Tigers pitchers to throw at opposing batters. When posing for his 1972 Tigers baseball card, he gave the photographer the finger and no one noticed it until the card was already out. During his career he would get in fistfights with two teams' traveling secretaries, a cabdriver, a marshmallow salesman, a sportswriter, two bouncers at a Texas topless joint—the list could go on. As a manager, Billy routinely screamed, waved his arms, kicked dirt on umpires—and while I think much of that was calculated, an attempt to help his team win through intimidation, it made him one of baseball's premier bad boys.

But unlike Steinbrenner and others, I wasn't convinced that Billy Martin or any manager was a draw for the fans.

I said as much on the air, on August 1, 1975, the day before Martin made his debut as Yankees manager during a four-game home stand against Cleveland. There was a rain delay, so to fill the air-time we invited veteran *New York Post* sportswriter Maury Allen into the broadcast booth to talk about the Yankees' new manager.

"I think the move will be great for the team," Allen said. "People will come see the Yankees now because Billy's such a fiery guy."

I shook my head.

"I don't think so, Maury. If fans came to the park to see a manager, then the stands in Washington would have been filled every game when Ted Williams was on the bench with the Senators in '69—and they weren't. It's great to have a good manager, but the reason fans come to the ball park is to see the players, not the manager."

Once again, I was just calling it as I saw it. But somewhere that day Billy Martin was listening to the broadcast—and he wasn't pleased.

"Billy's not happy with what you said," a reporter later told me. To which I responded, "I really don't care what he thinks." And I didn't.

Martin never confronted me directly about that or any other comments I made on the air. But he was noticeably cool toward me when I would see him at the stadium or on the plane on road trips.

Then Billy found out that I liked to fish.

We were on a plane heading to Minneapolis for a game when Martin brought it up. I like every kind of fishing—deep sea, surf, bait, lure, fly; every kind of fishing is my kind of fishing. Billy liked fishing, too, so we started talking about it, as fishermen will do.

I had also read somewhere that back in 1949, when he was playing in the minors with the Oakland Oaks in the Pacific Coast League, Martin had volunteered to be roommates with the team's only black player, Artie Wilson, a former Negro League player who later played briefly for the Giants. That took some guts to do back then—and given my own experiences with being shunned by teammates when I was in the minors, it increased my respect for Martin considerably.

The upshot was that Martin invited me to go bass fishing on Lake Minnetonka, outside Minneapolis.

You can learn a lot about a man when you're fishing with him. One thing I learned about Billy is how much he knew about base-ball. A lot of managers who are former players will kind of wing it, never expanding their knowledge much beyond the positions they played. But Billy seemed to understand the nuances of pitching, hitting, fielding, everything. Whatever his personal shortcomings, the man knew the game.

(I think Billy Martin was one of baseball's best managers, and later as a member of the Veterans Committee I campaigned to have him elected as a manager into the Hall of Fame. But few of the other committee members agreed.)

The other thing I learned about Billy was actually just a confir-mation of what I already knew—that is, how competitive he was. Before we started fishing, Billy bet me a dinner he would catch more fish than I would, and at first he did, pulling half a dozen fish into the boat and boasting about it all the while. But then my luck turned and I drew ahead of him.

Then it started to rain, not just a drizzle but a certified

downpour. I was ready to quit, but Billy wasn't—at least not until he got ahead of me in the fish count again. "Naw, naw, let's keep fishing," he insisted.

That's how competitive he was. He wouldn't quit until he beat me, or caught pneumonia in the attempt. In that sense, in their driving compulsion to win at everything, every time, Billy and Steinbrenner were exactly alike.

Billy didn't win that bet with me, but we occasionally fished together after that, and we had dinner from time to time. I went to his mother's birthday party, and to his latest wedding (he had already been married and divorced three times).

But one thing I would never do with Billy was go drinking with him. Billy Martin drunk was a trouble magnet—and I didn't need the trouble.

Everyone knows about Martin's on-again, off-again history as the Yankees manager—five times hired by Steinbrenner, five times fired by Steinbrenner. They were like an old couple who couldn't live with each other but couldn't live without each other.

Steinbrenner was considering hiring Martin for his sixth Yankees managerial slot when on Christmas Day, 1989, Martin, age sixty-one, was killed in a single-vehicle crash near Binghamton, New York. He and a pal had been drinking heavily, and on the way home the pickup truck his buddy was driving slid on ice and tumbled into a culvert, breaking Martin's neck.

I can't say that I was surprised when I heard the news. Billy always lived on the edge, so you always expected something to happen to him—and finally something did. They had a giant funeral for him at St. Patrick's Cathedral in New York, with sixty-five hundred people gathered outside and in the cathedral, including Steinbrenner, former president Richard Nixon, Mickey Mantle, Whitey Ford, and many others. As they gathered, a lot of people told a lot of stories about him from his playing and managing days.

Today most people remember Billy Martin for kicking dirt on umpires, for screaming in people's faces, and for his brawls and for his tumultuous relationships with just about everyone. But I have a different memory of him.

What I'll always remember about Billy Martin is him sitting in a boat on Lake Minnetonka, in the rain, soaking wet, for hours, trying to win a fishing contest.

Another player who took offense over something I said about him was Reggie Jackson.

Jackson had been drafted by the Kansas City Athletics in 1966, and had spent some time with their Birmingham, Alabama, AA team, where he had experienced some of the same racial harassment I had gone through in the Carolina League more than a decade earlier. He spent nine years with the A's in Kansas City and then Oakland, and put up some huge numbers, including 254 home runs. During that time he twice led the American League in homers, was the 1973 MVP, and had two World Series rings and six All-Star appearances.

After the Yankees lost the '76 World Series to the Cincinnati Reds in a sweep, George Steinbrenner decided he had to have Reggie Jackson.

But it was going to be expensive. Because the fundamental rules of the baseball business were changing.

When I was a player, and into the mid-1970s, almost every major league player, even the stars, had a one-year, annually renewable contract. Under the "reserve clause" of that contract, if a player refused to accept what the team offered him for the following year, no other team could sign him. Essentially it meant that once a team signed a player, the team owned him for as long as it wanted, and they could trade him to anyone they wanted. The system eliminated any competitive bidding among teams for a player's services, which naturally kept players' salaries down.

The first chink in the reserve clause came in 1969, when my old Cardinals teammate, Curt Flood, refused to be traded to the Philadelphia Phillies. In a letter to the commissioner, Curt said, "I do not feel I am a piece of property to be bought and sold." He later filed a lawsuit challenging the rule, which went all the way to the United States Supreme Court.

I publicly backed Curt in what he did, and even went out to St. Louis to do a story about him for Philadelphia TV station WFIL, where I was working at the time. As a former player, I thought that getting rid of the reserve clause would be a good thing for the players.

But privately I thought Curt was nuts. I didn't think he could win, and I was sure it would destroy what was left of his baseball career.

Which is exactly what happened. Curt eventually lost the lawsuit, and when he finally returned to baseball with the Washington Senators after a year-long hiatus, he simply couldn't play anymore. Still, court rulings in Curt's case helped to open up the reserve clause to arbitration between owners and the Major League Baseball Players Association.

From then on, Players Association executive director Marvin Miller relentlessly pursued elimination of the reserve clause, which eventually happened in 1975, when an arbitrator ruled that any player who played for a season without a new contract could then become a free agent. A year earlier, the same arbitrator had also ruled that the Oakland A's had violated their contract with pitcher Jim "Catfish" Hunter, thus making Hunter a free agent. After the first free agent bidding war in baseball history, Steinbrenner and the Yankees signed Hunter to a five-year, $3.35 million contract—

this for a guy who with the A's had been making just $100,000 a year. The era of multimillion-dollar free agents had begun.

(As a former player whose entire career was spent under the reserve clause, I'm often asked if I'm angry or resentful or envious of the eight-figure contracts that many players get these days. My answer is, not at all. I was a grown man, and it was my decision to play baseball; if I didn't like it, I could have walked away. And how can I resent some modern-day player making more money than I did when I was paid more for playing baseball than Jackie Robinson was?)

In any event, when Jackson became a free agent Steinbrenner wined and dined him, taking him to 21 and selling him on the benefits of living and playing in New York. Steinbrenner's persuasiveness, and his money, beat out the other teams that were vying for Jackson. He eventually signed a five-year, $2.9 million contract and became a Yankee.

Not everyone was happy about it. Billy Martin, for one, didn't like Reggie, thinking that Jackson didn't hustle on the field. In one 1977 incident, NBC-TV cameras picked up Jackson and Martin in a furious argument after Martin pulled Jackson from a game for not hustling on a fly ball and allowing the batter an extra base. Martin lunged at Jackson and had to be restrained.

The other Yankee players also weren't pleased when Jackson, who was not a modest man, said things to the press like "Sometimes I just underestimate the magnitude of me." In one infamous interview in *Sport* magazine early in the 1977 season, Jackson even bad-mouthed popular Yankees catcher Thurman Munson, saying, "This team, it all flows through me...I'm the straw that stirs the drink. Munson thinks he can be the straw that stirs the drink but he can only stir it bad."

Jackson later said he'd been quoted out of context about Munson. But it wasn't a good beginning.

Still, as a slugger Jackson produced. In 1977, he had thirty-two homers and 110 RBIs, which helped the Yankees to dominate the American League East and then win the pennant. The combination of performance and personal style made Jackson big news in the tabloids and other publications—including *Ebony* magazine.

An *Ebony* writer doing a story on Jackson interviewed me, and when he asked me if I thought Jackson was a "great" player, I responded honestly.

"Reggie Jackson is not a great player, he's a good player. I've seen Willie Mays, Hank Aaron, Roberto Clemente go out there every day and do it—bat .300 and knock in a hundred runs every year, steal thirty bases every year, throw guys out every year, win ball games every year, not just with the bat but with the glove. If Reggie Jackson is great, what is Willie Mays? What is Aaron? No, Reggie Jackson is a hell of a salesman. He's out there trying to make as much as he can make, and there's nothing wrong with that."

I didn't have any personal problem with Jackson. In fact, I was friends with his father, Martinez Clarence Jackson, a former second baseman with the Newark Eagles of the old Negro Leagues who ran a tailor and shoe-shine shop in downtown Philadelphia when I was working there.

But when Jackson read what I'd said about him in *Ebony,* he was livid.

We were on a road trip to Boston when the story came out, and Reggie bought a copy at the hotel. I was getting on an elevator when I ran into Maury Allen, the *New York Post* writer.

"Reggie saw something you said about him and he's furious," Allen told me. Allen said that Reggie was in the lobby, fuming.

So I went down to the lobby and when Jackson saw me he glared at me. He obviously wasn't happy.

"C'mon, let's talk about it," I said, leading a reluctant Jackson into the hotel bar. When we sat down I reiterated what I'd said to the *Ebony* reporter and explained why I said it. I didn't back down, and Jackson remained sullen, refusing even to look at me. When we finally left the bar, I considered the issue closed.

But Jackson obviously didn't. And a month later he let me know.

In 1977, the Yankees were in the World Series for the second year in a row, and with the addition of Reggie Jackson they were a better team than they'd been the previous year, when the Reds swept them. At the beginning of Game 6 against the LA Dodgers at Yankee Stadium, the Yankees were leading the series 3–2.

What Reggie Jackson did that day was one of the most amazing single-game performances in baseball history. In three straight at-bats, Jackson hit home runs, the last of which gave the Yankees an 8–3 lead, and eventually the game, and the series. It was the Yankees' first World Series victory since 1962.

I was working with ABC-TV that day, and was assigned to conduct the post-game interviews if the Yankees won. After the victory, the champagne was flying in the locker room. At one point when I was interviewing Yogi Berra, Yankees first base coach Elston Howard dumped what felt like an entire bottle of champagne on my head.

Soaking wet, I got Thurman Munson on camera, and after I finished with him I looked over and saw Jackson being mobbed by reporters and photographers. I bulled through the crowd— you can't be polite in situations like that—grabbed Jackson, and pulled him over to where we were set up for the camera. With the swarm pressing in around us, I put my hand on Jackson's shoulder to steady us, and then I congratulated him on his record-breaking performance.

As I talked I noticed a smirk spreading across his face. Although I had forgotten about our *Ebony* magazine flare-up, Jackson obviously had not.

"Well, Bill," he said, "it's a great feeling. A lot of people talk about great players. The word *superstar* is used a lot. You played in an era when the word really originated, with guys like Mays, Aaron, Clemente…"

Then Jackson smiled at me and said, "Now I can say that I had one day that was like those guys."

It was a jab at me, and yet at the same time I felt it was gracious, an acknowledgment that I had had a point. After my producer told me through my earpiece that Jackson had been named the series MVP—no surprise there—and I congratulated him on the air, we bear-hugged each other and Jackson moved away.

What Reggie Jackson did that day didn't change my opinion. I still think that a truly great player excels in all aspects of the game, on the field and in the batter's box.

But Reggie Jackson had an ability to come through in big ways in big games.

And on that day in the fall of 1977, there was a greatness about him.

I saw a lot of talented players during my years as a Yankees broadcaster: Catfish Hunter, Reggie Jackson, Goose Gossage, Rickey Henderson, and many others. But the consistently best Yankee player I ever knew was catcher Thurman Munson.

Like me, Munson came from a working-class family in Ohio. Unlike me, Munson had been a standout in every sport at his Canton, Ohio, high school, from basketball to football to baseball. He went to Kent State University on a scholarship, and was the fourth pick in the 1968 major league draft. Munson played just one full season in the minors, with the Binghamton (New York) Triplets, before being called up to the Yankees the next season.

By the 1971 season, he was an All-Star, allowing only nine passed balls and throwing out thirty-six of fifty-nine potential base stealers, for an outstanding "caught stealing" rate of 61 percent. During the entire season he made just one error, and that was only because he dropped the ball after Orioles catcher Andy Etchebarren knocked him unconscious when he barreled into him at the plate. During his ten-year career with the Yankees, the only major league team he ever played for, Munson would post a .292 batting average, be named American League Rookie of the Year in 1970 and MVP in 1976, win three Gold Glove Awards, and lead the Yankees as team captain from 1976 to 1979.

Munson was without question the most intelligent catcher in the American League, with a great sense of command in calling pitches and an ability to both challenge and calm the pitchers he worked with. He had those unique qualities that make a man a leader.

Not that he was a particularly impressive guy physically. Actually he was kind of dumpy looking, with short arms and stumpy legs— his teammates' nicknames for him were "Tugboat," "Squatty Body," and "the Wall"—and he sported one of those bushy, out-of-control 1970s mustaches that hung over the corners of his mouth and all the way down his chin. Munson's wife, Diana, liked to tell the story about how Munson, dressed as usual in beat-up jeans and a T-shirt, was pumping gas into his car one day when another customer, thinking he was the gas station attendant, yelled at him, "When you're finished with that, get mine, too." And Munson, at the time the second-highest-paid player on the New York Yankees, pumped the guy's gas for him.

Munson was an outstanding player. But unfortunately for him, there was another American League catcher named Carlton Fisk.

Fisk had joined the hated Boston Red Sox—hated by the Yankees and their fans, anyway—for his first full season in 1972, and was selected that year as the All-Star starting catcher, a position previously held by Munson. Fisk was also named 1972 American

League Rookie of the Year and was awarded a Gold Glove. He was, by any measure, a tremendous player.

In appearance, Fisk was also everything that Munson was not. Tall (six foot three), with chiseled good looks, Fisk was like something out of *Esquire* magazine. He was quickly dubbed "the Chosen One" by other league catchers, and the news media and the Boston fans loved the guy.

Munson, meanwhile, openly despised him. And Fisk returned the sentiment.

The friction between the two catchers went dramatically public in 1973 when, in a game in Boston, Munson found himself on third base as Yankee Gene Michael tried a suicide squeeze bunt. Michael missed the ball as Munson tore in toward home; it was almost comical to see Munson bearing down with those short, stumpy legs of his. Unfortunately, Red Sox catcher Fisk was waiting for him at the plate, ball in hand.

Munson slammed into Fisk, trying to knock the ball out of his hand, but Fisk held on and Munson was out. Munson and Fisk started swinging and soon both benches emptied for a memorable on-field brawl.

There was just something about Fisk that got under Munson's skin—his manner, his demeanor, something. In the news media, Munson could never come out on top in comparisons with golden boy Carlton Ernest Fisk. It ate away at Munson, to the point that when reporters tried to talk to him, Munson would basically tell them to leave him alone—which naturally resulted in even more positive attention being paid to Fisk.

By 1977, the always simmering Yankees–Red Sox rivalry was boiling over. (In the end, the Yankees would beat the Red Sox in the AL East and go on to win the World Series.) Just before a series against the Red Sox in June, there was a lot of talk in the sports media as to who was the better catcher, Munson or Fisk. During our broadcast of the first game, I took up the question—and came down solidly on Munson's side.

I wasn't being a homer. If I had thought Fisk was better, I would have said so. But as I told the listeners, Munson was more agile and had a quicker release than Fisk, and was a better all-around hitter. I noted that if Munson, like Fisk, had played at Fenway Park instead of the more difficult Yankee Stadium, he might have been one of the best right-handed hitters of his era.

And there were also the intangibles that to me made Munson superior. He called his own games, he knew the opposing batters, and he was a leader. He was the guy at the top of the dugout steps cheering his teammates on, the guy who led the team into battle when the benches cleared. He was the player the Yankees rallied behind.

I didn't think much about my comments at the time. But later I was walking by Munson's locker in the clubhouse, where he was sitting half dressed, and he called me over.

"I heard what you said about me on the broadcast the other night," he said, "that I was a better catcher than Fisk. I just wanted to say thanks."

I didn't want Munson, or any player or manager, to think that I was puffing him up on-air without good reason. If I ever did that for one guy, all the players would expect the same treatment, and would be pissed off if they didn't get it. So I told Munson, "No need to thank me. I said you're a better catcher because that's what I truly believe. And you know that if I thought you weren't the better catcher, I'd have said that, too."

Munson seemed to understand. Still, after that he was always a little warmer toward me, the broadcaster who had stood up for him against the hated Fisk. During those years I would sometimes go down to the field to throw batting practice for the Yankee bench-warmers, just as a way to help keep myself in shape. Whenever

Munson would see me down there, he'd call out, "Hey, Bill, throw me some, too," and I'd throw batting practice to him. We were never close—for professional reasons, I always tried to avoid getting too close to any player—but I liked and respected the guy.

On August 2, 1979, I was driving to a market near my home when I heard the news bulletin. We had just come off a six-game road trip, and I was looking forward to a calm day off. That calm ended when the radio announcer said, "New York Yankees catcher Thurman Munson was killed today in a plane crash in Akron, Ohio."

My first thought was, *Goddamn it, Munson! That goddamn plane!*

Munson had been flying small propeller planes for several years, but had recently upgraded to a $1.4 million Cessna Citation jet. I had to wonder if that damn plane was too complicated, and too powerful, for a relative novice pilot like Munson.

Munson had been practicing landings and takeoffs at an airport in Akron when the plane crashed. Munson's two passengers made it out alive; Munson did not. He was dead at age thirty-two.

The next day the Yankees were at home against the Orioles, and when I got to the stadium it seemed like everyone was in shock. Although Munson was withdrawn and distant from the press, and in fact from most outsiders, almost everyone within the Yankees organization loved the guy.

There was a memorial service before the game, and during it the Yankees players took their positions—all but one. The catcher's position remained empty as a tribute to Munson. Some fifty-one thousand fans joined in prayer and then in a thunderous standing ovation. From the broadcast booth Reggie Jackson could be seen in right field, wiping away tears with his sleeve—and his tears certainly weren't the only ones shed that night.

I was broadcasting that night and had to maintain my professional demeanor.

Still, that memorial service for Thurman Munson was one of the most moving things I ever saw in baseball.

And I'm convinced that when Thurman Munson died, part of what the Yankees were died with him.

My broadcasting work with the Yankees started every year at spring training and ended in the fall. That schedule left me plenty of time to try other things outside baseball.

One of the things I tried was a stint on the NBC *Today* show.

It was in the off season in 1973, and Joe Garagiola, the Cardinals-catcher-turned-broadcaster, was leaving after six years on the early-morning show. My voice coach, Lilyan Wilder, was encouraging me to apply for the job, and Garagiola, whom I had known since he called Cardinals games for KMOX radio in St. Louis, was also pushing me with the show's producers.

So I did a tryout interview with former Yankees president Mike Burke as my guest. Everybody in New York knew Mike, so the tryout went over well. Eventually the producers brought me on as a one-month temporary replacement for Joe, with plans to hire me full-time if it went well.

Unfortunately, it didn't.

There is an axiom in show business that says you should never follow any act that has children or animals in it. I would amend that to say you should never follow any act that has children, animals, or Joe Garagiola in it.

Joe had been enormously popular on the show. He was folksy, funny, and extremely personable on-air—a tough act for a guy like me to follow. And frankly, I didn't really like the job. I had to stay in a hotel in the city and get up at 3 AM every weekday—and I wasn't a morning person. Finally, to stay with the *Today* show I would have had to quit my Yankees broadcasting job, which I didn't want to do.

Although the full-time gig didn't work out, I did occasional sports-related pieces for the *Today* show—a segment about golfer Sam Snead, a segment about a new kind of ski boots, just about anything that interested me.

But then I did a segment on Paul Robeson, the great African American football star, singer, actor, and political activist.

It started with a call in 1976 from John Bateman, a former Rutgers University football coach. Paul Robeson had played for Rutgers in the early 1900s, and Bateman was trying to get Robeson's name reinstated on the 1918 All-American football team record. Robeson's name had been taken off that list in the 1950s during the McCarthy period, after he was accused of being a communist. He actually was a progressive, and a tireless fighter against racism, but at the time many people thought that was the same thing as being a communist. Robeson had died in January 1976, and Bateman thought it was past time to set things right.

I was intrigued by the story and started doing research. Finally I put together a segment on Robeson, co-hosted by my good friend Gene Shalit, showing photographs and talking with Robeson's son.

It was a good segment, one that I was proud of—and it was also far more controversial than the *Today* show producers wanted. A number of viewers complained that the show had "glorified a communist." The racists said it had glorified a "nigger communist." The complaints poured in.

The *Today* show producers may have wanted to stand behind me, but television, like baseball, is a game of numbers. After the Robeson report, my favorability rating among viewers dropped from the sixties to the thirties. *Today* show producer Stu Schulberg called me in and said, "Bill, .300 is good in baseball, but not in this business."

I thanked Stu and left. And to tell the truth, I wasn't that disappointed about getting fired.

I had some other memorable nonbaseball moments. For example, in 1980 I covered the Winter Olympics at Lake Placid for ABC radio, and was able to witness the famous "Miracle on Ice."

My primary job at the Olympics was to cover the "sliders"—the various luge and bobsled events. Although I was an avid skier, I didn't know much about bobsledding or luge, but as usual I found experts to guide me through it.

But at one point between slider events I ran into Lou Vairo, a future Olympic hockey coach who at the time was an advance scout for coach Herb Brooks's US Olympic team. The US team was just about to take on the powerhouse Soviet Union, which had won the hockey gold medal in every Olympics since 1964. Everybody expected the Americans to get slaughtered.

Vairo was a nice guy, but when he told me he thought the Americans had a good chance I thought he was dreaming. After the interview he gave me a hockey stick signed by all the US team members. I thanked him, but I didn't tell him that the piece of memorabilia I really wanted was a Mongolian Olympic team pin.

I'd been a dedicated knickknacks trader ever since my days with the Cardinals in St. Louis, operating "Bill White's Trading Post" in the team clubhouse. When I got to Lake Placid, I learned that the most sought-after item was the Mongolian pin—this because the Mongolian team had only three members, and the pins were scarce. So when I tried to trade the signed US hockey team stick for a Mongolian pin, I was laughed at.

Then came the Miracle on Ice.

Early in the game I wandered up to the ABC broadcast booth, where Al Michaels was calling the game for ABC-TV. As the time ticked down and the excitement grew, I found myself getting caught up in it. In the last few seconds, with the United States leading the Soviets 4–3, Michaels made his famous call—"Do you believe in miracles? YES!"—and suddenly I started screaming and jumping up and down like everyone else.

I had never done that at a sporting event, ever. I'm not sure why I did it then. It was just a great moment.

And an added benefit was that my signed US team hockey stick suddenly became one of the hottest trading items at the Olympics. Guys even offered me Mongolian team pins for it—and it was my turn to laugh at them. On the drive back to the hotel that night, I clutched that stick like it was made out of gold. I have it to this day.

I also covered the 1984 Winter Olympics in Sarajevo, once again focusing on the "slider" events. My most vivid memory of that is having to get up at 4 AM and ride in an SUV up a narrow mountain road to the site of the downhill events. I don't frighten easily, but driving along a narrow, icy road in the dark, with thousand-foot drop-offs a few feet from the blacktop and no guardrails, was something I wouldn't care to do again.

I also underwent some changes in my personal life during those years. Sadly, my wife and I separated and then divorced. Mildred was a good wife and a good mother, but we had grown apart over the years.

But I tried to remain a close and active presence in our children's lives, then and since.

I took an intense interest in their educations, as my mother and grandmother had done with me. My oldest daughter, Edna, attended several colleges and went on to a career in business before finally getting a degree from Penn State at the age of fifty-two. Debbie got a master's degree from Temple University and worked with special-education kids in Phoenix, Los Angeles, and now in Bucks County.

When they were growing up I would often take my boys, Tommy, Steve, and Mike, to Yankees games with me (the girls just weren't interested). While I was working in the broadcast booth I would park them in the owner's box, which was on the same level in the stadium, where I could keep an eye on them. George Steinbrenner was always nice to them and took an interest in their lives. Although Steve played baseball at the University of Delaware, none of the boys was interested in a professional baseball career—which was fine with me. I knew how hard it was to make it in the major leagues. Instead, they all went on to get business degrees and pursue successful careers in that field.

So it was a good life. I had five intelligent, well-grounded kids, and a job that gave me a lot of time off. The only problem was that by the late 1980s, I was starting to get bored with broadcasting baseball games.

Of course, there were always some exciting moments. For example, I was there in 1978 when Yankees shortstop Bucky Dent hit his famous home run in the American League East championship against the Red Sox—"Deep to left! Yastrzemski will not get it! It's a home run! A three-run home run for Bucky Dent and the Yankees now lead it by a score of 3–2!"

But those moments were rare. And really, how many times can you say "It's a ground ball to shortstop" with the interest level that viewers and listeners expect and deserve?

Yes, it was easy work. Because of changes in the Yankees broadcast contracts, I called only about sixty television games a year by then, which left plenty of time for other broadcast work that I did for CBS radio—and for fishing.

I was in my midfifties, and I had told myself that after twenty years I was going to leave broadcasting and do something else. I didn't know exactly what, but I thought it would be something in business and finance.

That was the plan. But as it turned out, baseball wasn't finished with me.

CHAPTER 12

April 1987 marked the fortieth anniversary of Jackie Robinson breaking the color line in Major League Baseball. As you would expect, in the days leading up to the anniversary of Jackie's first game with the Brooklyn Dodgers a number of media outlets devoted stories and news programs to the event.

One of them was ABC's *Nightline* with Ted Koppel, which planned a nostalgic, noncontroversial remembrance of Jackie and his career.

It didn't turn out that way. Instead, the news program dropped like a bombshell on baseball—and indirectly, it would have a profound effect on me.

The *Nightline* producers had asked Don Newcombe—the former Dodgers pitcher and the team's current director of community relations—to come on the show and talk about Jackie. At the last minute Newcombe couldn't make it—his plane was delayed—but the producers got Al Campanis, the LA Dodgers' general manager and vice president for player personnel, to appear by satellite from

Houston's Astrodome, where the Dodgers had just finished their season-opener game with the Astros.

Al had always been friendly. Whenever I ran into him at Dodgers spring training in Vero Beach, he always made a point of inviting me to his table at the team dining hall to sample some of his gourmet cooking. He was also well liked within the Dodgers organization.

And Al had been a good friend to Jackie Robinson. Before his major league debut, when Robinson had been playing second base for the Montreal Royals, one of the Dodgers' minor league teams, Branch Rickey had asked Al to room with Jackie and watch out for him. Al did, teaching Jackie how to avoid the high spikes and other abuses that were sure to come his way at second base. Once Al threw off his glove and offered to kick the ass of a player who was giving Robinson trouble.

As a player Al hadn't gotten far in the majors, playing in just seven Dodgers games. But he stayed with the Dodgers organization as a minor league manager, a scouting director, and from 1968 as the head of player personnel. Among other things, he was credited with bringing star pitchers Sandy Koufax and Fernando Valenzuela to the team.

The *Nightline* broadcast started off amiably enough, with mostly softball questions. But then baseball writer Roger Kahn, who was also on the show, raised the question of minorities—or the lack of them—in baseball's front offices and manager slots.

There had been a pathetically small number of African Americans in managerial positions. The first major league black manager, Hall of Fame player Frank Robinson, had been hired as player-manager with the Cleveland Indians in 1975 and later held the manager's slot with the Giants, Orioles, and Expos before retiring in 2006.

The first black general manager, Bill Lucas, a minor leaguer with the then Milwaukee Braves and later an executive with the Atlanta Braves, had been named Braves general manager in 1976.

But Bill Lucas had died of a brain hemorrhage in 1979, and in 1987 Frank was in between managing jobs. So at the time of the *Nightline* broadcast there were no—none, zero—black managers, general managers, or owners in Major League Baseball. At the time the highest-ranking blacks in baseball were Newcombe and Hank Aaron, director of player development for Atlanta.

Ted Koppel passed Kahn's question along to Campanis. Why the lack of African American managers, general managers, and owners in baseball?

"Mr. Koppel, there have been some black managers, but I really can't answer that question directly," Campanis said. "The only thing I can say is, you have to pay your dues when you become a manager. Generally you have to go to minor leagues, and there's not much pay involved. Some of the better-known black players have been able to get into other fields and make a pretty good living that way."

Koppel wasn't buying that.

Koppel: But you know in your heart of hearts that's a lot of baloney. There are a lot of black players, a lot of great black baseball men, who would dearly love to be in managerial positions...Is there still that much prejudice in baseball today?

Campanis: No, I don't believe it's prejudice. I truly believe they may not have some of the necessities to be, let's say, a field manager, or perhaps a general manager.

Koppel: Do you really believe that? That sounds like the same kind of garbage we were hearing forty years ago about players.

Campanis: It's not garbage Mr. Koppel . . . It just might be that—
why are black men or black people not good swimmers?
Because they don't have the buoyancy.

Koppel looked as if he couldn't believe what he was hearing. Necessities? Buoyancy? After a commercial break, Koppel came back and said that he was "flabbergasted" by Campanis's remarks and wanted to give him a chance to "dig yourself out." But Al just made it worse.

"I have never said that blacks are not intelligent," he said. "I think many of them are highly intelligent. But they may not have the desire to be in the front office . . . But they are outstanding athletes, very God-gifted and wonderful people . . . They are gifted with great musculature and various other things. They are fleet of foot, and this is why there are a lot of black ballplayers in the major leagues."

For Campanis it was a disaster—and by the end of the *Nightline* appearance he knew it. Shortly thereafter, looking shaken, he ran into Dodgers broadcaster Vin Scully and told him, "I think I screwed up."

Campanis apologized the next day, and a number of people came forward to defend him, including Don Newcombe, who later said that Al "does not have a prejudiced bone in his body." Others said the same.

But it was too late. Two days after the broadcast, Campanis was forced to resign.

I didn't see the initial *Nightline* broadcast. But when I heard the replays I was astonished.

On one hand, what Al had said seemed out of character. He was seventy years old and reportedly taking medication at the time. A couple of drinks may also have been involved.

On the other hand, the things Al said were the same ridiculous arguments that had been around for decades. Before 1947, they had said that blacks weren't intelligent enough to play baseball in the major leagues. When that was resoundingly disproved, they started saying that, yeah, blacks could play, but they weren't intelligent enough to manage or hold executive jobs.

And they kept using the same old bogus excuses. For example, Campanis's comment about managers needing minor league managing experience before they could move up to managing in the big leagues was absurd on its face.

Lou Piniella, the former Yankees player and then a batting coach, was named Yankees manager in 1986 and then general manager in 1988, and he had never managed in the minor leagues. Alvin Dark, who took over as Giants manager in 1961 and went on to manage four other teams, had never managed in the minors, either. Lou Boudreau, Joe Cronin, Joe Adcock—there had been numerous players who went straight from playing to managing jobs without "paying their dues" as managers in the minors.

(Alvin Dark had had his own "Campanis moment" in 1964. Although he later said he was misquoted, *Newsday* quoted Dark as saying of black and Latino players, "They are just not able to perform up to [the level of] the white ballplayers when it comes to mental alertness.")

In the end, I had to conclude that while Al Campanis was a basically decent man, he had said not only what he believed but what many other baseball executives of the time believed—that blacks in general lacked the ability to work in high-profile front office and managerial positions.

Later Frank Robinson said this of the Campanis incident: "Someone from the inner circle had let out what we'd known all along. That attitude had been something we had been trying to tell people about, that these things were going on, that these thoughts existed. Now the rest of the world heard it from someone who made decisions to hire or not to hire."

The backlash from Campanis's *Nightline* appearance was immediate. Baseball knew it faced a serious public relations problem. Baseball commissioner Peter Ueberroth quickly announced the formation of an affirmative action program headed by Harry Edwards, an African American sociology professor at the University of California at Berkeley, to seek out qualified blacks and Latinos to work in off-field baseball positions. And team executives suddenly were on notice that their hiring practices would be under a news media spotlight.

Over the next five years, baseball's hiring record improved somewhat. By 1992, six black or Latino managers had been hired by major league teams—but that was just six out of a total of forty-eight managerial hires. In the baseball front offices, minorities accounted for just 2 percent of employees in 1987, while by 1992 that figure had increased to 16 percent minority employees. Meanwhile, 17 percent of players on the field were black and another 15 percent Latino—which meant that black and Latino faces in the front offices were still only half as prevalent as they were on the field.

Often it seemed that the major league teams only wanted it to *appear* as if they were seriously considering blacks as managerial material. In the two years after the Campanis interview, I would occasionally pick up a newspaper and see that I was being considered for a field manager or general manager job by one team or another. This came as a surprise since none of the teams mentioned had ever contacted me. Most of the time it probably was just talk, but I couldn't help wondering if by throwing my name into the mix some baseball executives were giving themselves the ability to say, "See? We did consider a black guy for a manager's job."

Then, in late 1988, I got a call from Dodgers owner Peter O'Malley. Peter had taken over as owner of the Dodgers in 1979 from his father, Walter O'Malley, who had moved the Brooklyn team to Los Angeles in 1958—and had been hated by Brooklyn baseball fans ever since.

I didn't know Peter O'Malley very well at the time, so there was little small talk. He got right to the point.

"Bill, I'm on the search committee for a new National League president. We'd like to interview you for the job."

I had known the National League was looking for a new president. Longtime league president Chub Feeney, former general manager of the Giants, had held the job from 1970 to 1986, a period of remarkable stability within the league; there had been no expansions or franchise moves during his tenure. Chub had been succeeded in late 1986 by Yale University president A. Bartlett Giamatti, a lifelong baseball enthusiast, but now Giamatti was slated to become commissioner of baseball to replace the departing Peter Ueberroth.

So the National League search committee members—O'Malley, Mets co-owner Fred Wilpon, Atlanta Braves chairman Bill Bartholomay, and Chicago Cubs representative John Madigan—needed somebody to fill the slot. And given the heat over the minority hiring issue, I was pretty sure they wanted it to at least appear that they had considered someone who was black.

But when O'Malley first asked me about it, I was also certain that that someone wasn't going to be me.

"Are you serious?" I said. When O'Malley said he was, I told him, "Thanks, but I'm not interested."

"Okay, Bill, thanks for your time."

I meant what I said. Although I was getting a little bored with baseball broadcasting, taking an executive job like National League president was the farthest thing from my mind—even assuming that their interest in me was genuine and not just window dressing.

I didn't give it any more thought until a week later, when O'Malley called again.

"Bill, I know you said you weren't interested in the National League job. But the committee would still like to interview you."

I wasn't as instantly dismissive of O'Malley's second call.

"Okay, Peter," I said. I thought it wouldn't hurt to meet with them, even though I still wasn't interested in actually taking the job.

The interview took place a couple of weeks later at the Helmsley Palace Hotel in New York, not far from the Major League Baseball offices. As I passed through the hotel lobby, I noticed Joe Morgan, the Hall of Fame second baseman and sports broadcaster, off in the corner reading a newspaper. Apparently I wasn't the only African American player-turned-broadcaster who was being interviewed.

Waiting for me in a suite were O'Malley, Giamatti, Chub Feeney, Wilpon, and Bartholomay. John Madigan of the Cubs, the other search committee member, couldn't make it.

I was completely relaxed. As with almost every job I've ever had in my life, I had no emotional investment in the job prospect. I could take it or leave it—and at that point, I was still leaning toward leaving it.

We talked for about ninety minutes, longer than planned. At one point someone asked me about my method of conflict resolution. I summed it up this way: "I'd have the parties involved sit down together with me and try to work it out between themselves. If they can't do that, then I would make a decision—and I would stand by that decision."

I also stressed to the committee members that I did not want to be a so-called black hire. I wasn't naive. I knew that baseball was under a lot of pressure about minority hiring. But I insisted that if I were to take the job, I would want to be the president of the National League, not the *black* president of the National League— and I meant it. The committee members assured me that they would hire the best person, regardless of race.

Finally we all stood up, and I shook hands all around. But just before I got to the door, I stopped. There was something I hadn't mentioned to the committee members.

"I just want you guys to know that I'm divorced, and that I have a lady friend."

My lady friend was Nancy McKee, a woman I had known since she was a classmate of mine in junior high and high school in Warren, Ohio. We'd lost touch after that, and both of us went on to marry and have children. But several years after my wife and I divorced, I had renewed contact with Nancy, who also was divorced. We've been together ever since.

Ordinarily I wouldn't have felt compelled to mention anything about my personal life. But there was another factor in my relationship with Nancy that I felt the committee members might want to know about.

"And by the way," I told them, "she's not black."

The committee members sat there quietly for just a moment. Then Fred Wilpon said, "A lot of people are divorced. A lot of people have lady friends. I really don't see that as a problem." The other committee members nodded in agreement.

(Back then, and to this day, black–white relationships could be an issue with some people—from both racial groups. It was an issue with Nancy's mother when we first began our relationship, although in time she came around. And it certainly would have been an issue with my grandmother had she still been alive. Grandma wouldn't have liked it one bit.)

I didn't think about the interview, or the National League job in general, in the weeks after that. But then a few weeks later O'Malley called again and said the job was mine—if I would take it.

There were a lot of good reasons not to take it. I was well paid in my broadcasting work, and had plenty of free time for fishing, tennis, just enjoying life. I would be giving all that up for an executive job that promised long hours, extensive business travel, and constant headaches.

But in the end there was one overriding reason why I decided to accept the position as president of the National League.

It was a challenge. And throughout my life, a challenge has been something that is hard for me to resist.

From the moment my selection as the fifteenth president of the National League was announced in February 1989, the "firsts" began. In every newspaper and magazine and television report, it went something like this: "Bill White will be the first black president of baseball's National League..."

Again, I wasn't naive. I knew that after the spotlight the Campanis incident cast on baseball, the team owners wanted a black man for the job. I also knew that being the first African American to hold the position would be news in and of itself. That's the way the news business works; there was no escaping it.

But I felt the same way as I had when I was the "first full-time black broadcaster" in Major League Baseball. I didn't intend to fail, but if somehow I did, I wanted it to be Bill White who had failed, not a black man who had failed.

I also didn't want people to think that my entire emphasis would be on race-related issues. Did I want fairer treatment of minorities in baseball front offices? Absolutely. But was I going to get up on a public soapbox and demand that this team hire that guy and that team hire the other guy? No. I preferred to work behind the scenes, applying influence—and if necessary, pressure—to get the teams to do the right thing. My job was to promote the best interests of the National League, and of Major League Baseball in general, and it wouldn't help those interests if I was constantly speaking out in public about racism in the game, or if I concentrated on race issues to the exclusion of everything else.

Clifford Alexander, the former secretary of the army who was a consultant to baseball on minority hiring, probably put it best: "Bill isn't the president of the NAACP. He's the president of the National League."

So when the news media started talking about "firsts," I wish they had paid as much attention to another "first" that I represented: I was the first National League president in more than seventy years who had ever played baseball in the major leagues. Bart Giamatti had been an academic. Chub Feeney (National League president 1970–1986), the nephew of Giants owner Horace Stoneham, had been a batboy for the Giants before becoming a front office executive. Warren Giles (1951–1969) had been general manager and president of the Cincinnati Reds. Ford Frick (1934–1951) had been a sportswriter. John Heydler (1918–1934) had been an umpire and a sportswriter.

The point is that after thirteen years as a player and eighteen years as a baseball broadcaster, I knew the game and the people in it—players, managers, umpires, front office executives, reporters, public relations and marketing guys, even batboys. I knew the personalities; I knew the tricks of the trade. I think I knew as much or more about baseball as any of the dozen men who preceded me.

That knowledge and experience would be a big plus when dealing with some of baseball's stronger personalities. I remember once, early in my term as president, I was sitting in my office with Bart Giamatti, who had just moved up to the commissioner position, when LA Dodgers manager Tommy Lasorda called. As I put him on the speakerphone, Tommy started bitching and moaning about some baseballs he claimed had been doctored by a Houston Astros pitcher in a recent game against the Dodgers.

"I've got the balls right here, and I'm going to send Orel Hershiser over with them so you can see them!"

Tommy had balls, all right. He had balls pulling that sort of thing with me. I looked over at Bart and started laughing.

"Tommy, the umpires are the people who would have to give me the balls, not you. After you've had them, the balls aren't evidence anymore. And I want you to know that I used to hit against Don Drysdale and other Dodgers pitchers and I know for a fact that they doctored balls, too. So don't try to tell me this is something your team has never done."

Tommy was like a lot of good managers. He would lie awake at night trying to think of any little angle that would give his team an advantage. So as he blustered and bitched, I just laughed.

Finally Tommy hung up. By now Bart was looking at me with amazement.

"That's the advantage you have from being in the game so long," he said. "I never would have been able to talk to Lasorda like that."

I liked Bart a lot. The fact that he would be commissioner while I was league president had been a factor in my decision to take the job. A stout man with a trim salt-and-pepper beard, Bart had a brilliant mind, but he wasn't one of those smart guys who felt compelled to constantly advertise it. A product of America's best schools and former president of Yale University, he could talk comfortably with a cabbie or a CEO, and when necessary he could cuss like a sailor. One reason the owners had wanted him for league president and then commissioner was because while he was at Yale he had played hardball with the unions during a bitter strike by university clerical and technical workers.

Although Bart and I sometimes disagreed, there was never any rancor in it. Bart always conducted himself in a collegial fashion. I'm smiling as I write *collegial*. Defined as "marked by camaraderie among colleagues," it was one of Bart's favorite words. In the time I knew him, I can't remember a single conversation or memo in which he didn't use *collegial* at least once.

Far less collegial in spirit was Bart's deputy commissioner, Fay Vincent. Vincent, a former executive at Columbia Pictures and Coca-Cola, had been hired as deputy commissioner—a position that previously hadn't existed—because the owners wanted someone with business experience to assist Bart.

Although they were longtime friends, Vincent and Bart couldn't have been less alike. And Vincent and I were destined to butt heads on almost everything in the coming years.

Another source of annoyance was the sportswriters and others who dismissed the position of National League president as largely symbolic and ceremonial.

Sometimes I wish it had been ceremonial. Then all I would have had to do was go around and give speeches. But the president's job involved far more than that.

Some of the work, like the scheduling of games and umpire crews, was purely administrative. But I also was responsible for overseeing the league's thirty-two umpires; disciplining players; resolving disputes among players, coaches, and managers; and mediating disputes among team owners. During my tenure I had to deal with strikes, misbehaving players, rogue umpires, and guiding the league through a tumultuous expansion. It was an enormous responsibility, and it required an enormous amount of work.

(One odd little legend that surrounded my National League presidency was that I had actually taken a pay cut to leave broadcasting and become league president. I don't know where the press got that, and I never wasted time correcting it. But I often wondered: How stupid did they think I was that I would leave an easy, well-paying, low-stress job in broadcasting to take a difficult, high-stress baseball executive job that paid less money? Actually, my league job paid 30 percent more than I had been making in broadcasting, and with much better benefits.)

Fortunately, I had an outstanding staff in the league office, which was located on Park Avenue in New York, one floor above the Major League Baseball offices. Katy Feeney was in charge of media and public relations, and as Chub Feeney's daughter she had been around the game for her entire life; she knew baseball. Phyllis Collins was in charge of finances and budget; she had worked for years with the Atlanta Braves. Cathy Davis handled umpire issues and Nancy Crofts was the expert on league rules. Together they were the best staff that any league president could ever hope for.

Our head of umpires was Ed Vargo, with whom I'd had a long personal history—not all of it positive. Ed was one of only two umpires who had ejected me from a major league game.

It happened when I was with the Cardinals and we were playing the Astros in Houston. Ed had a habit of shifting left of the plate with a left-handed batter, and when I took a pitch that I thought was outside, Ed punched me out—that is, called a third strike. I usually didn't argue with umpires, but I thought Ed's position behind the plate had resulted in a bad call, so I said, "You little son-of-a-bitch! You need to keep your eyes on that outside corner!"

Boom! I was outta there. And I deserved it.

(My other major league ejection came when umpire Al Forman said I missed home plate after being batted in from second and I called him a "blind bastard." I was fined $50 by the league, but Cardinals manager Johnny Keane later gave me $50 to make up for it.)

When I first became league president, some of the umpires wanted me to fire Ed Vargo as head of umpires, saying he was too tough on them. But I looked at that as an endorsement. Ed was always kind of a cocky guy, but if the umpires wanted him out, I figured he must be doing his job.

So I had a good staff, an adequate budget—about $19 million, most of which was for umpires' pay and benefits—and a supportive ally in Commissioner Bart Giamatti. I was looking forward to starting work on some of my goals as league president.

My primary goal was to bring some fun back to the game of baseball—a game that in recent years had been ripped apart by acrimony among players, managers, umpires, and owners; a game that too often had become defined by what happened off the field—strikes, lockouts, free agent bidding wars—rather than by what happened on the field. I'll admit that it was an ambitious, perhaps even unattainable goal. But I was ready to try.

Even before I was officially installed as president, though, I got a taste of the sort of trouble that would punctuate my tenure with the National League.

The trouble's name was Pete Rose.

I didn't know Pete Rose very well when I was a player or a broadcaster. We were just nodding acquaintances. There were some things about "Charlie Hustle's" aggressive style of play that to me were a little annoying—like running to first base on a walk—but I admired Pete's passion for the game. As a player over twenty-four seasons, he had a .303 batting average and compiled a catalog of major league "mosts"—most career hits (4,256), most career games played (3,562), most career at-bats (14,053). And on and on. During his five years as the Reds' manager, he posted a win–loss record of 426–388. The guy was a shoo-in for the Hall of Fame in his first year of eligibility.

Unfortunately, as all the world now knows, Pete liked to gamble. And he made the mistake of gambling on baseball.

From his very first day in a major league organization, every player knows the rules on gambling; they are posted in every team clubhouse. A player might get off with a fine or a temporary suspension for other egregious off-field misbehavior (drug use, for example), but for any player, manager, umpire, or other baseball employee to get caught gambling on baseball is an automatic banishing offense—for a minimum of a year if he bets on other teams, and for life if he bets on any game in which he's a participant.

It's been that way ever since eight Chicago White Sox players were banned for conspiring with gamblers to throw the 1919 World Series. Of the eighteen additional people banned since then, ten were accused of gambling on baseball or associating with gamblers. Mickey Mantle and Willie Mays were even banned by Commissioner Bowie Kuhn in 1983 when they took post-retirement jobs as greeters at Atlantic City casinos after the commissioner told them not to. (They were reinstated by Ueberroth in 1985.)

Pete Rose knew all this as well as anybody. But he still gambled on baseball.

The first rumors about Rose's ties to gambling reached then commissioner Ueberroth in February 1989. Rose was ordered to fly to New York from spring training in Tampa to discuss the allegation. Rose denied it vehemently, and apparently persuasively. Ueberroth let it drop. Then a *Sports Illustrated* writer contacted the league office for comment on an impending story about Rose and betting on baseball.

Bart Giamatti was still league president at the time. His official start date as the new commissioner was April 1, the same day I would take over as league president. I was already on the National League payroll because we were beginning the transition. I was traveling with Bart and Fay Vincent to spring training in Arizona and Florida when the query from *Sports Illustrated* came in. Bart called an emergency meeting.

The meeting was held in Bart's hotel room in Scottsdale. Five of us were sitting around a table: Bart, Fay, Ueberroth, former National League president Chub Feeney, and me. No one was smiling. The mood was grim when the Cincinnati Reds resident agent joined us.

Each major league city had a "resident agent," usually a former FBI agent or other law enforcement investigator, whose job it was to keep an eye on baseball personnel and investigate any suspected wrongdoing by them or any threats against them. At that time, the agents were anonymous—the players didn't even know who they were—and they usually had extensive contacts with local police.

Sometimes the resident agent could get a player in trouble with things he found out, but sometimes the agent could get a player or other baseball official out of trouble. For example, once when I was league president I was called at 2 AM and informed that a certain umpire was about to be publicly accused of rape by a woman he'd been with in his hotel room. I called the umpire, who vehemently denied it. Meanwhile, the resident agent immediately got on the case and proved conclusively that the woman's story was bogus, that it was a shakedown for money. She decided not to make the allegation, and the umpire's reputation was protected.

The investigation of Pete Rose, however, came up with a different result.

"This does not look good," the Cincinnati resident agent told us as he gave each of us a packet several inches thick. "Based on this information, I'm almost positive that Pete Rose has been betting on baseball."

We all took our packets and retired to our separate rooms. It took us nearly three hours to go through it all, and the evidence was damning.

There were depositions from guys Pete hung out with at Gold's Gym in Cincinnati stating that Rose had bet thousands of dollars on baseball games, although not necessarily Reds games. There were xeroxed copies of betting slips apparently bearing Rose's signature. There were transcripts of tape recordings of bookies discussing Rose's bets, and much more.

I was shocked, and disappointed. It didn't matter whether Rose had bet on Reds games or other games. He knew the rules. And then he had lied about it.

Now Ueberroth and Bart Giamatti, as the incoming commissioner, had to decide what to do about it.

I still wasn't officially installed as National League president, and in any event, gambling allegations against a player was a commissioner-level matter. But I offered a suggestion.

"If we allow Pete to stay with the Reds, it's going to be a circus," I told the group. "Every time the Reds go into a new city and start a new series, all the talk is going to be about Pete and gambling, regardless of what's happening on the field. That won't help Pete, it won't help his team, and it certainly won't help baseball. So why not tell Pete he can have a leave of absence—make it a mandatory leave of absence if necessary—so he can have all the time he needs to clear himself. If he's cleared of the charges, we'll welcome him back to the game. And if he's not..."

I didn't have to finish the sentence. Everybody knew what would happen if the charges stood up.

I was the new guy, so my suggestion didn't carry much weight. Bart decided to take a different tack.

One day before the *Sports Illustrated* story appeared, under a headline called "The Rose Probe," Bart and Ueberroth jointly issued a statement:

"The office of the commissioner, which was founded to protect the integrity of baseball, has been conducting a full inquiry into serious allegations involving Mr. Pete Rose. Mr. Rose has cooperated with the commissioner's inquiry. When the commissioner's office has completed the inquiry, the commissioner will consider the information presented and take whatever action is warranted."

As I had predicted, Pete Rose became a traveling circus that summer. It was an issue that consumed major league baseball's attention for almost the entire season.

Three days after becoming commissioner, Bart Giamatti turned the investigation over to an attorney named John Dowd, a former marine captain and onetime chief of the Organized Crime Strike Force in the Justice Department. I liked Dowd, but a lot of people didn't, thinking he was eager to crucify Rose. Dowd certainly was a bulldog.

Dowd ultimately prepared a 225-page report, similar to the one we had seen in Scottsdale, that documented Rose's gambling on baseball in 1985 and 1986 and offered a day-by-day chronicle of Rose betting thousands of dollars on games in 1987, including bets on fifty-two Reds games. The report said there was no evidence that Rose had bet against his team, but that didn't matter. Placing bets on baseball was an unpardonable offense; placing bets on your own team, which could affect how you used your players, was even worse.

A lot of people criticized Dowd, and Giamatti, for the report, saying it was a hatchet job based on accusations by a bunch of low-lifes. Rose, for his part, was still denying the allegations, and a lot of fans wanted to believe him.

Unfortunately, even before the report came out, while Dowd was conducting his investigation, Bart made a mistake. He allowed a letter to go out, with his signature, addressed to a federal judge presiding over a drug trafficking and tax evasion case against one of Rose's bookie accusers, a guy named Ron Peters. The letter praised the bookie for his cooperation in the Rose investigation.

The letter may or may not have helped the bookie get a lighter sentence—he got just two years in prison—but it didn't help Bart. A Cincinnati state judge issued a temporary restraining order prohibiting Bart from holding a hearing on Rose. The judge said Bart's letter on the bookie's behalf had been inappropriate, and that it indicated Bart was prejudiced and had pre-judged the evidence against Rose. The issue went around and around, but eventually Bart and Rose entered into negotiations.

Finally, in August, Bart and Rose reached an agreement. Rose agreed to be permanently placed on baseball's "ineligible list"—in other words, banned—although he would be eligible to apply for future reinstatement. Rose also acknowledged that the commissioner had a "factual basis" to impose the ban, but he did not admit that he had bet on baseball games. In effect, Rose was pleading "no contest" to the allegations.

Bart, for his part, agreed that he would not make any "formal findings" that Rose had bet on baseball. But when Bart was asked at a press conference if he personally thought Rose had in fact bet on baseball and on Reds games, Bart, as was his way, responded honestly.

"Yes," Bart said.

I was at that press conference, and when Bart gave that answer I knew there was going to be trouble, that he would be accused of violating the agreement with Rose. And he was. More turmoil followed.

Rose later pleaded guilty to two charges of tax evasion on income derived from selling autographs and gambling on horse races; he served five months in a medium-security prison and paid more than $400,000 in fines and restitution. He continued to lie about his baseball gambling for fifteen years, in the process savaging Bart Giamatti and others for supposedly treating him unfairly. It wasn't until Rose published his second book in 2004—*My Prison Without Bars*—and went on the interview circuit that he finally admitted to betting on baseball while playing for and managing the Reds. He also admitted betting on the Reds, although he claimed he never bet against his team.

For Rose and for baseball in general, the whole thing was a sorry spectacle. And it may keep him out of the Hall of Fame forever, since in 1991 the Hall voted to exclude any player who is on the ineligible list—and so far, no commissioner has seemed inclined to take Rose's name off the list.

Of course, it's not up to me. But would I ever vote to put Pete Rose in the Hall of Fame?

My answer is no. He knew the rules, and he broke them. And for that he should have to pay the price.

Sadly, by the time Rose finally came clean, Bart Giamatti wasn't around to be vindicated.

On September 1, 1989, the Friday evening before the Labor Day weekend, I was driving west on I-78 back to Pennsylvania, looking forward to a long weekend, when I heard the news flash on the radio.

"Bart Giamatti, the former Yale president who earlier this year was named commissioner of Major League Baseball, died today of an apparent heart attack. He was fifty-one."

I could hardly believe it. Just a few hours earlier I had been talking to Bart in his office, and though he had seemed tired and worn after the tumultuous summer, he had been planning to relax over the long weekend at his vacation home in Martha's Vineyard. And now after just five months in office, and at a far-too-early age, this good man was suddenly dead.

I don't know if the flak Bart took over the Pete Rose issue had any direct effect on what happened. Bart was a heavy guy, and a smoker, and he suffered from hypertension. But I know that the pressures of the Rose scandal hadn't helped.

As I continued to listen to the radio reports, the voice of Deputy Commissioner Fay Vincent came on with his reaction to Bart's death. Vincent said all the right things about Bart, what a good guy he was, what a loss it was to his family and to baseball, and so on.

But then Vincent started talking about the future of Major League Baseball, and while I can't remember his exact words, I do remember mine.

"I'll be damned," I said aloud. "He's already campaigning to be commissioner."

And I was right.

CHAPTER 13

A month after Bart Giamatti's death, I walked downstairs to the Major League Baseball offices for a meeting with the newly appointed commissioner of baseball—Francis Thomas "Fay" Vincent Jr.

Just as I had suspected when I heard him talking about Bart's death on my car radio, Vincent had also almost immediately started angling to replace him. And unfortunately for the game, and for me, he had succeeded.

Within a day of Bart's death, the executive council of Major League Baseball had met in teleconference to name an interim commissioner. There was very little discussion about who to choose. As Bart's deputy, Vincent was the only person on the scene who could quickly step in to handle the day-to-day operations until a permanent commissioner could be found. The executive council, which consisted of three owners from each league and the presidents of the two leagues, me included, voted unanimously for Vincent as interim commissioner.

But Vincent made it clear that he wanted the job without the *interim* in front of the title—and his backers immediately began lobbying for him. Mets co-owner Fred Wilpon announced that Vincent was "perfectly capable" of handing the commissioner's job. And George Steinbrenner appealed to everyone's emotions when he said that moving Vincent up to commissioner was "what Bart would have wanted."

I don't know if Steinbrenner was right about that—and George almost certainly wouldn't have said it if he had known that the next year Vincent would ban him from baseball for the second time. Still, given his prior positions as an executive in the movie and soft-drink industries, I had to assume that Vincent knew something about how to run a business.

I just wasn't sure that he knew how to run baseball.

Vincent was fifty-one at the time, a pale, unassuming-looking man with thick glasses. He had once been a gifted student-athlete at Williams College, until a classmate locked him in his room as a prank and Vincent had tried to walk along a narrow ledge to the window of the room next door. He fell four stories, crushing his spine. Forever afterward he walked with a cane and seemed to be in almost constant pain. He later got a law degree at Yale, and went on to be an executive at Columbia Pictures and Coca-Cola before joining Bart Giamatti in the baseball commissioner's office.

I could never quite figure out the relationship between Bart and Vincent. To me they seemed like exact opposites. Bart had been open and gregarious and able to get along with anyone; Vincent was quiet, reclusive, and, in my opinion, manipulative.

But now Bart was dead. And Vincent wanted the top job in Major League Baseball.

In mid-September, the executive council met at the Pfister Hotel in Milwaukee, just prior to the regularly scheduled owners' meeting. Vincent was in the room with us as we discussed some general matters, but when the discussion turned to the commissioner's office we asked him to wait outside. As he left, he probably assumed that his elevation to permanent commissioner was mostly a formality.

Vincent had his backers. The three American League owners on the council—Jerry Reinsdorf of the Chicago White Sox, Haywood Sullivan of the Boston Red Sox, and Bud Selig of the Milwaukee Brewers—were all for him. So was American League president Dr. Bobby Brown, who had played third base for the Yankees for eight seasons in the late 1940s and early '50s while also studying to be a cardiologist.

Some of the National League owners on the committee were less enthusiastic about Vincent. There was discontent among the league owners about the course of National League expansion—discontent shared by me—and they were wary of Vincent's positions on that issue and others.

When the discussion turned to the commissioner's job, I spoke up. I suggested that instead of rushing into anything—again, Bart had been dead less than two weeks—we conduct a nationwide search for a new commissioner.

Later some of Vincent's supporters would suggest that I was trying to put myself forward for the commissioner's job, which was complete nonsense. I had been league president for only five months, and already the constant headaches that came with the job were starting to wear on me. There was absolutely no way I would have considered the even more high-pressure, high-profile job of commissioner.

Passing over my suggestion for a nationwide search, Reinsdorf said they didn't want to waste time. Someone called for a vote on recommending Vincent as the next commissioner to the full ownership. It passed 5–3, with two of the three National League owners on the committee, Doug Danforth of the Pirates and Peter O'Malley of the Dodgers, voting against. I was the third vote against Vincent. Reinsdorf suggested that the official vote be made unanimous, and reluctantly I agreed. If Vincent was to be the next commissioner, it was only fair to publicly give him unanimous support.

Vincent was summoned back into the room and when informed of the decision he told the owners on the committee, "I'm truly grateful for this opportunity to carry on what Bart started. And if it ever gets to the point where you don't want me, then I'll resign."

At the time I remember thinking, *What a strange thing for the new commissioner of baseball to say.*

The whole purpose of being commissioner of baseball was to stand above the narrow interests of team owners or players or anyone else and do what was best for baseball. In the early 1900s, baseball had been ruled by the National Commission, which consisted of the two league presidents and a commission chairman who simply mediated disputes between the two. But after the 1919 "Black Sox" gambling scandal, with much of the public thinking that baseball was controlled by gambling interests, the owners realized that they needed someone with no financial interest in baseball, someone with national standing and a reputation for incorruptibility, to administer baseball and restore public confidence in the game.

They chose Kenesaw Mountain Landis, a federal judge who had garnered national attention when he ruled against Standard Oil in a landmark anti-trust case. (Landis was named after the Civil War battle of Kennesaw Mountain, where his Union father had lost a leg; for some reason they dropped the second *n* in *Kennesaw.*) Landis said he would accept the job only if he was given virtually unlimited authority over all aspects of both the game and business of baseball. He and he alone would decide what was "in the best interests of baseball," with no appeal of his decisions. The owners reluctantly agreed.

Unfortunately, Landis was a racist who kept black players out of major league baseball for as long as he lived. (As a federal judge, he had also helped strip black heavyweight boxer Jack Johnson of his title.) He ruled baseball with an iron hand, often angering owners and players alike, for twenty-four years until his death in 1944. His racial attitudes aside, in standing up to special interests in the game he set the tone for what a commissioner of baseball was supposed to be.

Not all of the commissioners who followed Landis met the original standards of being men who were "outside of baseball" and had national reputations. Happy Chandler, commissioner from 1945 to 1951, had been governor of Kentucky and a US senator, but Ford Frick (1951–1965) had been a sportswriter and National League public relations director and then league president before becoming commissioner. William "Spike" Eckert (1965–1968) had been an air force lieutenant general, but he had had no national standing and little knowledge of baseball. When he became commissioner, he hadn't been to a baseball game in a decade. Dubbed "the Unknown Soldier," he was forced out just three years into his six-year term. Bowie Kuhn (1969–1984) had been the National League's lawyer, and although he had a reputation as an "owners' commissioner," he had sometimes stood up to the owners.

On the other hand, Peter Ueberroth (1984–1989) was an "outside baseball" man with national standing. A businessman who gained fame for organizing the 1984 Olympics in Los Angeles—the historically money-losing Olympics had actually showed a $250 million profit that year—he had been named *Time* magazine's Man of the Year for the feat. A strong commissioner, he had had no problem standing up to owners or players. Bart Giamatti had been president of Yale, and might have become a strong commissioner if he had lived.

The point is that with the exception of Spike Eckert, each of the previous commissioners had either a pre-baseball national reputation that enhanced his authority or years of experience with the inner workings of the baseball business.

Fay Vincent had neither.

In retrospect, I believe that in choosing Fay Vincent, Reinsdorf and Selig and others were setting the stage for a return to a dependably owner-controlled commissioner. They didn't want another Ueberroth—much less a modern-day Kenesaw Landis. It would take them some time to get exactly what they wanted. But in the meantime, they were perfectly content to let Vincent sit in the commissioner's chair.

The next day, September 13, 1989, the combined team owners accepted the executive committee's "unanimous" recommendation and unanimously approved Fay Vincent as the eighth commissioner of baseball.

My doubts about the new commissioner didn't end at that meeting. Instead, they soon got worse.

In a meeting with Vincent a month after Bart's death, I spent a few minutes going over routine details of National League business. Then, out of the blue, Vincent said, "Bill, I want you to fire Lou Hoynes."

I could hardly believe it. Lou, a graduate of Columbia and Harvard Law School, had been the National League attorney for the past nineteen years, and had been involved in league litigation from the Curt Flood "reserve clause" lawsuit to the Pete Rose controversy. In addition to being an excellent lawyer, he was a valuable source of corporate memory. I also liked Lou personally. He had welcomed me into the president's job and helped show me the lay of the land. We often played tennis together—I didn't hold it against Lou that he always beat me.

I'm not sure why Vincent wanted Lou fired. Maybe it was a personality conflict, or maybe Vincent wanted to bring his own lawyer into National League business. Vincent had already forced out of the commissioner's office several experienced employees who had been brought in by Ueberroth.

But whatever the reason, no way was I going to fire Lou Hoynes.

"No, Fay, I'm not going to come in on my first year in the job and fire someone with nearly twenty years of experience. Lou's done good work for the National League, and I'm not going to let him go."

Vincent didn't say anything at first. But then he leaned back in his chair and said something else I could hardly believe.

"You know Bill, this is all so new for the both of us. Neither one of us really knows what we are doing."

Maybe that was Vincent's way of trying to sound self-deprecating. My reaction was, *What do you mean* we *don't know what we're doing?* I had been in baseball for more than three decades as a player and a broadcaster, and I knew the game and the business of baseball as well as anybody. Vincent, on the other hand, had been in baseball exactly six months.

Maybe he didn't know what he was doing. But I certainly did.

I didn't hear any more from Vincent about firing Lou Hoynes. As he almost always did when we confronted each other on an issue, Vincent backed down. Although he liked to think of himself as a tough guy, a tough administrator, in my opinion he wasn't.

Vincent also seemed to have an uncanny ability to do exactly the wrong thing at precisely the wrong time. I found that out early on, in March 1990.

The owners had locked out the players for thirty-two days in a contract dispute, wiping out most of spring training. But after the owners made some concessions on arbitration, and raised the minimum player salary to $100,000, the two sides settled on a contract on March 19. They also agreed to move back opening day to

April 9 to squeeze in some spring training games, and to add three extra days to the regular season.

But the umpires union said they weren't consulted on the scheduling change, so on March 23 the umpires union head, Richie Phillips, announced that the umpires wouldn't work the spring training games.

Phillips was a big, loud bear of a guy who never missed an opportunity to throw the union's weight—and his—around. A streetwise West Philadelphia kid, the son of a policeman, Phillips had gone to law school and become a prosecutor under then Philadelphia district attorney (and later senator) Arlen Specter. As a private attorney, Phillips got into union organizing, helping to form a union for NBA referees before getting involved with baseball umpires. Although he was officially the umpire union's lawyer, not its president, he called all the shots.

Phillips liked to portray himself as a crusader, a guy defending the weak against the powerful. He claimed that in his youth he had organized an altar boys' strike at his church to protest a parish priest who was ripping off their tips, and he always described his union organizing as "doing God's work." But if he was working for God, he was getting well paid by the union members. Although a lot of umpires thought he had done a good job in raising salaries, others later protested his reported $300,000-plus annual salary—a lot of money for a union with fewer than a hundred members.

Richie also never missed an opportunity to get his mug prominently displayed in the news media. I was pretty certain that was what he was doing now with his threatened work stoppage by the umpires at the expanded spring training.

Phillips filed an unfair labor practice charge against the two leagues for altering the season schedule. But at the same time, he quietly promised that the umpires would be ready to work on opening day. He also said the union didn't care if we used minor league umpires to work the remaining spring training games.

As far as I was concerned, the umpires "work stoppage" was essentially meaningless. Who cared if we had minor league umpires at spring training games? As long as the regular umpires were ready to go on opening day, as the union had promised, what difference did it make? Besides, having the minor league umpires do some spring training games would give us an opportunity to see some of the up-and-coming young umps. So I wanted to just ignore Richie Phillips and his umpires' "mini strike."

But Vincent didn't see it that way. In a telephone conference call with me, American League president Bobby Brown and Chuck O'Connor of the Morgan, Lewis & Bockius law firm, which had represented baseball in the earlier negotiations with the players, Vincent said the umpire union's actions were violations of no-strike and grievance clauses in our contracts with them. He wanted to get a court order to force the umpires to work spring training.

"We're going to have to show the umpires who's boss," he said.

I was astonished.

"Fay, what did you say?"

"We're going to show them who's boss."

It was a foolish idea. In trying to look tough, Vincent was picking a fight that didn't need to be fought.

"Fay, that would be a big mistake," I told him. "What difference does it make if minor league umpires work spring training? And if for some reason the regular umpires don't show up on opening day, the contract says we can fire them. But they aren't going to take that chance. If you take them to court, it's just going to be a big publicity fest for Richie Phillips."

But no. Vincent wanted to "show them who's boss."

Against my better judgment, Bobby Brown and I went to the law offices of Morgan, Lewis to plan the strategy. To make matters worse than they already were, Chuck O'Connor, who was worn out after the negotiations with the players, was on vacation, so they trotted out two young associates to handle the legal work. They were nice young men but they were inexperienced. They didn't seem to have a clue as to what to do.

So when we went to federal court in Philadelphia, where the umpires union was headquartered, and made our request for an injunction against the union, we got killed. The judge refused to issue a preliminary injunction and scheduled a hearing on the following Tuesday. After that hearing the judge ordered both sides to try to work things out, so we spent two long, fruitless days and nights trying to settle the thing. But by this time Richie Phillips had been talking tough to his membership and to the news media. He wouldn't budge.

Then on Thursday, one of the young lawyers assigned to the case walked into our conference room and said, "Commissioner Vincent wants to settle."

I couldn't believe it.

"What do you mean he wants to settle? He's the one who started this mess in the first place. He sent us down here to walk the plank, now he's trying to make us look like fools. Get him on the phone and tell him I'm seriously pissed."

The kid left and came back a few minutes later. He shrugged.

"The commissioner wants to settle. He says to give them [the union] what they want."

I was furious. In fact, in more than three decades in baseball I don't think I had ever been angrier than I was at that moment. How could Vincent put Bobby and me in this position, insisting that we publicly fight the union over an essentially inconsequential matter and then, without ever attending a negotiating session or even talking it over with us, suddenly decide to reverse himself and unilaterally throw in the towel? I was fuming.

In the end the union got everything it wanted, including reimbursement for the umpires for the spring training games they missed. Richie Phillips went in front of the TV cameras and reporters and crowed about how he and the union had kicked our ass.

That was bad enough. But then the day after the settlement, I turned on the *Today* show on NBC and saw Fay Vincent talking about how he had settled the umpires' strike—and, by implication, how he had saved the baseball season from being ruined by the incompetent intransigence of league presidents Bobby Brown and Bill White. He never acknowledged that the court fight with the umpires had been his idea.

Way to go, Fay, I thought as I watched him on television. *You really showed those umpires who was boss.*

I was still angry about the whole thing a week later, when the settlement agreement with the umpires union came to me to be signed. I told the owners on the league executive committee that I wouldn't do it.

"It's Fay's agreement," I said. "Let him sign it."

It was my way of expressing my contempt—not so much for the agreement itself, but for the way Vincent had acted in getting it.

A short time later I was in Vincent's office for a meeting when I noticed a single book on his bookshelf. It was easy to spot, because while Bart Giamatti had his office bookshelves lined with scholarly works, Vincent had just one book on display. It was *Leadership Secrets of Attila the Hun*.

The book didn't have any factual connection to the ancient conqueror. It was actually a self-help, motivational book, written by a PhD, that became popular among executives in the late 1980s and early 1990s. (George Steinbrenner had several copies.) As far as I could tell, its primary appeal was in the title. Prominently placed on an executive office desk or bookshelf, it let high-level executives give the impression that they were tough guys, willing to pillage and slaughter to get their way, just like old Attila.

But if that was the image Vincent was trying to convey, he was wrong. When it came to standing up and digging in and not taking any crap, Fay Vincent wasn't Attila the Hun.

I was.

Despite my labor battles with the umpires union, the truth is that I had always respected umpires. I seldom argued with them as a player, and as a broadcaster I rarely second-guessed their calls. They had a tough job, and I knew it.

Of course, umpires are human, so even though their calls are accurate 95 percent of the time, it still leaves room for mistakes— an outside ball called a strike, a foul ball called fair. But baseball is a game of errors, and if an umpire blows a call against a team, chances are that sooner or later he'll blow another call in that team's favor. It all balances out—which is why I've always been opposed to using televised replays on umpire calls. Why waste the time?

The umpires I knew as a player and a broadcaster were professionals. And most of them did the best job they could in a professional manner.

But by the time I became National League president, the attitudes of some umpires seemed to be changing.

Until the 1940s, most major league umpires developed their skills through OJT—on the job training. They would start out calling amateur games, then work their way through the various minor league levels. If they were both good and lucky, they could move up to the majors. By the 1960s, virtually all major league umpires were graduates of professional umpire schools, but it was still hard to move up to the big leagues. Unlike players, umpires stayed on the job for years and years, often into their sixties, and job openings were rare.

In the old days, the pay disparity between players and umpires hadn't been that great. For example, in 1953 the top pay for a veteran major league umpire was $16,000—more than I made as a rookie major league player. In 1970, the Major League Umpires Association (MLUA) was formed, and after a series of strikes and labor negotiations, by the early 1990s top umpire pay was about $175,000.

That was good pay for a six-months-a-year job, but obviously it couldn't match the millions that free agent players were getting. No fan ever came to a baseball game to see an umpire, so who's going to get into a bidding war for one? The disparity may have caused resentment among some umpires, who may have taken that resentment onto the field with them. Maybe it gave them satisfaction to know that even though the guy swinging at the plate was making umpteen millions of dollars, he was still out when the umpire said he was out.

At the same time, under the leadership of MLUA head Phillips, and after winning big settlements in a series of strikes, a lot of umpires seemed to develop a superior attitude toward everyone else in the game. They seemed to think that the union made them bulletproof, no matter what they did on the field, and that they could rule without being questioned—by players, managers, owners, or me. They seemed to forget that they worked for, and were paid, by the National and American Leagues, not the MLUA.

That attitude had manifested itself on the field. Instead of remaining anonymous arbiters, the umpires demanded—and got—individual numbers on their uniforms, and some began showboating for the crowds and the cameras, exaggerating their call movements and generally calling attention to themselves. Some umpires started dancing around behind the plate like Mikhail Baryshnikov doing *The Nutcracker.* Pretty soon the umpires actually wanted the power to levy fines against players, managers, even owners if they publicly criticized them. Obviously they didn't get that power, but it made me wonder, *What will they want next? The power to fine the fans for booing them?* It got so bad that one umpire actually filed a $5 million slander lawsuit against Reds manager Lou Piniella after Piniella publicly called him "biased." He dropped the lawsuit after Piniella reluctantly apologized.

Another thing the newer umpires seemed to be doing too much of was needlessly arguing with players. When a player or manager started arguing and shouting at an umpire, the umpire would start arguing and shouting back, sometimes even following the player, still shouting, as the player walked away. That wouldn't have happened in my playing days. An umpire wouldn't try to justify a call, because he knew he didn't have to.

Take Dusty Boggess, for example, a National League umpire from World War II through the early 1960s. Just about everybody liked Dusty, but it was well known that he occasionally would show up for work with a few drinks in him—and as a result, he might easily call a strike on a pitch that was two feet off the plate. (When that happened, players would tell one another, "Dusty's feeling good today; swing at anything!") Sure, you could argue with him about an obviously bad call, but Dusty would just calmly say, "You may be right"—and that was the end of it.

The point is that most umpires back then did not get angry or emotional over a disputed call.

Of course, when it came to professional demeanor and attitude on the field, some umpires I dealt with as National League president were better than others.

In that respect, and although I liked him personally, Joe West was not one of the better ones.

I had first met West when I was a broadcaster. I was calling a game in Pittsburgh for CBS radio, and while at dinner one night I ran into John Kibler, a veteran umpire I'd known since my days as a player. Kibler called me over to his table and introduced me to West.

"This guy is going to be a great umpire," Kibler said. "He's got a great eye for the game. All he has to do is calm down a bit."

Unfortunately, by the time I became league president, West still hadn't calmed down.

One day in August 1990, I arrived at my office in National League headquarters and found a videotape on my desk. Whenever there had been an incident in a game—a fight, a prolonged argument with an umpire, whatever—I would get a report and a videotape on it. I assumed this videotape would show just another routine scuffle.

But when I watched it, what I saw was pretty disturbing.

The tape was of a recent game between the Mets and the Phillies at Shea Stadium. In the bottom of the fifth, Phillies pitcher Pat Combs hit the Mets' Doc Gooden in the knee and Gooden charged the mound, sparking a bench-clearing brawl that delayed the game for twenty minutes.

Believe it or not, I can't remember ever being in an on-field fight when I was a player; it always seemed like a silly thing for a professional ballplayer to do. But I'd seen plenty of brawls in my days as a broadcaster, and I knew the drill. Except for the two guys who were initially pissed at each other—and maybe not even them—almost no one really wanted to fight. A player came out of the dugout or the bullpen to support his teammates, but all he really wanted to do was find a friend, hold on to each other, and avoid getting hurt. Most of the time, even the guys who were really mad would just wrestle around and throw halfhearted punches. Serious injuries in on-field fights were extremely rare.

But what was disturbing on this videotape wasn't the players. It was second base umpire Joe West. As Phillies pitcher Dennis Cook came out of the bullpen and ran toward the pileup, West grabbed

Cook by the neck from behind, lifted him up, and body-slammed him to the ground. It was like something out of WrestleMania.

Cook wasn't a little guy, standing six three and maybe 190 pounds. But West, a former college football star, was a massive guy, weighing in at about 270 pounds. By slamming Cook to the ground that way, West could have ended the kid's career.

West had clearly overstepped the bounds. When there's an on-field fight, an umpire should use his "command voice" and "command presence" to try to make the fighters knock it off; usually that's enough. If it isn't, an umpire may interject himself between two players if he can do so without getting hurt. But an umpire should never, ever become part of the fight like Joe West had.

As I said, I liked West, but this wasn't the first problem I'd had with his on-field behavior. Earlier in my term as president, in August 1989, West had been involved in an on-field shoving match with Cincinnati Reds manager Pete Rose and Reds second baseman Ron Oester. Oester had been called out on strikes, ending the game, and had angrily thrown his bat along the first base line and started arguing with home plate umpire Bill Hohn. West, who was umpiring at first, got involved and allegedly shoved Oester. By this time the TV cameras had been turned off, but apparently Rose, who was already under pressure from the gambling allegations, stepped in and pushed West. Although there wasn't any videotape of the incident, the accounts I heard sounded serious enough for me to fly out to Cincinnati the next day.

When I went to the umpires' dressing room before the game, I asked the other umpires what had happened. They all answered with some variant of "Who, me? I didn't see nothing." Eventually I got West and Oester into a private room to talk it over. I fined Oester $100 for throwing his bat, and while I didn't demand that West apologize, I made it clear to both of them I wanted the feud to be over. They agreed and shook hands. Later I contacted Rose, who had been demanding that I reprimand West, and said that the matter was closed and I didn't want it discussed further.

That was the way I preferred to handle things like that. Bring the two sides together and deal with it quietly and privately.

But now, a year later, in the Mets–Phillies brawl, Joe West was involved in another serious on-field incident. And this time, because of the unnecessary confrontation between union head Richie Phillips and Fay Vincent, it was about to become a media event.

A week and a half after the Cook body-slamming incident, Joe West got into another beef involving the Phillies. In a game against the Dodgers, Phillies outfielder Von Hayes made it to first on a fielder's choice, and when he got there he started talking trash to the first base coach about the home plate umpire. He was just blowing off steam, but West, the first base umpire, overheard it and ejected him from the game.

The Phillies were seriously pissed. Members of the team publicly called West "unprofessional and biased," and the team filed a complaint against West with the National League, asking me to take action against the umpire. The umpires union also filed a complaint with the league, demanding that I punish the Phillies guys for their comments about West.

It was a mess. And like the earlier body-slamming incident, it was all because West couldn't control his emotions on the field.

As I looked into the ejection of Hayes, I interviewed Dodgers first baseman Eddie Murray, the only unbiased witness. Murray told me what I had already begun to suspect.

"Bill, Hayes didn't do anything over the top," he said. "Joe West is a good umpire, but he has a bad attitude."

A week later, I drove to Philadelphia to meet with West and Richie Phillips about the Hayes and Cook incidents. When I got to Phillips's office building, there were reporters and TV crews waiting in the lobby, having been alerted by Phillips that I was coming. Phillips never missed the opportunity to turn a routine meeting into a media circus. I didn't speak to the reporters, but I was annoyed that Phillips had set up the media "ambush."

It didn't improve my mood when I walked into Phillips's office and saw Joe West sitting there with a smirk on his face—a smirk that said, *The hell with you, there's nothing you can do to me.* That immediately ticked me off.

I had never intended to suspend West for his actions. Although I had the authority to do so, I didn't like to do that with umpires because any public punishment of an umpire would tend to undermine his authority with the players on the field. But I was certainly going to set Joe West straight.

"Listen, Joe," I told him, "as long as I am president of this league you will not touch another player! You body-slammed Dennis Cook. What if you had wrecked that kid's shoulder and he couldn't pitch again? Or what if he had gotten up and blindly hit you? If there's a fight on the field, I want you to let the other three umpires handle it."

Then I asked about the Von Hayes ejection.

"For the umpires it's always about protecting each other," West said. "When Hayes came to first base, cussing up a storm, I just felt like I had to protect my guy."

That was nonsense, and I told him so.

"If a player's in your face, that's one thing. If he's cussing at you directly, okay, eject him. But if a guy's just letting off steam, let it go. Hayes wasn't cussing you at first base, so you should have just let it go. Don't take everything so personally."

West wasn't alone among umpires in his lack of emotional control. It was a problem that I would face again and again. Instead of calmly ignoring players who argued with them, instead of just walking away, they would get angry and prolong the argument.

Sometimes they would even instigate it, taunting players and demanding to have the last word.

For example, there was umpire Jerry Crawford, the son of retired umpire Shag Crawford. Shag had been known for his hot temper—and so, increasingly, was his son. In one game, Jerry had engaged in an ugly, nose-to-nose, spit-spraying argument with Lou Piniella that went on for far too long and ended up with Jerry ejecting Piniella. So later I sent Jerry a videotape of the argument and a note that said simply, "Please watch this."

Unlike Joe West, Jerry seemed to get it. Later he called and told me he'd watched the tape.

"I see what you mean, Bill," Jerry said.

Jerry calmed down for the rest of the season and wound up being named the National League's best umpire in a private survey of players and managers. The survey results were supposed to be secret, but I called his father, Shag Crawford, and told him about it. Shag appreciated that.

But Joe West couldn't seem to get it through his head that maybe he, not the players, might be causing the problems.

At one point during the meeting with West and Phillips I took a men's room break, and Phillips followed me in.

"C'mon, Bill," he said, "you know Joe's a good umpire."

"Yes, he's a good umpire, but that's not the point. The point is that he will never touch another player. Period."

That should have ended it. But after I left the meeting in Phillips's office and pushed my way through the press mob without commenting, Phillips and West went down and basked in the warm light of the news cameras. In the next day's papers, Phillips made it sound as if he and West had brushed me back, and that I had "admitted" that West was a good umpire. To me it was an egregious misrepresentation of what I had actually said.

Now I was angry. In an interview with a reporter, I suggested that either Phillips was lying or I was—and I knew I wasn't. I also issued a statement saying again that "Joe West will never touch another player while I'm president."

The whole thing might have blown over in a day or two. But then Fay Vincent had to stick his nose in it.

Vincent knew, or should have known, that umpire issues were the purview of the two league presidents. At that time, umpires worked for the respective leagues, not for Major League Baseball. Except under the most extraordinary circumstances, the commissioner's role in this sort of thing was to back up the league president and otherwise keep his mouth shut.

As former American League president Lee MacPhail put it in an interview, "In on-field matters of this nature, the league president has full and complete authority. The commissioner should have said, 'I support Bill White 100 percent in this case' and then left it at that."

At one point I even told Vincent, "Look, if you want the umpires under your control, take 'em. Then I'll do what you do, just travel around and give speeches."

But Vincent wouldn't let it go. After the White–Phillips–West controversy became public, he called me to a meeting in which he questioned my version of events, and thus my integrity. He told me that I should have taken a witness with me to the meeting with Phillips and West—as if my word alone wasn't good enough—and tried to scold me for calling Phillips a liar. Then instead of backing me publicly, he issued a statement saying the matter was "under investigation" by the commissioner.

It was exactly the wrong tack to take with me. I valued my reputation for integrity and honesty—brutally blunt honesty when necessary—more than anything else. I had spent more than three decades building up that reputation in baseball, and I wasn't going to let Vincent call it into question.

I told the news media that either Vincent would publicly support me or "It's good-bye, I'm going home."

Would I have actually quit? You bet. I don't bluff.

Finally, under pressure, Vincent issued a statement that supported my actions in the Joe West case. He also stated that in the future, disputes between umpires and the leagues would be handled by the league presidents, and that we would work out a joint policy on what actions umpires should take in on-field fights. It was the least amount of support for the league presidents that he could get away with.

As far as I was concerned, that ended it. But again, it was an ending to a problem that never should have been a problem in the first place.

The dispute over Joe West and the public wrangling with Richie Phillips, along with my playing background, prompted some people, Phillips included, to portray me as being anti-umpire. That wasn't the truth. As I said, I respected umpires in general, and I supported them when I could.

I never wanted an umpire to feel unreasonable fear for his job. I always thought that a scared umpire was a bad umpire.

Still, there were some umpires who simply failed to live up to what was expected of them.

One of them was an umpire crew chief—there's no need to name him—who had been caught shoplifting seven boxes of baseball cards at a Target store. We found out about it when Katy Feeney was checking box scores and noticed there were only three umpires working a game instead of four. When she investigated, she learned of the crew chief's arrest.

I could hardly believe it. I had known this guy since my days as a player, and here he was, with almost a quarter century as a major league umpire, making more than $100,000 a year, caught stuffing

$144 worth of baseball cards into his pants. Later we learned that he had also tried to steal more baseball cards from a Costco store. The story made it into the papers.

I immediately called him, and he asked to be allowed to keep umpiring.

To me that was not an option. For an umpire, integrity and honesty are essential.

I didn't want to just cut the guy loose. But I insisted he take a leave of absence until the case was resolved. I had the league pay for his lawyer, and the umpire eventually pleaded no contest and got three years' probation. We also paid his salary for the rest of the season and let him quietly retire with full pension rights. It was the right thing to do—but it was also very sad.

As in any group of people, there were umpires who had personal failings, and personal secrets. During my time as president, there were two umpires who allegedly had connections to gamblers, but it was never shown that they had bet on baseball, so they were only warned. Just before I started with the league, another umpire, Dave Pallone, was investigated in connection with a gay prostitution ring, and although he was never charged with a crime, then president Giamatti reluctantly decided that given the current attitudes it was best that he resign. He got a severance package, and later wrote a book about his life as a gay umpire.

(Although there may have been others, only one major league player ever "came out" as being gay during his career. Glenn Burke played for the Dodgers and the Athletics in the late 1970s, and the controversy over his sexual orientation forced him out of the game. He died in 1995 of an AIDS-related illness.)

We even had gender issues to deal with. After a dozen years umpiring in the minors, Pam Postema became the first female to umpire a major league spring training game. But later, she was one of seven umpires who were released from the minors, and in

1991 she filed a sex discrimination lawsuit against baseball. I didn't believe she had been fired because of her gender, but our lawyers told us it would cost $600,000 to fight it in court, so we settled out of court for about $300,000.

Some other umpires simply weren't physically up to the demands of the job. No one expects an umpire to be able to run like a Rickey Henderson or a Lou Brock, but he has to be able to follow the action on the field. And some of the umpires had simply stayed in the game past their ability to do that.

One umpire who was having trouble getting around on the field was Fred Brocklander, who had been hired as a replacement during the 1979 umpire strike. After hearing reports about Brocklander, I sent Ed Vargo, the league's supervisor of umpires, to check him out. Ed's report was pointedly brief: "This guy can't move."

Ed was right. I went to Shea Stadium for a game that Brocklander was umpiring at third base, and when a fly went out to left field, Brocklander took two steps and stopped. His knees were gone, and the medication he was taking for his knee problems were causing other issues. Brocklander finally agreed that it was time to leave.

Umpire Doug Harvey, who was called "God" by the players, and later became one of only nine umpires to be inducted into the Hall of Fame, had two often-stated goals: He wanted to umpire until he was sixty-five, and he wanted to work five thousand major league games. But by 1992, it was clear he could not achieve either goal. At age sixty-two, his knees were going, and it was painful for him to get around—and almost as painful to watch him try. He called me to talk about his knee problems, and I told him that if he decided it was time to go we'd give him a big send-off. Doug agreed, so we had a press conference before the All-Star Game in San Diego at which Doug announced his retirement after the season and I thanked him for his many years of service. Doug's last game was number 4,673—short of his goal, but Doug was always grateful that we helped him leave umpiring with dignity and style.

Since baseball began, an umpire's visual acuity has been the subject of discussion. It's such a traditionally sensitive issue that until the mid-1950s umpires were forbidden to wear eyeglasses on the field. An umpire can, of course, expect to hear some variation on the phrase "What are you, blind?" thousands of times from fans and players during his career.

For veteran umpire Dutch Rennert, later in his career, it was a legitimate question. Dutch was a good umpire, but in 1990 we started getting complaints about him missing obvious calls, complaints that continued into the next season.

One questionable call prompted a nasty confrontation with Reds manager Lou Piniella. Dutch was working first base in a Reds–Giants game when Reds batter Bill Doran hit a long ball that Dutch ruled a home run. But then Dutch, unsure of his call, consulted with home plate umpire Gary Darling, who ruled the ball foul. Darling was right—Dutch had missed the call—but Piniella was furious and got into a shouting match with Dutch and Darling. Obviously, Dutch wasn't seeing the balls the way he should have. Then someone sent me a magazine story about Dutch, and in one of the photos of him it was clear that there was major swelling on one of his eyelids, which can cause vision complications. I didn't know if that had anything to do with his bad calls, but I flew down to Florida to talk to him.

"C'mon, Bill," Dutch said, "you're upset because you're a Piniella guy and both of you had years together with the Yankees. I really want to do twenty years and I'm at eighteen now. Give me another chance."

I did, but there were more complaints about missed calls, and finally I told Dutch to get me a report from his ophthalmologist. The report indicated that he was uncorrectably deficient in one eye, and at my insistence he finally retired in 1992 after nineteen seasons. Later I saw him on a golf course at Vero Beach, and he thanked me for doing him a favor.

Often it wasn't advancing age that created problems for umpires, but rather their weight. Unlike football and basketball referees who are constantly on the move, baseball umpires are stationary most of the time. The practice of having a big food spread in the umpires' dressing room before and after every game didn't help.

Of course, it was one thing if an umpire simply had a few extra pounds on him. But umpires Eric Gregg and John McSherry were way beyond that. They each weighed in at close to four hundred pounds.

Gregg, known as "the Plump Ump"—*plump* was a serious understatement—started major league umpiring in 1975, only the third black umpire in major league history. (The first was Emmett Ashford in 1966; it took umpires a long time to catch up to players in breaking baseball color barriers.) His girth was the subject of a lot of jokes and stories over the years, and Eric, a jocular guy with a big smile, laughed along with everybody else.

One famous Eric Gregg story involves the Loma Prieta earthquake, which happened just before Game 3 of the 1989 World Series at Candlestick Park in San Francisco. When the earthquake hit, most of the umpires ran out of the dressing room for safety. Eric, however, crawled under the pre-game food table, and as the stadium rattled and shook, his hand was observed reaching out from under the table to grab for some chow. Eric didn't deny the story.

But Eric's weight problem wasn't just a joke, and neither was John McSherry's. To me they were serious physical issues.

Before spring training in 1990, I said as much to Eric, and I later told McSherry the same thing.

"We need to find a way to get this under control," I told them.

"If you don't lose weight by opening day I'm going to delay your assignment. And if you don't have significant weight loss by mid-season, I'll have to let you go."

I'm not sure my threat to fire them would have survived a union challenge. But John and Eric both eventually agreed to participate in the weight loss program at Duke University—the league even paid for Eric's program—and both made some progress. Eric lost fifty pounds, not nearly enough to put him in shape, but still it was something.

But the diet and exercise regime didn't last for either of them. John McSherry, still seriously overweight, died at age fifty-one, collapsing on the field seven pitches into the opening day game in Cincinnati in 1996. Eric Gregg, who got even bigger after he left umpiring, died of a massive stroke when he was fifty-five years old.

It's difficult not to conclude that Eric's and John's weight problems at least contributed to their deaths. And while I'm not saying that every umpire should be forced to step on a scale before he takes the field, union rules that prevent or discourage intervention when there's a clear health hazard don't make much sense to me.

I also tried to help out some older umpires whom I had known when I was a player and who had retired before the union negotiated better pension plans. When we looked into it, we found that the retired umpires' health benefits were woefully inadequate. We also discovered five widows of umpires who were receiving just $200 a month from their husbands' pension plans.

I didn't think that was right. I couldn't solve all the problems, but I got the National League owners to pay for six retired umpires' supplemental Medicare premiums. I also got the five widows' monthly stipends increased to $700 a month by the time I left the league. It wasn't much when you consider that baseball was a multibillion-dollar business, but it supplemented their Social Security checks, and they appreciated it. I was proud of that accomplishment.

There were other things we did in the National League office to help umpires. Phillips and the union may have won significant salary increases for umpires. But when it came to treating umpires like human beings, I truly believe that we at the league cared more about the umpires than he did.

Eventually he went too far. In July 1999, Phillips announced that more than fifty major league umpires had signed resignation letters effective September 2—before the play-offs and World Series. The idea behind the threatened mass resignation was to put pressure on the team owners during new contract negotiations.

Unfortunately for the umpires, they learned a lesson about their relative importance in the game when the league presidents accepted twenty-two of the resignations and brought up minor league umpires to replace them. For the leagues, it was a golden opportunity to get rid of some of the umpire deadwood. When the umpires tried to rescind their resignations, both leagues said no.

All this happened long after I had left the league presidency. But if I had been there, I would have accepted *all* of the umpires' resignations and then made them reapply for their jobs—and kept only the best.

Eventually about half of the umpires whose resignations were accepted were hired back. But in the meantime, most of the umpires were furious at Phillips and voted to decertify the union, putting Phillips out of his job. They then formed a new union, the World Umpires Association.

When I knew him, Richie Phillips had always liked to boast that he had never lost a battle for the umpires. But his overconfidence and aggressive, in-your-face style finally caused him to lose his most important battle—his last one.

Of course, it wasn't just umpires who gave me headaches as league president. Players and managers certainly contributed their share.

And when they stepped out of line, it was my job to hand out fines and suspensions.

As you might guess, at a time when the average player salary was about $800,000, and when the star players made millions, a fine of $250 or $500 was pretty much a joke, especially since the teams, not the player or manager, usually paid the fines. Ninety-five percent of the time, when I imposed a fine the player or manager would simply pay up.

But I was amazed at how some players or managers would bitch and moan and fight over a few hundred bucks.

Dodgers manager Tommy Lasorda was one. Once he had a spit-flying, chest-bumping argument with an umpire and then threatened to kick his ass. After I got a report from the umpire and reviewed the videotape, I imposed a $500 fine on Lasorda.

I never publicized my fines against players or managers, never announced them to the press, so the Dodgers could have just paid Tommy's fine and been done with it. But no. Tommy, being Tommy, had to make a big deal out of it and tell reporters he wasn't going to pay the fine.

Players and managers had seven days to pay their fines, and on the sixth day there still wasn't a check from Lasorda on my desk. I called Lasorda and Fred Claire, the Dodgers' general manager, and told them if the check wasn't there the next day Lasorda couldn't put on a uniform—and of course, the next day I got the check. It was a waste of everybody's time—but that was Tommy Lasorda.

Although the piddling fines didn't really have much impact, suspensions were another matter. For a player whose contract has certain bonus provisions in it, or a relief pitcher whose pay was based on his number of game appearances, a suspension could actually hurt. And it could hurt the team that had to do without him during the suspension.

In 1993, I started getting a lot of complaints from owners and general managers about pitchers throwing at batters. They wanted me to do something about it.

When I was a player, brushing back batters was an accepted part of the game. For example, if you showboated a home run, strutting around the bases to taunt the pitcher, you knew that your next time at bat he was going to put you in the dirt. It was a given. And while a knockdown pitch might prompt a charge at the mound, nobody ever mounted a campaign to eliminate the practice.

Personally, I never saw anything wrong with a pitcher throwing inside as long as he wasn't "head-hunting"—that is, throwing directly at a batter's head, which could cause serious injuries. And I always thought that a good player who was keeping his eyes open could avoid getting hit.

But things changed when players started making millions of dollars. They were a big investment, and owners and general managers didn't want them getting hurt. Even a hairline fracture of a finger, which in the old days we would have ignored, would put a modern-day player on the disabled list.

So the owners and general managers started demanding that I do something about intentional pitches at batters. Fred Claire of the Dodgers was particularly vocal on the subject.

Okay, I told the owners and GMs, if that's what you want, here's what I'll do. I'll send a letter to all the teams announcing that if I see a pitcher throwing at a batter, I'll fine him $500 and suspend him for up to seven days. No exceptions.

Good, great, outstanding, the owners and GMs said. We have to stop this.

So I sent out the letter, which I'm sure few if any pitchers actually read, and the suspensions started to fly. I suspended Dodgers pitcher Ricky Trlicek for three games for hitting Gary Sheffield of the Padres. I suspended pitcher Jose Bautista of the Cubs for three games for hitting Mark Carreon of the Giants. I suspended

Dodgers pitcher Ramon Martinez for five games for hitting Charlie Hayes of Colorado, and I suspended Rockies pitcher Keith Shepherd for seven games for hitting Cory Snyder of LA. And that was just in the first two weeks of June 1993.

Of course, nobody wanted *their* pitchers suspended for throwing at batters. They just wanted the *other guy's* pitchers suspended for throwing at batters.

For example, Dodgers GM Fred Claire called me up and said he thought the punishment for Martinez was excessive. I chuckled and reminded him that he had been one of the loudest voices in favor of getting knockdowns under control. Fred, who's a good guy, had to admit that that was true.

In baseball, as in life, sometimes you have to be careful what you wish for.

Any player or manager who was fined or suspended had the right to appeal. But under the rules at the time, the league president was the final judge and jury for fines of $1,000 or less or suspensions of seven days or less. In other words, they had to appeal to the guy who'd imposed the fine or suspension in the first place—which in the National League was me.

Sometimes the appeals worked. A player appealing a $500 fine might come in to my office, usually with a representative from the players association, sometimes with his agent as well, and try to get me to knock it down to $250 or even $100. I knew the money didn't really matter. They just wanted to feel like they'd won something. But it seemed silly to me. Here we were, three or four well-paid professionals—the player, the union rep, the agent, and me—spending an hour or two of our time wrangling over a hundred or two hundred bucks.

On occasion, I actually decided that I'd been wrong in fining or suspending a player. I remember getting an umpire's report about a Cardinals player who allegedly had thrown a bat at an umpire after being called out on strikes. There was a delay in getting the videotape of it, but the guy already had a reputation for fighting with umpires, so I fined him $300 and suspended him for three days. He appealed.

But before the appeal hearing, I finally got to look at the videotape. Sure enough, the player had been getting in the umpire's face and cussing, and as he had walked toward the dugout he had tossed the bat over his shoulder, narrowly missing the umpire. But the tape showed that the umpire shouldn't have been anywhere near that bat. As the player walked away the umpire had followed him, wanting to continue the argument. I didn't think the player even knew the umpire was there when he tossed the bat.

So when the player and the players association lawyer showed up for the appeal hearing, I told him what I'd seen on the tape and said, "I'm still fining you $300 for cussing at the umpire. But you didn't throw the bat at him, so I'm dropping the suspension."

But then the player said, "I don't want that."

His lawyer and I looked at each other. Well, what do you want?

"Cut the fine in half and keep the suspension," the guy said. "I need the rest."

Okay. Done.

Of course, I never imagined that any amount of fines or suspensions would ever completely eliminate brawls or screaming matches or other such behavior on the field.

That was part of baseball, and I knew it would never change.

CHAPTER 14

The team owners and CEOs I dealt with as president of the National League had several things in common: They were almost all men; they were all white; and they all had a lot more money than most people. But they all had their own distinct characters and backgrounds.

Some of them grew up inside baseball. There was Peter O'Malley of the Dodgers, son of Walter O'Malley; and Bill Giles of the Phillies, whose father, Warren Giles, had been general manager and president of the Cincinnati Reds before being named National League president. Bill Giles had worked for the Reds in the 1950s, and helped found the Houston Astros (then called the Colt .45s) in 1962 before moving to the Phillies and putting together a group that bought the team in 1981.

Other owners and CEOs were businessmen who had become wealthy in other fields before turning to baseball. Doug Danforth, chairman of the Pirates, had been the top executive at Westinghouse. Fred Wilpon, co-owner of the Mets with publishing heir

Nelson Doubleday Jr., was a tough, calculating businessman whose most notable connection to baseball before he bought into the Mets in 1980 was that he played with Sandy Koufax on the Lafayette High School baseball team in Brooklyn. Bill Bartholomay of the Braves was a Chicago insurance executive who assembled a consortium to buy the team in 1962 and then later moved them from Milwaukee to Atlanta. Although he later sold the controlling interest to Ted Turner, Bartholomay stayed on as chairman.

Bob Lurie of the Giants was a San Francisco real estate magnate who put together a group that bought the team from Horace Stoneham for $8 million in 1976, saving the team from being moved to Canada. Bob was a great guy, but he struggled with bad teams and an even worse park—Candlestick—that he couldn't manage to replace. When Bob announced in late 1992 that the Giants were up for sale, he broke down and cried.

Joan Kroc had inherited the San Diego Padres after her husband, McDonald's empire founder Ray Kroc, died in 1984. Joan, a truly nice woman, really didn't have much interest in being a team owner. She had wanted to donate the team to the city of San Diego, but league rules prohibited municipal ownership. In 1990, she sold the team to a group headed by Tom Werner, a TV executive who had helped create *The Cosby Show, Mork and Mindy,* and other popular shows.

John McMullen, owner of the Astros until 1993, was a Naval Academy graduate and marine engineer who had been one of George Steinbrenner's limited partners when George bought the Yankees. (It was McMullen who had said, "Nothing in life is so limited as being the limited partner of George Steinbrenner.") John was an irascible guy, a staunch conservative who had been active in Republican Party affairs.

Some new owners were wealthy guys who bought baseball teams without really knowing much about what they were getting into. For example, Wayne Huizenga, who had built from scratch such companies as Waste Management, Blockbuster Video, and AutoNation, owned the 1993 expansion team Florida Marlins. And once at an owners' committee meeting he wondered aloud what was so important about baseball's exemption from anti-trust laws.

The other owners could hardly believe it. The series of court decisions dating back to the 1920s that effectively exempted baseball from anti-trust laws were the bedrock foundation of the business. For an owner to question that was like a multimillion-dollar free agent player standing up in a players association meeting and pining for the good old days of the reserve clause. Still, Huizenga was an extremely smart guy with a lot of fresh ideas. I thought it was too bad that he sold the Marlins in 1998.

Naturally, I had less contact with American League owners, but I would still encounter them at owners' meetings or other functions.

There was George Steinbrenner of the Yankees, of course, although in 1990 Fay Vincent banned him for life after Steinbrenner paid $40,000 to a small-time gambler for allegedly providing inside information against Yankees outfielder Dave Winfield, with whom Steinbrenner was having one of his many, many intra-team battles. At the time I asked George why he accepted the ban—to me the punishment didn't seem to fit the alleged "crime"—and George said he was involved in the Olympics at the time and didn't want to endanger that position with a drawn-out fight. He soon regretted that decision, however, and engineered a series of lawsuits against Vincent. He was reinstated in 1993 after Vincent left, but he had mellowed somewhat since the raucous "Bronx Zoo" days and generally left day-to-day team operations to others. He died in July 2010 at age eighty.

Jerry Reinsdorf of the White Sox was another notable American League owner. A onetime tax attorney with the IRS, Reinsdorf had gotten rich setting up real estate partnership tax shelters before assembling a limited partnership to buy the White Sox in 1981 for $19 million. (Later Reinsdorf also bought the Chicago Bulls basketball franchise.) Reinsdorf was a militantly anti-players-union guy who once complained to me that "players are greedy"—a strange thing to hear from a multimillionaire who got rich exploiting tax loopholes. He was unswervingly devoted to the bottom line. Once after the White Sox won the pennant Jerry started complaining that the victory was going to cost him money on the next year's salary structure.

Carl Pohlad of the Minnesota Twins, a World War II combat veteran, had started his banking career foreclosing on farms during the Great Depression and built a banking empire before buying the Twins in 1984.

Bud Selig had worked in the car leasing business before buying the bankrupt Seattle Pilots and moving them to Milwaukee to become the Milwaukee Brewers.

Gene Autry, the former singing cowboy who owned the California Angels, was always cordial when I would see him on trips to the West Coast. He and his wife, Jackie, would often invite me to dinner. But Gene was in his early eighties then, and often in poor health, so Jackie, who was in her late forties, usually attended the various owners' meetings alone. She always claimed to be just "a simple little Polish girl from New Jersey," but she was actually a very savvy businesswoman.

Another American League owner whom I'm often asked about now—although not so much back then—was the relatively young and largely unknown general managing partner of the Texas Rangers. His name was George W. Bush.

I had met his father, President George H. W. Bush, before I met the son. President Bush had once invited Nancy and me to the White House for an informal dinner with some other people.

While the president and I were on different sides of the political aisle, I found him to be a friendly, personable man. Bush had been a first baseman for the Yale baseball team, playing in the 1947 and 1948 College World Series, and later he sent me an autographed photo that said, "To Bill White, a better first baseman than I was."

I first met the younger George Bush in 1989, after he and a group of investors bought the Texas Rangers for $89 million. Although Bush's investment was small, about $600,000, he was named the co–managing general partner with Dallas businessman Rusty Rose. Bush, then forty-three, was the public face of the team while Rose handled the financial side.

Shortly after the sale, American League president Bobby Brown decided to invite Bush and Rose to New York for a kind of orientation meeting to fill them in on league rules and in general explain how the business of Major League Baseball worked. I heard about it and asked if I could sit in, since the National League was planning to expand and I wanted to see how they handled a new owners' orientation.

Bobby said it was okay, so I went to the meeting in the Major League Baseball conference room, which was one floor below the league offices. Dick Wagner, a former general manager of the Cincinnati Reds and a special assistant to Bobby Brown, was running the meeting while Bush and Rose and some other people sat around a conference table.

Dick Wagner was one of the most knowledgeable men in baseball. But about five minutes into the presentation I looked over and saw George Bush and Rusty Rose leaning back in their chairs, with their expensive cowboy boots propped up on the conference table, and they were both reading copies of *The Wall Street Journal*.

It wasn't my meeting, so I didn't say anything. Maybe that was just the way they did things down in Texas. And of course I never imagined that this then unknown Texas oilman and new baseball team owner would someday become the governor of Texas and then the president of the United States.

But I know this: If it had been my meeting, I would have politely told those Texans to take their damn cowboy boots off my conference table and pay some attention.

Still, despite that initial display of disengagement, Bush went on to become a popular guy among the other baseball owners. He was personable, easygoing, and liked to joke around. On a personal level, everybody seemed to like him.

So as I said, other than their racial makeup—there has never been a black owner in Major League Baseball, and it wasn't until 2003 that Arte Moreno of the Angels became the first Hispanic owner—the baseball owners I dealt with represented a broad mix of backgrounds, personalities, and styles.

And then, in a category all her own, there was Marge Schott.

Margaret Unnewehr Schott always said she was just a typical middle-aged housewife when her husband, Charles, died in 1968. It was true she had been a housewife, but she wasn't quite typical. She was the daughter of a Cincinnati lumber tycoon, and her husband, who owned a Buick dealership and other businesses, also came from a wealthy family. When he died, they were living in a twelve-thousand-square-foot stone mansion on seventy acres outside the city. Marge, who had no children, continued to live there for the rest of her life.

Marge had known a number of Cincinnati Reds players and executives through her charitable fund-raising work, and while she didn't know a lot about baseball she was a longtime fan of the team. She bought a small stake in the team in 1981, and in 1984, when it appeared the Reds might be bought and moved, she bought a 33 percent controlling interest for $11 million and became the president and CEO.

She was a popular and very visible owner with the fans, a local hero. She kept ticket prices at Riverfront Stadium the lowest in the league—just $12 for a box seat—and sold hot dogs for a dollar each. During games she usually sat in a regular box seat, as opposed to a private executive luxury box, and cheerfully signed autographs for fans. By the time I came on as National League president, she was a fairly stout, gray-haired sixty-year-old who chain-smoked cigarettes and favored red-and-white sweaters and red slacks—the Reds' team colors.

Eventually Marge Schott would be vilified as a racist and an anti-Semite and a disgrace to baseball. Newspapers and sports magazine would dub her "the Red Menace" and "Baseball's Big Red Headache," and civil rights groups would demand that she be driven out of the game. But I had no hint of that when I first became league president.

Instead, my first official contact with her came after she banned a reporter from the stadium's news media dining room.

The reporter was Ritter Collett, a longtime sportswriter, editor, and columnist for the *Dayton Daily News*. Age sixty-eight at the time, Ritter, who had covered every World Series since 1946, had written some things in his column that were critical of Marge. Marge, being an autocrat at heart, retaliated by revoking Collett's news media dining room privileges at Riverfront Stadium.

Marge had no right to do that. Although she owned the team, the city of Cincinnati owned the stadium. So when Collett called me and asked for help, I told him, "I'll take care of the problem, Ritter. Just sit tight until I get back to you."

Then I called Marge. Although we'd briefly spoken at some owners' meetings, I didn't know her well. She immediately started venting about how sportswriters were always taking cheap shots at her and she was tired of it.

"Those reporters have the *privilege* of eating in my dining room," she insisted. "They don't have a *right* to be there."

I tried to explain to her that it wasn't her dining room; it was the *city's* dining room. But talking to Marge when she had her back up was like talking to a wall; she stubbornly refused to listen. Finally, after what seemed like hours, I was getting annoyed.

"Marge, we're wasting time. Ritter's going to come to your office tomorrow and the two of you are going to talk about it. And when you two are done, I want you to give Ritter his dining room pass back."

Ritter met with Marge the next day and left the meeting with his dining pass reinstated. Reds employees were shocked that I had managed to get Marge to change her mind, and over the next few days I got three calls from team employees complaining about everything from low wages to lack of annual raises, and asking me if I could intervene with Marge.

I couldn't really help them with that. But after the Collett episode, Marge and I developed an unusual relationship—particularly in light of what came later. Marge would often call me before owners' meetings to ask how she should vote on an issue, and at the luncheons during the meetings she usually sat at my table. She felt, rightly, that the other owners looked down on her, dismissed her as an oddball, and that I was the only one who treated her with respect.

She *was* a certified oddball—particularly when it came to her dog, a giant, 170-pound St. Bernard named Schottzie that she turned into an unofficial symbol of the team. (The original Schottzie died in 1991 and was replaced with "Schottzie 02.") Her stadium office was crammed with stuffed St. Bernards, and players and managers were often embarrassed when they were required to pose for pictures with stuffed likenesses of Schottzie on their baseball caps. Marge's practice of letting Schottzie have the run of the stadium, including the field, forced players to dodge huge piles of dog droppings—and when they complained Marge said the players "should be happy I don't have a horse." I finally had to order her to keep her dog off the field, or at least put him on a leash.

Marge's cheapness was legendary. There were stories about how she collected the leftover doughnuts at business meetings and then sold them to her employees the next day for 35 cents each (a story she denied), and about how she once charged manager Lou Piniella for the cost of three bats he had donated to a local charity—which she did not deny. She was a hoarder who kept a room at the stadium packed with outdated "Schottzie" calendars and undistributed "give-away day" bats and hats and candy bars, some of them reportedly as much as eight years old.

I first came face-to-face with Marge's tight-fisted ways during the Reds' 1990 World Series against Oakland. The host teams are supposed to provide office space for league employees, but when we got to Riverfront Stadium, Marge had us crammed into the public relations office, where some of our senior employees actually had to do their paperwork while sitting on the floor. Marge's way of making it up to them was to bring them a bag of Biscoff cookies, the little airline in-flight snacks that she had gathered up on various flights. The National League staff was delighted when the Reds wrapped up the series in Oakland after a four-game sweep—not only because the National League team won, but because it meant they wouldn't have to go back to Cincinnati and deal with Marge.

That same World Series highlighted Marge's cheapness in other, more public ways. In the first inning of the last game in Oakland, Reds outfielder Eric Davis suffered a severely bruised kidney while diving for a ball. Davis spent the next six days in an Oakland hospital. Because of his injuries Davis couldn't fly on a commercial airliner, so he had to charter a $15,000 medical evacuation flight to get back home to Cincinnati—a cost that Marge publicly refused to pay.

It wasn't so much the money that upset Davis—he was making more than $3 million a year—as the fact that Marge had never even called him while he was in the hospital.

"I got calls from Bill White and Jesse Jackson," Davis told reporters, but not from Schott. "If I were a dog I would have gotten more care, and that's the truth." Certainly if the dog had been Schottzie, that would have been true.

(Marge was known for being unsympathetic to injured players on her payroll. Once when Reds pitcher and 1990 World Series MVP Jose Rijo was put on the disabled list, Marge complained that she was "paying him $3 million to sit on his butt.")

Marge and the Reds eventually paid for Davis's medical flight—which is what they should have done in the first place. Selling day-old doughnuts and hoarding free baseball caps may have been eccentrically funny, but Marge took a hammering in the news media and among many fans for her treatment of Davis. It caused her trouble she could have avoided.

In fact, it was Marge's miserly ways that indirectly led her to becoming the most reviled person in baseball.

Despite the low ticket prices, the Cincinnati Reds were one of the most profitable teams in the league. Unfortunately, Marge had a habit of refusing to divide up the profits with the team's other limited investors.

Marge didn't keep the money for herself. Instead, she put the profits—including her own 33 percent share of them—into an escrow account and kept them there as a kind of "rainy day" fund. By 1991, she reportedly had $53 million in the escrow account—and not surprisingly, the other investors were suing to get their share.

Before the lawsuit went to trial, I scheduled a meeting in Cincinnati with Marge and the investors. National League lawyers were defending Schott in the lawsuit, so I explained to the investors that the league had a responsibility to defend our owners, and that if they persisted with the lawsuit our lawyers would fight them as hard as they could. But I also explained to Marge that we wouldn't keep footing her legal expenses, and suggested that she hold back enough money for projected payroll expenses for the next year and distribute the rest of the escrow account. Marge didn't like it—she hated to let go of money—but she finally relented and the lawsuit was settled out of court in May 1991.

The problem was that during the lengthy period of depositions in the investors' lawsuit, one of the Reds' employees, team controller Tim Sabo, gave what Marge thought was damaging testimony against her. Marge responded by firing Sabo from his $25,000-a-year job—like all Reds employees, he was woefully underpaid—so Sabo filed a $2.5 million lawsuit against her for wrongful termination.

In his lawsuit, Sabo, who was white, alleged that one reason he was fired was because he objected to Marge Schott's use of racial slurs and her unwritten policy not to hire black employees. In a deposition in Sabo's case, another former Reds employee, marketing director Charles "Cal" Levy, said that he had heard Schott refer to outfielders Eric Davis and Dave Parker as her "million dollar niggers" and say that "sneaky goddamn Jews are all alike."

Marge didn't help her cause when in another deposition in the same case, when asked if she had ever used the word *nigger,* she said, "Sure, everybody's used the word once in their lifetime... Very seldom do I use that word...That's mainly a Southern term." Asked if she had ever referred to the Martin Luther King Jr. holiday as "nigger day," Marge said, "I don't believe so. I wouldn't even know when Martin Luther King Day is."

Asked if she was prejudiced against Jews, Marge said, "No. They are not smarter than us, just sharper." She also acknowledged keeping a Nazi swastika armband in her home, but said it was just a World War II souvenir that an employee from one of her other businesses had given her. "I keep it in a drawer with Christmas decorations," she said. (Later, after the storm broke, she also told a reporter that "Hitler was good in the beginning but he went too far.")

The depositions containing Marge's outrageous remarks didn't become public until November 1992, shortly before Sabo's lawsuit against Schott was dismissed. When they were revealed, they set off a firestorm.

Marge issued a statement saying she didn't mean to offend anyone. She said she had used the word *nigger* only in jest. She met with Cincinnati African American and Jewish groups to apologize. Still, the media was in an uproar, and there were calls for an investigation by the league and Major League Baseball.

I decided I'd better get out to Cincinnati.

I drove Marge to lunch at the Queen City Club. She told me that the allegations against her in Sabo's lawsuit were overblown, that he'd just been mad because he wasn't making enough money. She told me about apologizing to the local Jewish and African American groups, and said they had accepted the apology.

I tried to impress upon Marge that her remarks in the depositions had been at best insensitive and hurtful, that they not only hurt other people but could also seriously damage her. I also reminded her of an earlier problem with her making insensitive racial remarks.

In the three years that I had known her, I had never heard Marge use racist terms in referring to blacks or Jews. But at an owners' meeting in January 1992, long before her racially charged statements in the depositions had come out, Marge had been telling the other owners about a goodwill baseball tour she had been on in Japan. Throughout her talk, Marge had said things like, "The Jap prime minister said this," or "the Japs gave me that." Finally I had to break into her talk and tell her, "Marge, they're Japanese, not *Japs.*" It had been more than a little embarrassing.

Now at the lunch at the Queen City Club, I reminded her of that incident and insisted she not say anything like that again—about blacks, Asians, Hispanics, anybody. For once, Marge was receptive; she seemed to understand that she had screwed up.

After lunch I drove her back to her stadium office, but when I started to leave she insisted that I come inside. We went to her office and talked about the team for a while, and then as I was leaving she said, "Wait Bill, I want to show you something."

She took me over to a big trophy case that contained team memorabilia and pointed at a plaque inside.

"That's what the Japs gave me," Marge said.

The receptionist sitting nearby had to put her face in her hands to hide her laughter. I threw up my hands in frustration. After three hours of talking about stupid and insensitive comments Marge had made, she went and made another one—and she didn't even seem to realize it!

Later that day, Marge told a *New York Times* reporter about her meeting with me.

"He didn't yell at me. Bill never yells at me," Marge said. Asked if she hoped the controversy was over, Marge said, "I certainly hope so...I've never been racial in my life. I watch out for those people in my businesses. I got a letter from two black ladies today. The people who know me know this [the lawsuit] was just a cheap ploy."

One problem with that statement was that there were virtually none of "those people" in Marge's businesses—or at least not in her baseball business. Of forty-five Reds nonplayer personnel, only two were black—one of them a groundskeeper who later quit, the other a woman who worked in the ticket office.

Marge even told another *New York Times* reporter about her meeting with me and her use of the word *Jap*.

"Bill said to me, Marge, you quit that!" she laughingly told the reporter. "I said, 'Bill, I didn't know it was so bad, but I'll stop.' I didn't mean to insult the Japanese. I love them..."

If Marge had been able to keep her mouth shut, maybe the whole thing would have blown over. But then a woman in California read a newspaper story about my meeting with Schott and dropped another bombshell.

The woman was Sharon Jones, who had worked as the executive assistant to Oakland A's president Roy Eisenhardt. Jones told reporters that in the late 1980s, she wasn't sure exactly when, she had helped arrange a conference call between the owners and then commissioner Peter Ueberroth, apparently to discuss minority hiring issues. While some of the other owners were on the line, but before Ueberroth came on, Jones said she heard Marge Schott speaking.

"I wonder what the commissioner wants this time," Jones quoted Schott as saying. "Is it this race thing? I'm sick and tired of talking about this race thing. I once had a nigger work for me. He couldn't do the job. I had to put him in the mailroom and he couldn't even handle that. I later found out the nigger couldn't read or write...I would never hire another nigger. I'd rather have a trained monkey working for me than a nigger."

Jones, who had left the A's after twelve years to work for a college, said she decided to go public after reading Schott's remarks about her meeting with me—remarks that Jones, who was black, said "made me cry."

Although Marge denied Jones's allegations, it was clear that Major League Baseball had to do something. Within a week, a four-member committee was named to investigate Marge's comments and actions. The committee members were Jackie Autry of the

Angels, Doug Danforth of the Pirates, American League president Bobby Brown, and me.

Part of our investigation was easy. There was no question about Marge's remarks in the lawsuit depositions. We also determined that Schott had frequently used racial slurs in the presence of other Reds employees. But Sharon Jones's allegations about Schott's "trained monkey" comments on the conference call were harder to pin down. I had no reason to doubt Jones's sincerity. In fact, from what I had learned about Marge, the comments actually sounded like the sort of stupid thing she would say, especially if she'd been drinking, which she did often. But we couldn't find anyone else who was able—or willing—to corroborate the story.

Meanwhile, the investigation committee and Major League Baseball in general were being assailed from all sides of the issue.

Ohio senator Howard Metzenbaum called the appointment of the investigation committee a stalling tactic. Jesse Jackson described the in-house committee as "the chickens guarding the henhouse." The NAACP, the Southern Christian Leadership Conference, the National Urban League, the Anti-Defamation League of B'nai B'rith, and the players associations of Major League Baseball, the NBA, and the NFL were all calling for Schott to be severely disciplined. The press was going crazy. *Sports Illustrated* put an angry-looking Marge Schott on the cover under the headline "Red Menace." *The New York Times* called her "Baseball's Big Red Headache."

At the same time, others were calling our investigation of Schott a "witch-hunt." A lot of Cincinnati fans still loved Marge, and thought the other owners were picking on her. Other people argued that no matter what Schott had said, she had a First Amendment right to say it.

Through it all, Marge was defiant. She hired the influential Washington, DC, attorney Robert Bennett to defend her and threatened to sue if the other owners tried to ban her from baseball. At one point, Marge even employed what might be called the "gender defense." In a statement concerning the investigation, Marge said, "As a woman in this male-dominated 'fraternity,' I have never been fully accepted as an equal. Now, once again, I feel as though I'm being discriminated against."

Noting that racial and ethnic comments were common when she was growing up, Schott said, "Perhaps subconsciously, I may even have thought that these words made me sound tough, aggressive, or masculine to my male competitors in the business world."

In the meantime, Marge tried to enlist—or perhaps buy—support by donating money to various black schools and churches in Cincinnati. She gave $100,000 to a predominantly black school, and smaller but still substantial amounts to black churches. I got letters from church members saying what a nice woman she was. When Marge Schott started handing out wads of precious money, you knew she realized she was in trouble.

The whole thing was an unmitigated mess. And for months it overwhelmed everything else connected with baseball.

Finally it came time for Major League Baseball to mete out punishment.

I had suggested that we ban Schott from Riverfront Stadium for a year and require her to undergo cultural sensitivity training. I didn't know how much good the sensitivity training would have done, but I knew how much Marge loved going to the games and basking in the adoration of the fans. So it seemed to me that that would be the one thing that might actually impress on her that she had to change her ways. It would also keep her, I hoped, out of the public eye. I was certain that if given the opportunity, Marge would shoot her mouth off and the controversy would flare up again.

But the owners' executive council disagreed. In a deal worked out with Marge's lawyer, they decided that Marge would be banned from day-to-day operations of the Reds for one year but could participate in long-range planning. She was also fined $25,000—the maximum allowable under baseball rules—and required to take sensitivity training.

But she wasn't banned from the stadium. For the first month of the season she had to stay out of sight in her executive box, but after that she could return to her regular box seat in the stands—which is all that Marge really wanted anyway. She wanted to wave and blow kisses and be adored by the fans—which for the most part she still was.

The agreement was widely denounced as a slap on the wrist. Most of the critics had wanted her driven permanently from baseball.

And eventually she would be—once again as an indirect result not only of her unstoppable mouth but also of her cheapskate behavior.

On April 1, 1996, after an unseasonable snowfall earlier in the day, the Reds kicked off their season opener with the Montreal Expos. Seven pitches into the game, umpire John McSherry, whom I had once pressured to lose weight, called a time-out and started walking toward the Reds dugout. After a few steps he collapsed and fell facedown to the ground, dead of an apparent heart attack at age fifty-one. After the other umpires postponed the game until the next day, Marge was caught on videotape looking visibly upset with the postponement and reportedly saying, "Snow this morning and now this. I don't believe it. I feel cheated."

The remark infuriated umpires and alienated a lot of fans. Later it was reported that a bouquet of sympathy flowers Marge sent to the umpires' dressing room after McSherry's death had actually been given to her as an opening day gift by the Reds' television affiliate. Marge, cheap as ever, had "regifted" the flowers. Soon thereafter, in an interview with ESPN, Marge repeated her earlier remarks about how Hitler "was good in the beginning but he went too far."

That was it. Major League Baseball again banned her from the Reds' day-to-day operations through the 1998 season. Many of the Reds fans, tired of the controversies, had turned against her, and her limited partners in the Reds were planning to oust her. In 1999, she sold her controlling interest in the team for $67 million.

A year later, I saw Marge when former Reds star first baseman Tony Perez was inducted into the Hall of Fame in 2000. I was walking through a hotel lobby when I spotted her coming toward me, looking tired and worn and older than her years. I think Marge had always held me partly to blame for what had happened in 1992–93; after that she had stopped calling me for advice on how to vote at the owners' meetings, and she voted against me on a number of occasions.

"Hi, Marge," I said.

"Hi, honey," she said, which is what she said to everybody, and then she walked past me. I don't think she even recognized me.

I never saw her again. Marge Schott died in Cincinnati in 2004 at age seventy-five.

In the years since the Marge Schott controversy, a lot of people have asked me if I was personally angered or offended by the things she said. The answer, perhaps surprisingly, is no.

You have to understand that starting when I was nineteen years old and playing in the Carolina League, I had been subjected to some of the worst imaginable racial taunts and insults. After being called a "nigger" to my face by crowds of angry, ignorant rednecks, the behind-the-scenes racist mutterings of a Marge Schott couldn't hurt me. Sure, sometimes I wondered if Marge had ever used racist epithets to refer to me behind my back—but I never asked her. It didn't matter to me.

The truth is that Marge Schott was simply an angry, lonely old woman who talked too much and drank too much and couldn't control herself.

In some ways, I felt sorry for her.

Besides, Marge certainly wasn't the only baseball owner to drag her feet on hiring minorities for front office positions. And there had certainly been other owners who shared Marge's beliefs about black people's abilities.

It was just that, unlike Marge, they were smart enough not to say it out loud.

During the Schott controversy, I had made it a policy to say as little as possible to the news media. But that was nothing new. I already had a reputation for being inaccessible to most reporters.

That reputation was well deserved. And there were good reasons for it.

There were some reporters I admired, particularly some of the black reporters from the early days. A. S. "Doc" Young, a reporter and editor for *Jet* and *Ebony* and a host of other publications; Sam Lacy, a reporter who helped bring Jackie Robinson into the big leagues; Wendell Smith, who wrote about segregation in spring training; Mal Goode, a longtime Pittsburgh newscaster who became the first black network television correspondent on ABC. These were guys who understood the struggles that the early black major league players were going through.

As far as the mainstream press went, I never had much of a problem during my playing days. When I was with the Giants in the 1950s, I knew the New York news media could be tough, but I was just a rookie so they didn't pay much attention to me. When the Giants moved to San Francisco, I was there for only a month before I was traded, and I spent most of my time on the bench, so again the local reporters pretty much left me alone.

After I joined the Cardinals in 1959, I was in a town that

embraced its team in good times and bad. Sure, St. Louis reporters would point out a player's weak spots—like the time Harry Caray said I couldn't hit a curve ball with a canoe paddle—but they generally weren't snide or sarcastic about it. Legendary reporter Bob Broeg of the *St. Louis Post-Dispatch* would also take note if a player was in a slump, but he would do it matter-of-factly, without any wiseass commentary.

It was a little different when I went to Philadelphia. The Phillies were in a long slump, and both the Philadelphia fans and the Philadelphia sportswriters were notoriously unforgiving. I remember once in 1968, Bill Conlin of the *Philadelphia Daily News* wrote a column before the season even began saying that we had no chance for a winning season. I always wondered why a guy would trash the home team before a single batter had stepped up to the plate—but then, that was Conlin.

A lot of the Philadelphia sportswriters were like Conlin—angry, sarcastic, opinionated. One notable exception was Frank Dolson of *The Philadelphia Inquirer*. When Frank criticized me in print I paid attention, because Frank was always fair. In fact, Frank and I actually became friends, especially after I learned that he was a Yankees fan. When I was broadcasting for the Yankees we'd often drive up to New York together for a game, and after he retired from the newspaper business Frank took a job with the team as an adviser to George Steinbrenner. When Frank died of cancer in 2006, he left behind a legacy of honest professionalism.

I tried to emulate that when I was a sports reporter for WFIL-TV in Philadelphia. I reported the facts about what I was covering and didn't try to second-guess a player or manager or coach, or kick him when he was down. Maybe it was because I'd been a player, but I never understood why so many reporters seemed to actually enjoy hammering on some kid who was 0–15 at the start of a season. I'm not a psychiatrist, but maybe it was because most of the reporters had never actually played the sports they covered, and they were trying to get even for their lack of athletic skills.

It was the same thing when I was a broadcaster for the Yankees. I wasn't flashy or controversial or overly colorful—Phil Rizzuto was colorful enough for the both of us—and I tried not to second-guess or ridicule people.

In truth, I seldom had any serious run-ins with reporters in the playing and broadcasting phases of my career. Nobody expected me to deal with the press on a regular basis, or to be a public spokesman for anything.

That changed when I became president of the National League.

Shortly after my appointment was announced, I gave a number of press interviews. The problem was that all the reporters and broadcast interviewers always seemed to ask the exact same questions. For some reason, reporters seem to develop a kind of group-think when they approach a story; they all pursue the same theme, relentlessly.

I guess it has always been that way. I remember back in 1961, after I'd spoken out against segregation in spring training, I was approached by an endless string of reporters who wanted to interview me about it. It got so bad that when writer Alex Haley showed up to interview me—this was before he became famous for writing *Roots*—I wouldn't talk to him about it. I was polite to him, and tried to set him up with other black players to talk to. But I was just tired of saying the same thing over and over.

So during my term as president I avoided most reporters whenever I could, speaking only to those I knew and trusted to be both accurate and fair. I didn't need to talk with reporters to get my job done. If I had something to say concerning the National League, whenever possible I issued a written statement. That way I could be sure I was quoted accurately, and I didn't have to give the same answers to the same questions from twenty different reporters on twenty different phone calls.

Unfortunately, some reporters will pursue their own agendas even if they have to make things up to do it.

A good example was a story that appeared in a New York paper in May 1992. I had spoken at a meeting of the Black Coaches Association in Atlanta, and during the speech I talked about the impact of Jackie Robinson, desegregation in spring training, and my behind-the-scenes efforts as league president to encourage minority hiring. At one point, one of the coaches asked if baseball owners were racist. In response I gave a brief history of racism in baseball, and mentioned some of the teams that had been most reluctant to hire black players—the Yankees, the Tigers, the Phillies, and the Red Sox. I noted that the Major League Baseball owners had voted 15–1 against allowing Jackie Robinson to be signed by the Dodgers in the 1940s. I also said that I sometimes still felt bitter about my experiences with racism in the minor leagues.

I didn't think anything about it until the next day when I picked up a paper in my office in New York and saw a story headlined something like: "NL's White: Team Owners 'Racist.'" The accompanying article, which was based on an inaccurate wire service story out of Atlanta, said that I was "bitter" about working with racist baseball owners.

I almost fell out of my chair. Where the hell did that come from?

I soon got a call from Bob Lurie, owner of the San Francisco Giants and one of my biggest supporters as league president.

"Bill, what happened?" he said.

"Bob, I never said anything close to what appeared in that story."

Like anyone who knew me, Bob understood that I would never have said anything like that. It was not only wrong—not all team owners were racists, and Bob certainly wasn't—but to say it publicly would have been incredibly stupid on my part.

The problem is that people who don't know you will see something like that and assume it must be true.

"I can't believe you said that!" Fay Vincent said when I stepped into his office—but his tone made it clear that he certainly could believe I had said that. "I want you to apologize."

"I'm not going to apologize to anyone, Fay. What that article said wasn't accurate."

Then Vincent wanted me to explain my version of the story at a press conference. I refused. I'd been around reporters for three decades as a player and broadcaster, and I had been one myself; I knew how they operated. If I responded to the inaccurate story it would just give them another story, and then they'd want me to respond to that story, and on and on.

"If I respond it'll just drag it out," I told Vincent. "If I don't say anything it will go away."

I was right. The story faded away in a day. But for me it was another lesson learned about the news media.

Of course, a lot of reporters bitched and moaned about my inaccessibility. Even some of the owners privately criticized my low-visibility approach to my job. I sometimes wondered if some of them felt cheated by the fact that having hired a black man for the president's job, I wasn't advertising their progressive attitudes toward minorities by getting my face on television all the time.

But some of the owners understood. John McMullen of the Astros put it this way in a newspaper story: "Bill understands that if you live by the media, you die by the media. You can't win. Everything goes into extra innings."

John had it right. Too often the news media doesn't play fair, and they always want the last word.

You can't win their game. So why play it?

CHAPTER 15

In June 1989, at a press conference during an owners' meeting in Kansas City, I was standing next to then commissioner Bart Giamatti and American League president Bobby Brown when a reporter asked Bart a question.

"There's been talk about expansion for years," the reporter said. "Has the National League voted to expand?"

The reporter's question was expected. Bart's answer was not.

"Yes," Bart said, smiling.

The instant that "yes" passed Bart's lips, I did a double take. We'd been talking for months about increasing the number of teams in the league, but the idea that we had already formally voted on it was news to me.

I leaned over and whispered to Bart, "When did we take a vote on expansion?"

Bart, still smiling, whispered back: "We didn't."

But vote or no vote, Bart was in it now. By the end of the press conference, Bart had announced that we would soon be releasing a timetable for adding two teams to the National League.

Bart had jumped the gun on this one, but it didn't really matter. We all knew that expansion was coming. Over the past few years, the pressure to add more teams—political pressure and later financial pressure—had become enormous.

For sixty years, from 1901 to 1960, there had been sixteen teams in major league baseball—eight in the National League, eight in the American League, with no divisions within the leagues. Simple.

By the 1960s, however, the US population had grown dramatically, demographics had shifted, and the demand for more teams was increasing. In 1961, the American League expanded to include the Los Angeles Angels, and that same year, after the Washington Senators left that city to become the Minnesota Twins, the American League added another franchise, the new Washington Senators. The next year, 1962, the National League added the Houston Colt .45s (renamed the Astros in 1965) and the New York Mets. In the number of teams, the score was National League ten, American League ten.

In 1969, the San Diego Padres and the Montreal Expos joined the National League, and the American League enfranchised the Kansas City Royals and the Seattle Pilots, who soon moved to Milwaukee and became the Brewers. There were then twelve teams in each league, with the leagues divided into East and West Divisions. In 1977, the American League expanded yet again, adding the Seattle Mariners and the Toronto Blue Jays. There were now twenty-six teams—fourteen in the American League, twelve in the National League.

After the 1977 American League expansion, everyone thought that the National League would soon follow and add two more teams of its own. But the National League, which was the older and probably the more conservative of the two leagues—it was some-times known as "the Senior Circuit," as opposed to the "Junior Cir-cuit" American League—was really in no hurry to expand further. Although the National League said in 1985 that it would eventually add two more teams, it didn't say when.

The problem was that a lot of cities wanted a major league base-ball team. And the politicians who represented those cities wanted to be able to point to a baseball team and say to the voters at elec-tion time, "Vote for me—I brought you Major League Baseball!"

(It wasn't just politicians who were desperate for major league teams. I was constantly amazed at how passionate some fans were to get a team—and how angry they could become when they didn't. To cite one extreme example, in 1992, after I blocked efforts by a group of Florida investors to buy the San Francisco Giants and move the team to the St. Petersburg–Tampa area, I got a let-ter from a Tampa obstetrician. In the letter he called me "an igno-rant ex-jock/ex-TV announcer" and "a rotten human being," and he closed by saying "I can only hope you have a long, slow, painful death." And this guy was a doctor! I can only imagine what the cab-drivers and bartenders were saying about me.)

Anyway, when baseball seemed to be dragging its feet on expansion, the politicians got ticked off. In 1987, Colorado senator Tim Wirth, who desperately wanted a team for the Denver area, created a US Senate task force on the expansion of Major League Baseball. The task force was made up of senators from eight poten-tial expansion states—Colorado, Arizona, Florida, Louisiana, Indi-ana, Tennessee, Virginia, and New Jersey—as well as the nonvoting congressional delegate from Washington, DC, and Congressman (and later Senator) Jim Bunning of Kentucky, one of my old team-mates from the Phillies.

In other circumstances, a task force like that might have just been political window dressing, a venue for politicians to spout off without having any actual power to do anything. But this task force, and Congress in general, held a very big club over Major League Baseball—that is, the threat to remove baseball's exemption from anti-trust laws.

Beginning in the 1920s, various court decisions had exempted baseball from antitrust laws, giving the two leagues a monopoly over the game in America. Baseball had the power to say when and where to add new teams, to determine whether existing teams could move to other cities, to collectively negotiate TV contracts, and so on. Because of the anti-trust exemption, coordinated actions among team owners that would have been illegal in any other industry were allowed in baseball.

In 1972, however, in the anti-reserve clause lawsuit brought by my fellow Cardinal Curt Flood, the Supreme Court said that Congress had the power to impose anti-trust restrictions on Major League Baseball. So far Congress hadn't done anything, but the very thought that the politicians could take away, or severely restrict, their monopoly terrified the baseball owners.

So when the Senate task force on expansion demanded action from baseball, baseball had to respond—or at least act like it was responding. The baseball commissioner—first Peter Ueberroth and then Bart Giamatti—kept assuring the increasingly impatient politicians that expansion was coming.

Meanwhile, there was another source of pressure for baseball to expand—money. Like any franchise business, whether it's McDonald's or Blockbuster or whatever, new franchisees are required to pay a fee to join the organization. Some owners whose teams were losing money were looking to those franchise fees to help get them out of the red.

Given all the political and financial pressures pushing for expansion, maybe it's not surprising Bart Giamatti was eager to announce expansion plans at that press conference in 1989.

But the big questions were still to be answered: How much money would new franchises bring in? How much of that money would each team get? And most important to baseball fans, which cities would get to join the ranks of Major League Baseball?

Even before Bart made his surprise announcement, I had appointed a National League committee to study expansion. Doug Danforth of the Pittsburgh Pirates favored it. Fred Wilpon of the Mets did as well. I also appointed the Houston Astros' John McMullen to the committee because he was opposed to expansion, and I thought it would be good to have an opposing voice heard.

We quickly found out that the economics of expansion had changed since 1977. Back then, Seattle had paid $6.3 million and Toronto had paid $7 million to join the American League. But with Major League Baseball now bringing in bigger revenues, including more than half a billion dollars in TV broadcasting fees, the value of a baseball franchise had skyrocketed. Our analysis indicated that we could charge anywhere from $40 million to $120 million per expansion team. Eventually we decided to charge $95 million in expansion fees per team, or $190 million total from the two-team expansion.

It was a lot of money. And as always happens with a lot of money, a lot of people wanted a piece of it.

Early on in my term as league president, Bart and I had clashed on whether to involve the American League in our expansion plans. Bart repeatedly insisted that the expansion process be conducted in a spirit of—his favorite word—"collegiality," and that the American League be included in all discussions and decisions.

But I wasn't feeling collegial. I knew what those guys in the American League were up to. When they enfranchised Seattle and Toronto in 1977, they hadn't consulted with the National League. And they certainly hadn't shared the $13 million in franchise fees with us.

But now they wanted to do both. They wanted to be involved in the expansion process, and they wanted part of the money the National League expansion brought in. Red Sox owner Haywood Sullivan, a former Red Sox catcher and general manager, had admitted as much.

"I'm going to be honest here," he told us during a meeting. "You're getting money through expansion and we want some of it."

Eventually we agreed, as a courtesy, to keep the commissioner's office updated on our progress. But I was damned if I was going to give those guys any of our money—at least not without a serious fight.

In any event, in early 1990 we announced the expansion timetable. By the end of the year, we would have met with all the potential ownership groups and cut the list to five cities. In early 1991, we would begin on-site inspections. By the end of 1991, we'd be ready to name the two winners, and by the start of the 1993 season we'd have two new expansion teams playing in the National League.

The expansion sweepstakes was off and running.

The National League expansion committee accepted preliminary applications from eighteen prospective owners and investors groups in ten cities: Buffalo, Denver, Washington, DC, Charlotte, Phoenix, Nashville, Sacramento, and three Florida cities—Miami, Orlando, and St. Petersburg–Tampa.

Some of the cities were long shots from the start for a simple reason: The investors groups just didn't have the money. Obviously, starting up a baseball team is an expensive proposition, and we didn't want an expansion team to go belly-up after just a year or two. In fact, one potential owner in Orlando dropped out after he took a good long look at the numbers. He concluded that if he got a major league team, he would lose $12 million a year.

Even if they'd had the money, some cities just didn't seem like the right fit. Sacramento was too close to the Bay Area, which already had two major league teams, the Giants and the Oakland Athletics. Nashville seemed to be too small a market to sustain a major league club; same thing with Charlotte, North Carolina.

Phoenix also was a long shot. Arizona senator John McCain, a member of the Senate task force on expansion, desperately wanted a team in Phoenix—he had called for Major League Baseball to expand by *six* teams in order to increase Phoenix's chances—but once again, the expansion committee members worried that there wasn't enough financial backing.

Meanwhile, I had other concerns about Arizona.

In 1990, a ballot measure to establish a state Martin Luther King Day holiday had been defeated, which meant that Arizona and New Hampshire were the only two states that didn't recognize the holiday. I couldn't do anything about New Hampshire, but when a delegation of Arizona civic leaders and politicians—including McCain and Governor Rose Mofford—came to New York to lobby for a team, I could certainly put a little pressure on Arizona.

After discussing other aspects of the franchise application, I asked the Arizona delegation straight out: "What's being done by the state on establishing a King holiday, and what are your thoughts on the issue?"

There was an uncomfortable silence. Then Astros owner John McMullen, who was on the league expansion committee, muttered in the background.

"Do we really want to mix politics and business here?" McMullen said. "I really don't think that's an appropriate question."

Maybe it didn't seem appropriate to John, but it certainly seemed appropriate to me. My personal feelings aside, it was a sensitive matter among black and other minority athletes and in professional sports in general. After the 1990 ballot rejection of the

King holiday, the NFL announced that a scheduled Super Bowl in Phoenix would be moved to Pasadena. Who knew what impact a continued rejection of the holiday by Arizona might have on Major League Baseball if Phoenix actually got a team?

I never would have publicly browbeaten the Arizona delegation over the issue. As I've said, to the annoyance of some civil rights groups and others, that simply wasn't my style as league president. But it was my style, and my job, to let the Arizona delegation know that it was a significant issue.

Finally Senator McCain spoke up. "We're working on that," he said. "The climate is changing. We're confident it's going to be done."

I don't know if my question to the delegation had any impact on their thinking, but Arizona voters enacted a King holiday in 1992. In 1996, the Super Bowl was played in Tempe, and in 1998 Arizona finally got its baseball team, the Arizona Diamondbacks.

Although we had planned to narrow the list of contending cities to five, we finally made it six: Denver, Buffalo, Orlando, Miami, Tampa–St. Petersburg, and Washington, DC.

Washington was on the list primarily for political reasons. Congressmen from across the country wanted a DC team (they probably figured they'd be able to get free tickets), and there was still great concern about baseball's anti-trust exemption. Also, former baseball commissioner Bowie Kuhn, who had grown up in Washington and had been a fan of the old Senators team, was lobbying hard behind the scenes to bring a team to that city.

But it was still a long shot for Washington. Its investors group was having a hard time meeting our "60–40 rule"—investors had to have at least 60 percent of the $95 million expansion fee in cash, and could borrow only 40 percent. Besides that, the city was close to Baltimore and the Orioles, and baseball had already failed twice in Washington. We just didn't think it would work.

Buffalo was in the running because while it was a relatively small city, people there were clearly baseball fans. Buffalo's AAA minor league team, the Bisons, drew a million fans a season to their twenty-thousand-seat downtown stadium, which could be expanded to forty-two thousand seats if a major league team came in. And let's be honest, it didn't hurt Buffalo's chances that the Bisons were an affiliate of the Pirates organization, and the chairman of our expansion committee was Pirates owner Doug Danforth.

Three Buffalo groups were vying for a shot. One, a wealthy family group, soon dropped out. Another group was headed by Malcolm Glazer, a Tampa-based businessman who would later become owner of the Tampa Bay Buccaneers and the Manchester United soccer team in England. Glazer visited with the expansion committee in New York and offered a unique proposal. His idea was to base a team in Buffalo but have it play its home games in four different cities.

"We want to create a traveling baseball team," Glazer told us—and he was dead serious. We were polite, but we thought the guy was nuts.

We finally chose Bob Rich Jr., who ran the Bisons, to represent Buffalo in the final selection process. However, Buffalo had one strike against them after Bob Rich Sr., who controlled the money, said publicly, "We do not believe in baseball at any cost." He was referring to the high price of free agents and the $95 million franchise fee. It wasn't exactly what we wanted to hear from a prospective owner.

Of the three Florida cities in the final selection process, we decided against Orlando and Tampa–St. Petersburg. We figured that people came to Orlando for Disney World and other attractions and then went home. Tampa–St. Petersburg was a good spring training city, but the fans were transients who went home after spring training ended. And in both cases, financing was an issue.

In the end, we picked the investors group from Miami to represent Florida, largely because of Wayne Huizenga. The Waste Management and Blockbuster founder had $95 million in cash—"I can write you a check right now," he told us—and he also had Joe Robbie Stadium, an outdoor football stadium that could be converted to baseball. Given Florida's summer weather, we worried about excessive rain delays, but Huizenga promised in writing that if he got a team he would build a domed stadium.

And finally there was Denver, which to my mind was always at the top of the list for a new team. I had played there in the minor leagues and knew it was a great baseball town. Independent surveys had shown that people in Colorado would drive three hours to see a major league game. It was also geographically perfect for Major League Baseball because it was situated in the middle of the as-yet-untapped Rocky Mountain states. Initially there was some financing difficulty when a local investor dropped out, but other investors then stepped in. I was sure Denver would get one of the two expansion teams.

But if Denver got the franchise, it wasn't because of Bob Howsam.

Howsam had been the general manager of the Cardinals who had traded me to the Phillies in 1965 and then lied about my age to reporters and other teams. Now he was working with the Colorado Baseball Commission, a booster group, to help bring baseball to Denver.

I try not to hold grudges—but I'm not always successful at it. I still had no respect for him. Howsam, on the other hand, always tried to act like he was one of my old buddies. He tried to call me often during the expansion selection process, but on my instructions my assistant always told him I was out, even when I was in.

Once in 1990, Howsam had called my hotel room when we were both in Cooperstown at a Hall of Fame induction ceremony and said he desperately needed to talk to me. I told him that at that early stage it wouldn't be proper for me to talk to him or anyone else about expansion, but he assured me that wasn't the subject.

"I don't want to talk to you about expansion," he said. "I just want to talk to you."

Reluctantly I agreed to meet him in his hotel room. And the first thing he said to me when I walked in was, "You know, Bill, I'm working with this expansion group in Denver..."

I turned and walked out.

Of course, I never would have let my personal antipathy to Howsam change how I would vote on Denver for expansion.

But he probably had some anxious moments worrying that I would.

While all this was going on, we were still battling the attempts by the American League to take—I would actually say "steal"— some of our $190 million in expansion fees.

The American League wanted the expansion money divided up equally among all the major league teams—which meant that, since they had fourteen teams and we had twelve, they would actually get more than half of it. But I didn't care if they wanted only a penny. There was no precedent for one league sharing its expansion fees with the other league, and I didn't want to start one.

Finally Commissioner Fay Vincent stepped in.

In May 1991, representatives from both leagues met with the commissioner to argue their cases on the expansion fees. But before the meeting even began, Vincent said, "I'm going to listen to both sides and then decide how this will be split."

Split? What did he mean, split? Obviously he had already made up his mind on the most important question—that is, whether to break precedent and give the American League anything at all. Now he just wanted us to haggle over the final price.

All that being said, I was a realist. I knew the American League was probably going to get something. But I was still seething as we made our presentation.

Basically, our argument was this: They didn't pay us when they expanded, so we shouldn't have to pay them now. The American League argued that if the National League kept all the expansion fees, our teams would have an unfair advantage.

A week and a half later, Vincent announced his decision. The National League would take 78 percent of the $190 million in expansion fees, or about $12 million per team, and the American League would get 22 percent, or about $3 million per team. He also declared that each team would provide three players in the expansion draft, and that in any future expansion the leagues would split all expansion fees equally.

It was the sort of compromise that pissed off everybody. American League owners thought they'd gotten too little, National League owners thought they'd lost too much. And it didn't help that in his written decision Vincent had scolded us all.

"The squabbling within baseball," he wrote, "the finger-pointing, the tendency to see economic issues as moral ones . . . all of these are contributing to our joint fall from grace."

That was the way Vincent was. He couldn't just make a decision; he had to preach and pontificate about it.

Finally on July 5, 1991, after the owners formally approved the expansion committee's final choices, we announced the two winners of the National League expansion competition—Denver and Miami. The Denver group named their team the Colorado Rockies, giving it statewide appeal, and the Miami group went with the Florida Marlins for the same reason.

It had been a long and difficult and sometimes acrimonious process. But I honestly believed that we had fairly evaluated all of the applicants and found the two best. On a personal level, I think that guiding the National League through the expansion was my biggest accomplishment as president.

Of course, there were still some issues that needed to be addressed before the teams were ready to actually take the field. One of them was minority hiring.

It was true that baseball's record on hiring minorities for front office jobs had been dismal. But in fairness, the turnover in non-managerial front office jobs was slow. People loved working in baseball and generally stayed for a long time. I didn't want teams to create phony, make-work positions simply so they could be filled with minorities. And I certainly didn't want experienced, qualified, and loyal nonminority front office employees to be fired so minorities could take their places. That wouldn't have been right. So while I quietly urged team owners to give minorities an equal shot at jobs when openings occurred, I understood that changing the face of the existing teams' workforces would take time.

But with two new teams in the National League, we now had two clean slates. And I was determined that their front office workforces would reflect the communities in which they operated.

With every group that applied for an expansion team, minority hiring had been a topic of discussion with the expansion committee. Both of the expansion groups we selected had promised that fair hiring practices would be a top priority.

For example, before Miami was selected, Wayne Huizenga had assured me that at least 40 percent of his new hires would be minorities. Since Miami-Dade County was about 20 percent African American and 50 percent Hispanic, I knew there would be a large pool of minority applicants to choose from.

Denver was a slightly different situation. It was only about 10 percent black, but it also had a large Hispanic population—and I wanted its off-the-field workforce to reflect that.

"Just make sure your staff looks like your local population," I told the Denver group.

"No problem," they said.

Given all that, I was surprised to find out during the start-up phase that none of the Marlins' upper-level employees was black. I was equally surprised, and annoyed, that when the Colorado Rockies hired their first six upper-level executives, every one of them was white.

I let the team owners know how I felt—and to his credit, so did Fay Vincent. Despite my many problems with him, Vincent was diligent on minority hiring issues. After I told him what was happening in Denver and Miami, Vincent spoke out publicly, demanding that the two new teams improve their minority hiring—and they did.

The Rockies' workforce became at least slightly more diverse, and the Marlins hired more black employees, including hiring a young black businessman named Jonathan Mariner as the team's executive vice president and chief financial officer. Mariner later became chief financial officer for Major League Baseball.

So in 1993, after years of hard work and planning, the Colorado Rockies and the Florida Marlins took the field as the two newest teams in Major League Baseball. It was, I thought, a great accomplishment.

But Commissioner Fay Vincent wasn't around to see it.

From almost the moment Vincent became commissioner after Bart Giamatti's death, I felt that his lack of experience in baseball was causing him to make some ill-considered moves. His attempt to get rid of Lou Hoynes; his intrusion into the umpires' spring training mini strike and the Joe West controversy; his high-handed scolding of us for trying to protect the National League's rights during expansion—those were just a few examples that I was directly involved in.

I wasn't the only one who doubted Vincent's effectiveness as commissioner. Some of the team owners who had supported his selection as commissioner were turning against him as well.

A few of the owners were annoyed with Vincent when he very publicly injected himself into contract negotiations during the owners' lockout of players during spring training in 1990—just as he injected himself into the umpires' mini strike that I had to deal with the same year. The perception among some owners, particular the hard-line anti-union guys like Reinsdorf and Selig, was that Vincent was straying out of his lane—professional negotiators, not commissioners, were supposed to handle labor negotiations—and that he had been far too favorable toward the players.

Over my many years in baseball, I noticed a funny thing about owners and players. During contract negotiation time, players would shout and scream and fight like hell, but once the contract was signed they went back to work and forgot about it. For a lot of owners, on the other hand, the anger during negotiations became a festering sore that wouldn't go away. Maybe because they had to sign the checks, their anger and resentment would smolder for years—and anyone who had been against them, or even not completely for them, won a permanent place on their mental enemies lists.

In any event, the lockout caused some owners to turn against Vincent. And then, as mentioned earlier, Vincent suspended George Steinbrenner from the Yankees for paying that small-time gambler $40,000 during Steinbrenner's dispute with Dave Winfield.

Many of the other team owners were quietly pleased that Steinbrenner had been kicked out of baseball. They didn't like him, partly because his free-spending ways had driven up salaries throughout the game, and partly because—well, because he was George Steinbrenner, with all that that encompassed.

But they also didn't like the way Vincent had handled the matter. Many believed that during the Steinbrenner investigation, Vincent had flouted baseball procedures and basic rules of fairness. If Vincent could do that to Steinbrenner, what would keep him from doing it to one of them?

A few weeks after Steinbrenner's banishment, some of the owners took up the issue during an executive council meeting in Chicago. With Vincent in the room, Jerry Reinsdorf of the White Sox made a motion.

"There are some concerns about how you handled this entire affair," Reinsdorf said, referring to the Steinbrenner case. "I'd like to move that we form a committee to look into the powers of the commissioner."

Vincent didn't show any emotion; he never did. But it was clear that some of the owners wanted to gut the commissioner's authority.

The discussion went around the room, with Vincent's action being thoroughly criticized. Then it was my turn to speak.

Everyone knew about my disdain for Vincent—it was no secret—so they probably expected me to be in favor of Reinsdorf's proposal.

But while I disdained the man who was commissioner, I respected the *concept* of the commissioner. If the owners succeeded in curtailing the commissioner's authority, even after Vincent was gone, the commissioner's office would never get that authority back. What the owners wanted to do was not in the best interests of baseball.

"What are you going to do," I asked the owners, "form a committee on every ruling the commissioner makes? If you do that, we'll be forming committees every other week. I'm not sure that's the best way to spend our time."

Reinsdorf's motion eventually died. And later I got a short hand-written note from Vincent.

"Dear Bill," it said. "Thank you for your help, patience and humility. You are a very good man and partner. I just hope I can do better at being useful to you. I'll try harder. Sincerely, Fay."

Despite the "sincerely," I don't know if Vincent was being sincere. I do know that he had seriously missed the point. I hadn't been defending Fay Vincent. I'd been defending the authority of the office of the commissioner.

Despite that small victory for Vincent, the Steinbrenner issue didn't go away. Six months later, after Steinbrenner's lawyers delivered a report on the way Vincent had handled Steinbrenner, the executive council reopened the issue—and they didn't like what they found. Reinsdorf said there was "significant concern" among some owners about the way Steinbrenner had been treated.

That should have been a warning to Vincent. If he had managed to create sympathy for *George Steinbrenner,* he must have seriously screwed up. Vincent eventually agreed to reinstate Steinbrenner after the Yankees owner dropped the lawsuit he had engineered against the commissioner.

Soon Vincent would face more challenges from the owners.

In June 1992, Reinsdorf, Milwaukee Brewers owner Bud Selig, and other members of the Player Relations Committee, which oversaw contract negotiations, tried to force Vincent to give up the commissioner's traditional "best interests of baseball" powers. Vincent properly refused, but later, at the regular owners' meetings, he agreed not to intercede in contract negotiations. It bought him some time—but then came the final straw.

Earlier that year, as we were planning to add two new teams, we had had to deal with a geographic anomaly within the National League structure. The basic problem was that when the league was divided into East and West Divisions, Chicago and St. Louis were put in the East while Atlanta and Cincinnati were in the West. Geographically, of course, it should have been just the opposite.

So in March 1992, I suggested at an owners' meeting that we "realign" the teams. Atlanta, Cincinnati, and St. Louis all said that was fine, but Chicago Cubs chairman Stan Cook said no. Cook was worried that playing against teams in the West Division would mean more games on the West Coast and thus later local start-times for Cubs games. Not only would later start-times mean fewer viewers for Cubs games on superstation WGN—which, like the Cubs, was owned by the Tribune Company—but it might also cut into the station's lucrative local evening news broadcasts.

I had tried hard to work out a solution, getting West Coast teams to agree to earlier start-times and so on. But Cook was adamant. Under National League rules, any team affected by realignment had to agree to it, so Cook's opposition constituted a veto.

I thought the realignment was best for baseball, but I understood Cook's point. And besides, rules are rules. But Vincent didn't see it that way.

I had just landed in Los Angeles for a meeting when my office called and said that Vincent, out of the blue, had made a decision: He was going to order the Cubs realignment to take place under his "best interests of baseball" authority. I canceled the meeting and caught the next flight back to New York.

"That's not a good idea, Fay," I told Vincent. "The Cubs are going to sue you. And if they get a trial in Chicago, with a Chicago judge, chances are they're going to win."

But Vincent wouldn't listen. A month later he formally ordered the realignment, and as predicted, the Cubs sued.

Injecting himself into contract negotiations, the Steinbrenner suspension, the Cubs lawsuit—it was all too much. The tide had turned against Fay Vincent.

In August, the owners asked Vincent to convene a special

meeting to discuss his powers as commissioner. Vincent refused, so Jerry Reinsdorf asked American League president Bobby Brown and me to call the meeting.

The meeting was held in Chicago on September 3, 1992; Vincent declined to attend. After some discussion, the owners called for a vote on a "no confidence" resolution. The resolution stated in part: "The major league clubs do not have confidence in the ability of the present Commissioner... under his direction it is impossible for baseball to move forward effectively and constructively."

In the end the anti-Vincent faction, led by Reinsdorf, Selig, Cook of the Chicago Cubs, and Carl Pohlad of the Twins, won out. The owners voted 18–9, with one abstention, in favor of the no-confidence resolution.

(The abstention came from Marge Schott, whose trouble with racism allegations was still several months in the future. Marge told me during the meeting that she planned to abstain, but that she had to leave early because if she changed her flight reservation it would cost her an extra $50. Meanwhile, one of the pro-Vincent votes came from George W. Bush, who told me before the meeting that he had to vote for Vincent, not because he necessarily liked what he was doing as commissioner, but out of personal family loyalty. It seems that in his youth, before his accident, Vincent had worked for a summer in the Texas oil fields with Bush's uncle, William H. T. Bush.)

I hadn't taken part in the meeting except to enter Schott's abstention for her. But after the vote someone suggested that I call Vincent and give him the news.

In retrospect I should have refused. After all, the owners had hired Vincent; they should have been the ones to fire him. Nevertheless, I left the room and made my way to a pay telephone in the hall.

"Commissioner," I said when I got Vincent on the line, "the

owners just took a vote of no confidence against you. They want
you to resign."

Vincent asked me to read the no-confidence resolution to him,
and I did.

"Thank you," Vincent said, and then he hung up.

I never spoke with him again.

At first Vincent refused to resign, hiring a lawyer and proclaim-
ing that he would take his fight against dismissal to the courts. In
typical fashion, a few days later he backed down and submitted his
resignation.

"People have said, 'You're the last commissioner,'" Vincent told
reporters. "Well, if I'm the last commissioner, that's a sad thing."
He added in his resignation statement, "I can only hope owners
will realize that a strong Commissioner, a person of experience
and stature in the community, is integral to baseball. I hope they
learn this lesson before too much damage is done to the game, to
the players, umpires and others who work in the game, and most
importantly, to the fans."

Fay still didn't get it. He still didn't understand that he, even
more than the owners, was responsible for the damage done to
baseball.

Despite my personal feelings about Vincent, I took no joy in his
downfall. Although I hadn't voted in the no-confidence meeting,
I had agreed that Vincent had to go, that he simply was not, as
he put it in his resignation statement, "a person of experience and
stature in the community." But at the same time, I was worried that
getting rid of him would create a dangerous situation for baseball.

In later years, Vincent would continue to style himself as "The
Last Commissioner"—that was even the title of one of his books—
meaning he was the last true "outside" commissioner before the
game was taken over by powerful internal interests. Again, that
was typical Vincent.

But in my opinion, Bart Giamatti was the actual "last true commissioner"—or at least he would have been if he had lived. From his very first day, when he told the owners he would leave whenever they wanted him to, Fay Vincent had shown weakness, indecisiveness, and an inability to lead—and thus he made it easy for the enemies of a strong commissioner's office to take over baseball.

That was what they had intended all along. And with Fay Vincent's unwitting help, they had succeeded.

I never regretted taking the job of National League president, and I never regretted leaving it.

I only wish that I had left it a little earlier.

Within days of Fay Vincent's forced resignation from the commissioner's office, Brewers owner Bud Selig was named chairman of the owners' executive council and took over as de facto interim commissioner. At the time, I didn't worry about it too much. Everyone assumed that a new commissioner would be quickly chosen, and besides, I was on my way out.

From the moment I took over the National League president's job in 1989, I had intended to leave when my four-year appointment ended in early 1993. I had already accomplished most of what I'd wanted to do, most notably guiding the league through expansion, keeping the Giants in San Francisco—I had arranged for a Bay Area investors group to buy the team when it looked like they would be sold—and reestablishing the authority of the league president over the umpires union. I was looking forward to other things—including a lot more fishing. I'd had four years of constant meetings and travel and decisions, and it frankly was starting to wear on me. I wanted to start enjoying life.

Some people didn't want me to leave. For example, once before an All-Star Game, Willie Mays, Ernie Banks, and Earl Wilson came to my hotel room and asked me to stay on as league president.

"We need you here, Bill," Willie said. "It's important for the league and it's important for baseball."

Ernie said pretty much the same thing—and kept on saying it. He called me just about every week after that to tell me how important it was that I stay on.

Receiving support and encouraging words from guys like that was gratifying. But I was still looking forward to leaving.

Then, just before my term expired, Bud Selig called and asked me to stay on with the league for another year. The owners' executive council had just named Braves chairman Bill Bartholomay to be the head of a search committee for the new commissioner and there was concern about having the league president position open, especially since American League president Bobby Brown was also leaving. To ensure a smooth transition to a new commissioner, Selig wanted both of us to stay.

Reluctantly, I agreed to stay until a new commissioner took over and got settled into the job. (Bobby did, too.) And since I assumed that would be a relatively short process, I also started looking for my replacement.

I talked to several people I thought might be considered for the job. One of them was Bob Watson, a former player for the Astros, Red Sox, and Yankees who at the time was an assistant general manager for the Astros. But Watson said he was happy where he was—and later he became the first African American general manager in major league history.

I also called Jim Bunning, my former Phillies teammate who was then a Republican congressman from Kentucky. He obviously knew a lot about baseball and, having been a member of the Senate task force on expansion, he knew a lot about the politics surrounding baseball. But Jim had also been active in the Players Association during his career, and he knew that team owners had long memories.

"Are you crazy?" Jim said when I asked him if he was interested. "I was anti-owner when I was playing. There's no way those guys would want me around."

There were a few other former players I spoke with about the league president's job: Tom Seaver, Reggie Jackson, former Phillies outfielder Garry Maddox, former second baseman Ted Sizemore, who was then working for the Rawlings sports equipment company. For one reason or another, none worked out.

At one point, I had what I thought was an inspiration: General Colin Powell, who was then nearing the end of his term as chairman of the Joint Chiefs of Staff. Although I doubted that Powell would be interested in being a league president, I thought maybe he could serve for just a few months to learn the ropes and then take over as commissioner.

Colin Powell, Commissioner of Baseball. It would have been perfect, exactly what a commissioner should be. He was both "outside of baseball" and a person of national standing, at the time perhaps the most popular and respected public figure in America. He had the integrity and the moral authority to do what was best for baseball, and no one could have intimidated him. He was also African American, which I thought was important. With front office hiring in baseball still an issue, having an African American in the commissioner's job—the first in major league history—would send a powerful signal.

The question was, would Powell, who had commanded armies, be interested in commanding baseball?

I called Clifford Alexander, the former secretary of the army under Jimmy Carter, and arranged a meeting with General Powell.

I had met Powell briefly once before, in the clubhouse at Yankee Stadium at an opening day game. At the time, I had kidded him about not really being a Yankees fan, even though he had been raised in the Bronx in the late 1940s and early 1950s.

"You had to be a Brooklyn Dodgers fan, like the rest of us," I said to him. By *the rest of us,* I meant the young black kids who had been thrilled by Jackie Robinson's debut with the Dodgers. Powell was too good a politician to admit being a Dodgers fan in the Yankees clubhouse, so he had just smiled knowingly.

Anyway, as I was escorted into Powell's impressive, flag-bedecked office in the Pentagon, he stood up and extended his hand. He had an aura of authority that filled the room. We chatted for a while about baseball and then, not wanting to waste his time, I got down to business. Would he be interested in becoming National League president for a few months and then becoming commissioner of baseball?

He didn't jump at the opportunity.

For one thing, Powell said, he wasn't sure if baseball could afford him financially. He explained that he hadn't made a lot of money during his military career. Despite their awesome responsibilities, four-star generals at the time made only about $125,000 a year in base pay. For the first time in his life he was looking forward to earning some real money for himself and his family. At the time the commissioner's job paid about $650,000 a year, and although Powell didn't say so, I knew that after his retirement he could make that much by giving just half a dozen speeches.

I could certainly understand Powell's desire to provide financial security for his family. After so many years of service to the country, he deserved it.

But then Powell said something that, in retrospect, was alarming.

"Besides," he said, "I've heard there are going to be changes that won't allow the baseball commissioner to function independently. It's going to be hard to get someone if he really doesn't have authority."

Powell was extremely well connected and well informed. It made me wonder: *Does Colin Powell know something that I don't?*

Eventually Powell turned the commissioner's job down flat. And eventually I realized the truth. It wasn't just that the owners didn't want a strong and authoritative figure like Colin Powell as commissioner. The truth was that the most powerful faction within the owners' ranks didn't want a commissioner at all.

While I was sounding out Powell and the others, Bartholomay's commissioner search committee was looking at its own candidates. But I had the feeling they weren't looking too hard.

The committee had hired a head-hunting firm in Dallas to screen applicants and nominees for the position. Almost two hundred applications, most of them unsolicited, were considered, ranging from a thirteen-year-old girl in Georgia (unsolicited) to such well-known names as Ross Perot and Lee Iacocca. One potential candidate was Rangers managing partner George W. Bush, although he eventually decided to run for the Texas governorship.

Eventually the list was narrowed to ten people, including Northwestern University president Arnold Weber, US Olympic Committee executive director Harvey Schiller, Senator George Mitchell, former secretary of defense Donald Rumsfeld, and NBC Sports president Dick Ebersol. There were also two women on the list, former secretary of labor Lynn Martin and Anita DeFrantz of the International Olympic Committee, but it was widely assumed that they were just politically correct window dressing, that no way were the almost exclusively male baseball owners going to seriously consider a woman.

Eventually the list was again narrowed, to just two: Northwestern's Weber and the Olympic committee's Schiller. With all due respect to both of them, I wasn't sure either had the national standing to be a strong commissioner. Nevertheless, in January 1994, the executive council met to choose the candidate it would recommend to the full ownership as the next commissioner. Everybody—the press, the other owners, and the candidates themselves—expected that by the end of the day there would be a new commissioner of baseball.

Then the owners pulled the rug out. Eleven team owners signed a resolution to indefinitely delay choosing a new commissioner.

The two finalists were angry, and with good reason. Although Schiller was publicly gracious about it, Weber angrily withdrew his candidacy and reportedly told Major League Baseball to, in effect, stuff it.

I felt the same way. I had reluctantly agreed to stay on as league president until a new commissioner was chosen, and now it was apparent that there was no intention of doing that, and probably never had been. The search committee, the interviews, the selection process—it had all been a sham. Executive council chairman Bud Selig would continue to call the shots in baseball, along with Reinsdorf and others.

And in my opinion, their agenda was simple: They were going to fundamentally change the system that had governed baseball for the previous seventy years.

Almost from the moment he took over as interim commissioner, Selig and Reinsdorf and others had been planning to "restructure" baseball. The authority of the commissioner's office would be reduced, and his "best interests of baseball" powers would be eliminated. The authority of the two league presidents would also be reduced, and their staffs eliminated, until eventually they would become merely symbolic positions. Major League Baseball would be organized as a single corporation, with the most powerful faction among the twenty-eight owners making all the decisions. There would be no "outside baseball" interference.

As you might expect, I objected to the plan. I not only supported the independence of the commissioner's office, but also respected the traditional roles of the two leagues, and the competitiveness between them. Naturally, I thought the National League was the better of the two, and I had worked hard to protect its interests. I didn't want to see it reduced to just a name and a memory.

So at a joint meeting of the owners, I introduced a resolution that called for the separate roles and functions of the two leagues to continue as they traditionally had. If it passed, it would at least delay part of Selig's restructuring plans.

It didn't pass. The vote was 14–14, and a tie meant that it failed. But what particularly disappointed me is that seven of the National League owners had voted against the resolution, and thus against me. Then, later that same day, I nominated Peter O'Malley to the executive council. In the past such a nomination by me would have been unanimously approved, but this time the National League owners voted 10–4 in favor of another candidate.

For five years I had worked hard for those guys, trying to protect their interests and the interests of their league. And now they were refusing to back me up.

I realized then that I was tired of the politics, tired of the behind-the-scenes maneuverings, tired of the lies. I was tired of dealing with people who claimed to care about baseball but who cared only for the bottom line, people who would rather have a losing season and make a profit than win a pennant and just break even.

I was done.

I went back to my office in New York to clear up a few things. Then I walked out of the National League office for the last time.

I went to the spring owners' meetings in Scottsdale to formally hand over the office of National League president to Leonard Coleman, who had been selected to succeed me. Leonard had been an athlete at Princeton, a missionary in Africa, and most recently Major League Baseball's director of market development, one of the few African Americans in a high-level MLB position. I liked Leonard, but I knew that his presidency would be one of steadily diminished authority.

That night the owners were having a big group dinner, and they wanted me to attend. But I didn't want to have to sit there and listen to a lot of phony remarks about what a great guy I was from people I no longer trusted. I declined. And as noted earlier, a few months later, when Leonard Coleman called me and said the owners wanted to have a special dinner in my honor, I told him what the owners could do with that dinner as well.

Everything that I had feared would happen in baseball eventually did. Using the lure of increased sharing of revenues—that is, making the big-market "have" teams like the Yankees and the Red Sox share more money with the more numerous smaller-market "have-not" teams—Selig and Reinsdorf built up a power base within the owners' group. They then pushed through their baseball restructuring plan, turning Major League Baseball into a single corporate entity and effectively limiting the powers of the commissioner.

In 1998, after five years as interim commissioner, Selig was formally named commissioner of baseball—and he's been there ever since. To maintain the appearance of neutrality, Selig resigned as owner of the Brewers, but he named his daughter as the team CEO and reportedly continued to exercise control over the team until it was sold in 2005. (Meanwhile, Selig collected a salary of more than $16 million a year as commissioner. Vincent had been paid just $650,000 a year.)

In effect, it meant that an owner had become the commissioner of baseball. No longer was there even the pretense that an objective "outside baseball" authority was watching over the best interests of the game.

A few years after I left the league presidency, I was in Cooperstown for a Hall of Fame ceremony. In the dining room of the Otesaga Hotel I ran into Jerry Reinsdorf, the White Sox owner and architect of the owners' takeover. Reinsdorf said to me, "You think we're assholes, don't you?"

My honest answer was no. On a personal level I had always gotten along with the baseball owners I'd known, Selig and Reinsdorf included. I recognized them as smart, savvy businessmen, guys who focused on the bottom line.

And that was the problem. They understood the *business* of baseball.

But I don't think they ever truly understood the game.

As soon as word got around that I would be leaving the National League president's office, I started getting offers to stay in baseball.

In 1993, I met in St. Louis with August Busch III, the son of Gussie Busch, who had owned the Cardinals when I was a player. The younger Busch was a straight shooter. He looked me right in the eye and said that Anheuser-Busch was planning to sell the team in a few years, but before they did they wanted to make it competitive to increase its market value. He wanted me to take over as chief operating officer, with the same powers as a team owner or managing general partner, and rebuild the Cardinals into a top team.

It was tempting. I had always thought of the Cardinals as my team, the organization that had given me a chance to shine as a player and that had backed me up during some tough times. And then there was the one incentive that I had always been unable to ignore: It would be a challenge. The Cardinals hadn't won a division title in six years.

I initially told Busch that I would take the job. But before I left the league president's job, I had to reconsider.

By that time my relationships with Bud Selig and Jerry Reinsdorf, who were in effect running baseball, had soured. As the Cardinals' COO, I would have to work with them regularly, which didn't hold much appeal. And since the owners would have to approve any eventual sale of the Cardinals, I was concerned that my presence with St. Louis might adversely affect that. It just wouldn't be fair to the team.

So I called Busch and explained the situation. He understood, and in the end it worked out for the Cardinals. Under new leadership, with Walt Jocketty as general manager until 2007 and Tony La Russa as manager, as of 2010, the Cardinals have won a World Series, won the National League Championship Series twice, and won eight division titles.

There were other offers. In 1995, Tampa Bay Devil Rays owner Vince Naimoli talked to me about becoming chief executive of the Rays, which had just been awarded an American League expansion franchise. But I turned it down for the same reason I had turned down the Cardinals. I just didn't think I could effectively work with Reinsdorf and Selig. The Phillies offered me a job in an advisory capacity, but I turned that down, too. I even got an offer from WPIX, my old New York station, to come back to broadcasting and work with my old pal Phil Rizzuto.

That last one was an easy call. As much as I cared about Phil, I was certain that after so many years we wouldn't be able to re-create the old on-air excitement. You have to move forward, not back.

I did stay on for a while as a member of the Baseball Hall of Fame board and the Hall's Veterans Committee, during which time I was glad to see guys like Phil Rizzuto and Larry Doby be honored as Hall of Famers. But eventually the politics involved, the constant controversy over who should be in and who should be left out, got to be too much, and I quietly made my exit.

So in the end, after thirteen years as a player, eighteen years as a broadcaster, and five years as National League president, I walked away from baseball.

And I've never regretted it.

Chapter 16

Somewhere in my home there's a little gold card, encased in a nice leather wallet, that Major League Baseball gave me when I was National League president. It's a lifetime free pass to any baseball game in any stadium in any city in America.

It was a nice gift, the sort of thing they often give to guys who've been around the game a long time, and I appreciated it. But I really have no need for it.

Because I hardly ever go to baseball games anymore.

It's not that I'm angry at baseball, or bitter about my time in the game. Far from it. Baseball did a lot of good things for me, giving me an opportunity to do something I was good at and provide for myself and my family. And I like to think that over the years, I did some good things for baseball as well.

It's just that things are different now.

Maybe I don't go to baseball games because I played so many of them. According to the stats, during my thirteen-year major league career I played in 1,673 regular-season baseball games, including

every single one of the 162 games in the 1963 season—and that's
not even counting the games I played in high school and college
and in the minor leagues and in spring training. During my eighteen years as a broadcaster I also watched almost three thousand
baseball games, and I don't even know how many others I watched
when I was league president.

That's a lot of baseball.

Or maybe I don't go to games because I never really learned
how to just relax and watch a game for its own sake. When I was
a player, if I was watching it meant I wasn't playing—and I wanted
to play. As a broadcaster and league official, there was always some
professional aspect to watching a baseball game—how a certain
player was playing, how a certain manager was managing, how a
certain ump was umping. For all those years, baseball was work.

Or maybe there's an even simpler explanation. Maybe it's
because now, more than half a century after I started in baseball,
it's just not my game anymore.

In some ways maybe today's game is better. With improved
physical conditioning techniques, better nutrition, and developments in sports medicine, certainly the players are bigger, stronger, faster, and in general better athletes than most of us ever were.
For example, a 150-pound, five-foot-six shortstop like Phil Rizzuto
would have a hard time beating out an equally talented 196-pound,
six-foot-three shortstop like Derek Jeter. And an eighteen-year-old
Bill White who was a benchwarmer on his high school baseball
team could never compete with an eighteen-year-old high school
star who had been playing Little League and going to professionally run baseball clinics since he was six.

But even though the players of today may be better athletes,
to me the game of baseball is just not as exciting to watch—or to
play—as it was when I was playing. It's become more of an entertainment than a competition.

I don't mean that in an insulting way. There's nothing wrong with entertainment. And I guess the old guys in every field of endeavor always say that things were better back in their day.

But for a lot of reasons, in baseball's case I think it's true.

For one thing, we had to play harder and more aggressively than the players today. When I was a player, under the reserve clause, we survived year-to-year in the baseball business. With no long-term, multi-year contracts, every player, the stars included, had to go out there every game and fight and claw to be the best he possibly could be. You didn't think much about your long-term career, because you never knew if you were going to have one. Guys like me just wanted to make it through the season.

And back then the nature of the game *allowed* players to be aggressive, which isn't the case in today's game. The economics of today's game simply don't permit star players, or even average players, to get hurt. It's bad business for even a $3-million-a-year infielder to get intentionally run over at second, much less to let a pitcher throw a knockdown at a $20-million-a-year slugger.

So the players are protected. These days if you throw at a batter once, you get warned; throw at him a second time and chances are you'll get ejected, or even suspended. Remember, as National League president I suspended a bunch of pitchers for throwing at batters. That's what the owners wanted, and I understood the economics involved. The upshot is that pitchers now have to hold back, not throw inside pitches, and let the sluggers lean into the plate and swing for the fences.

It was different when I played. If you were running into a double play, you'd do whatever it took to break it up—knock down the second baseman, slide in with spikes high, whatever was required. It was expected of you, and nobody complained about it, not even the guy you knocked down—although you could be certain that before he even slapped the dust off his uniform he was planning some payback. And if you challenged a Bob Gibson or a Don Drysdale, if you crowded the plate or tried to show him up, you knew he'd put you in the dirt. Pitchers were expected to do that. And if a pitcher wasn't aggressive enough, his own teammates would get on his case.

I remember once when I was playing first base during a Cardinals-versus-Giants game in St. Louis in 1964, when the Cardinals were in a hard battle for the pennant. Willie Mays was at the plate for the Giants, taking big swings—"swinging from his ass," as we used to say—and trying to hit one out of the park, which could have cost us the game, and maybe the pennant, and maybe that sweet World Series payout. I walked halfway to the mound from first and yelled to our pitcher, so that Willie could hear, "Don't you let him swing on you like that! Knock his ass down!"

Willie Mays was like a big brother to me. But I was still willing to see him knocked in the dirt when he tried to take advantage of my team—and Willie understood completely.

Again, that sort of aggressive attitude was expected, not only by the players and the fans but by the managers as well. A guy like Billy Martin, who was notorious for ordering pitchers to throw at batters or telling base runners to slide in with spikes up high, wouldn't be allowed to do that in today's game. And frankly, today's star players don't really have to listen to their managers anyway. If you've got a ten-year, $200 million contract, you really don't have to take orders from anybody. What's the manager going to do? Bench you? Let you sit on your butt for $20 million a year?

As I've said, I don't begrudge modern players their astronomical salaries. The most I was ever paid for playing baseball was about $72,000 a year, which with inflation taken into account works out to about $500,000 in today's dollars. But that was still a pretty good income, far above what the average guy made for breaking his back in a steel mill all year long. So I didn't complain then—and I'm not about to complain now.

Besides, Major League Baseball, with record gross revenues of $6.6 billion in 2009, can afford the big salaries. Somebody has to get that money—and if the players don't get it, the owners will. Besides, the owners wouldn't pay those high salaries if they couldn't afford them.

It's true that money has hurt some parts of today's game. Take autographs and memorabilia, for example. When I was a player we never thought twice about giving some kid an autograph, or handing out signed baseballs. And we didn't expect a lot of money—or sometimes any money—from somebody using our name or image. When I signed a contract with Topps to put out my baseball card—all the players did—I got five bucks and a set of golf clubs in payment. These days, of course, a lot of the big-name players have six-figure contracts with agents to market their autographs, and professional dealers have squeezed out the kids. If you give somebody an autographed baseball these days, you can probably expect to see it on eBay a week later.

I guess business is business. But it does seem to have taken some of the innocence out of the game.

On the other hand, when I hear people say that the big salaries have increased the pressure on players to perform, I say that's just nonsense. The pressure to play well was just as great on players making $16,000 a year in 1956 as it is on players today—maybe even greater, since we lacked the job security most players have these days. With fewer teams, and with more players in the minors, and with the reserve clause tying you to one team, in the old days you had to constantly worry that some young kid on the team's AAA club would replace you, or that if you weren't the best at your position you'd get stuck behind a better player, maybe for years. So we would do whatever it took to be competitive.

For some players in recent times, being competitive has meant using steroids. For us, it often meant taking greenies.

"Greenies" were amphetamines. They'd been used in World War II to help pilots and others stay awake and alert, and they started coming into baseball in the late 1940s and 1950s. And they're still in baseball. Although testing for amphetamine use in Major League Baseball began in 2006, with suspensions for testing positive, a lot of players get around that by claiming they have attention deficit disorder and getting a therapeutic-use exemption to take Adderall or other amphetamine-like drugs.

When I was a player, "attention deficit disorder" was when you got picked off at first. We took greenies because we simply couldn't afford to be tired.

Maybe I was naive, but I had never heard of them until one day in the early 1960s, when my six-year-old daughter Debbie got sick and had to stay in Children's Hospital in St. Louis. The Cardinals were playing at home at the time, so I would play a game and then go to the hospital to stay overnight with my daughter while my wife was taking care of our other kids. Then the next day I'd head back to the ballpark for another game. After three days of that I was beat—and I looked it.

"Here," the Cardinals trainer said, handing me two little green pills. "Take a couple of these."

I didn't even know what they were, but I took them and almost immediately felt better—not stronger or faster, just wide awake. After that, whenever I felt really tired before a game I'd say to the trainer, "Hey, Doc, give me a couple of greenies, will you?"

It was only an occasional thing, and I never used them for recreational purposes.

And while many people disagree, I never thought of them as performance-enhancing drugs. They helped me stay alert, but they didn't help me hit a curveball. I finally gave them up for good when I took some before a game when I was with the Phillies and couldn't sleep for two nights.

But greenies weren't the only drugs and medications that other players and I used to stay competitive. I remember once when I was with the Cardinals, I had sprained my ankle so badly that I couldn't walk from my car to the clubhouse. A couple of the stadium ushers carried me up the stairs to the clubhouse and the trainers gave me a shot of Novocain in the ankle. I went out and played six innings, and then they gave me another shot.

Another time I was having problems with a torn rotator cuff in my shoulder, and a friend of mine took me to New York to see Dr. Hans Kraus, the so-called father of sports medicine and the man who treated President John Kennedy's back problems. He said the team trainers were giving me shots in the wrong place, and showed me where they should go. I went back to the trainers and they gave me the shots—and they worked. I had only thirty RBIs in the first half of the season, but after getting the shots, my shoulder got better and I had seventy-three RBIs in the second half.

I didn't even know what was in those shots—I think it was cortisone, which is to say, a steroid—and I really didn't care. I just wanted to play.

The point here is that given all that, I'm not going to be judgmental about players who used steroids—especially before they were banned and made illegal, and before their dangers were fully understood.

Steroids weren't even being discussed when I was playing, and they were barely on the radar when I became league president. I remember seeing Jose Canseco in the 1990 World Series and noticing he was a hell of a lot bigger than when he'd first come up to the majors. Same thing with Mark McGwire when I saw him taking batting practice before an All-Star Game. I had never seen anyone swing a bat with such speed and power. But I assumed that McGwire and Canseco had just been working their asses off in the gym.

Both McGwire and Canseco later acknowledged that they had used steroids, although McGwire said it was only to help him recover from injuries. Many other players have also acknowledged using the drugs during the so-called steroid era, while others, like Barry Bonds, have not.

There's no question that using steroids or human growth hormone is dangerous. Putting them in your body is as foolish as smoking two packs of Marlboros a day or constantly having a pinch of Copenhagen in your lip.

But should having used steroids before they were illegal, or before their dangers were fully understood, keep a guy out of the Hall of Fame? Should it require an asterisk to be placed next to any record he may have set?

I don't think so. If you're going to do that, you might as well do it to every record ever set by a player who used greenies—which would require a hell of a lot of asterisks. While you're at it, why not differentiate between pitching records before and after 1969, when in response to pitchers like my friend Bob Gibson, who'd had an astonishing 1.12 ERA the year before, the pitcher's mound was lowered and the strike zone reduced? Why not differentiate between home runs hit in the old stadiums and ones hit in the newer, slugger-friendly ones?

The fact is that baseball changes. And you have to take it as it comes.

Another change since I was a player, one that's close to my heart, is in the number of black baseball players. Near the end of my playing days, almost one of every four major league players was black. Today it's less than one in ten, with Hispanic players constituting the largest minority group in the game.

There's nothing wrong with that. And there are a lot of reasons why young black athletes gravitate more to basketball and football than baseball. For example, it's a lot easier to put a basketball court in an inner city than it is to put in a baseball field.

But back then, in the old days, the black players like Jackie Robinson and Larry Doby and Willie Mays and many others accomplished something important. Martin Luther King and Rosa Parks and many others forced America to deal with the moral and legal aspects of segregation and racism. But it was black athletes, in baseball and other sports, who put a close-up, personal face on black people for millions of sports fans. They saw us on the field, they read about us in the papers, they watched us on TV. They saw us compete with white men and they saw that we were as good as and often better than they were—and if anyone disputed it, the stats were there to prove it.

I'm not equating baseball players with Dr. King or Mrs. Parks. But I've always felt that if a guy took his kids to a baseball game and cheered for a black player on the field, it made it a little bit harder for him to go home and call that black man a "nigger."

Today that contribution is largely forgotten. People may remember Jackie Robinson (current Yankees second baseman Robinson Cano was named after Jackie), but most people, even young black baseball players, have forgotten guys like Larry Doby.

And maybe that's another reason I don't go to baseball games anymore. Maybe it would just be a reminder that the guys I played with and against now belong to another, largely forgotten time.

We're all getting old now, those of us who have survived. I'm fortunate to still be healthy and relatively fit, but a lot of the guys whom I remember as strong and vital young men are now confined to wheelchairs or counting down the days in nursing homes.

It makes me sad to see it. People my age will understand when I say that I hope that when I die, I'm able to die healthy.

And many of the players I knew have already gone on. Jackie Robinson, Curt Flood, Phil Rizzuto, Ken Boyer, Roy Campanella, Earl Wilson, Willie Stargell—the list could go on and on. They've all left baseball forever behind.

And so have I. Now I go fishing and work in my yard and travel in my motor home. I play tennis and golf—badly in the latter case—and enjoy dinners with friends. I try to spend as much time as I can with my children and grandchildren.

And that lifetime baseball stadium pass still sits unused in a drawer someplace.

It doesn't mean that I've forgotten baseball, any more than I've forgotten my life. Sometimes, when I'm sitting in a small boat, on a still lake, with a fishing line in the water and the sun going down, I'll think about baseball, and what I was, and where I've been.

I think about being a kid in Warren, Ohio, in a family that taught me the values that have guided me throughout my life, and about being a young ballplayer in the Deep South and vowing that the racists who were calling me "nigger" were never going to break me. I think about Willie Mays and Jackie Robinson and nights in Harlem, and about the struggle over desegregation in spring training, about the white guys who called me uppity and the other white guys who put a hand on my shoulder and told me to hang in there. I think about Phil Rizzuto and the Bronx Zoo, and about being president of the National League and the battles I fought. I think about it all.

And when I do that, when I turn it over in my mind, I realize something about baseball, and about life.

I realize that in baseball, and in life, I may not have been a great player.

But it was always a great game to play.

INDEX

ABOUT THE AUTHORS

WILLIAM DEKOVA "BILL" WHITE led three lives in Major League Baseball. He was a star first baseman for the New York Giants, the St. Louis Cardinals, and the Philadelphia Phillies from 1956 to 1969—with two years out for US Army service—during which time he received six Gold Glove Awards and was selected to the All-Star Game five times. After his retirement as a player he was a reporter and sports anchor for WFIL-TV in Philadelphia, and from 1971 to 1989 he announced New York Yankees games for television and radio as part of the legendary broadcast team that included Phil Rizzuto and Frank Messer. From 1989 to 1994 he was president of Major League Baseball's National League. Born in Florida in 1934, he was raised in Warren, Ohio, and attended Hiram College before embarking on his baseball career. He is the father of five children and the grandfather of two. He lives in Bucks County, Pennsylvania.

GORDON DILLOW is a veteran journalist who worked as a reporter and columnist for a number of newspapers, including the *Los Angeles Herald Examiner*, the *Los Angeles Times*, and the *Orange County Register*. As an embedded reporter with a marine infantry unit in 2003, Dillow was one of the first journalists to enter Iraq on the first night of the war. He is the co-author (with retired FBI special agent William J. Rehder) of the true-crime book, *Where the Money Is: True Tales from the Bank Robbery Capital of the World*. Dillow served as a US Army sergeant in Vietnam and is a graduate of the University of Montana journalism school. He lives in Scottsdale, Arizona.